his code name was
The Fox

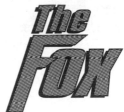

Other FoxTrot Books by Bill Amend

FoxTrot
Pass the Loot
Black Bart Says Draw
Eight Yards, Down and Out
Bury My Heart at Fun-Fun Mountain
Say Hello to Cactus Flats
May the Force Be with Us, Please
Take Us to Your Mall
The Return of the Lone Iguana
At Least This Place Sells T-shirts
Come Closer, Roger, There's a Mosquito on Your Nose
Welcome to Jasorassic Park
I'm Flying, Jack . . . I Mean, Roger
Think iFruity
Death By Field Trip
Encyclopedias Brown and White

Anthologies

FoxTrot: The Works
FoxTrot *en masse*
Enormously FoxTrot
Wildly FoxTrot
FoxTrot Beyond a Doubt
Camp FoxTrot
Assorted FoxTrot

his code name was

by Bill Amend

Andrews McMeel
Publishing

Kansas City

FoxTrot is distributed internationally by Universal Press Syndicate.

His Code Name Was The Fox copyright © 2002 by Bill Amend. All rights reserved. Printed in the United States of America. No part of this book may be used or reproduced in any manner whatsoever without written permission except in the case of reprints in the context of reviews. For information, write Andrews McMeel Publishing, LLC, 4520 Main Street, Kansas City, Missouri 64111.

06 07 08 BAH 10 9 8 7 6 5 4

ISBN 13: 978-0-7407-2191-5
ISBN 10: 0-7407-2191-7

Library of Congress Control Number: 2001095892

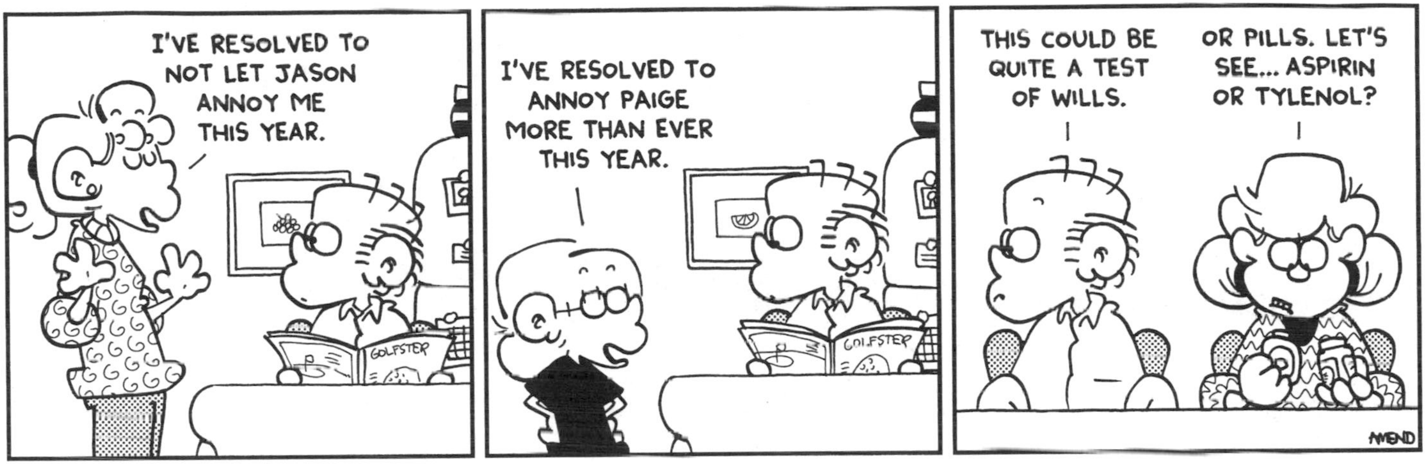
I'VE RESOLVED TO NOT LET JASON ANNOY ME THIS YEAR.
GOLFSTER
I'VE RESOLVED TO ANNOY PAIGE MORE THAN EVER THIS YEAR.
GOLFSTER
THIS COULD BE QUITE A TEST OF WILLS.
OR PILLS. LET'S SEE... ASPIRIN OR TYLENOL?
AMEND

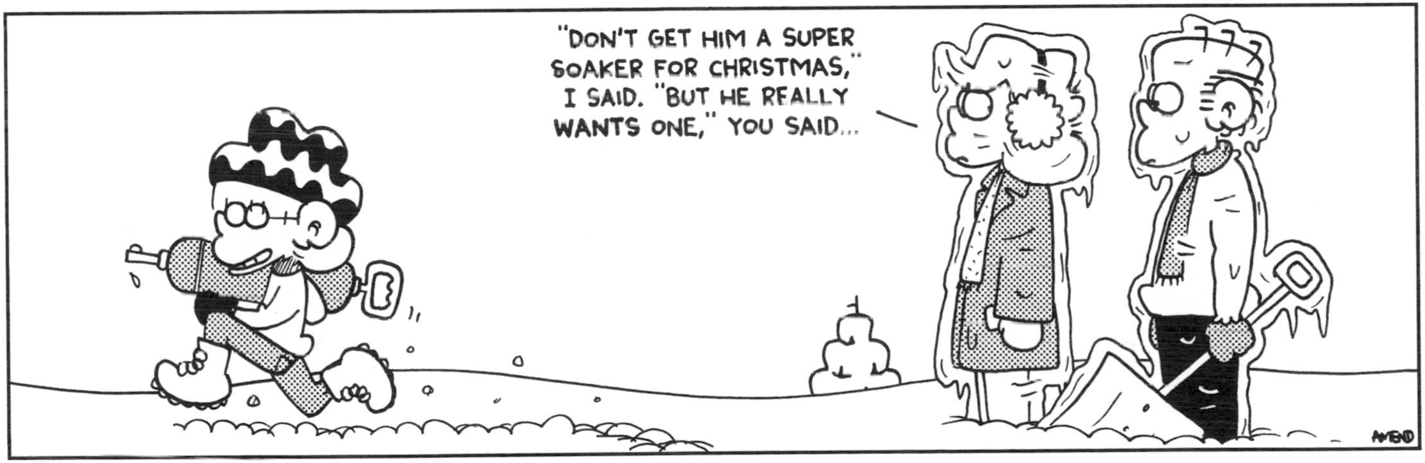
"DON'T GET HIM A SUPER SOAKER FOR CHRISTMAS," I SAID. "BUT HE REALLY WANTS ONE," YOU SAID...
AMEND

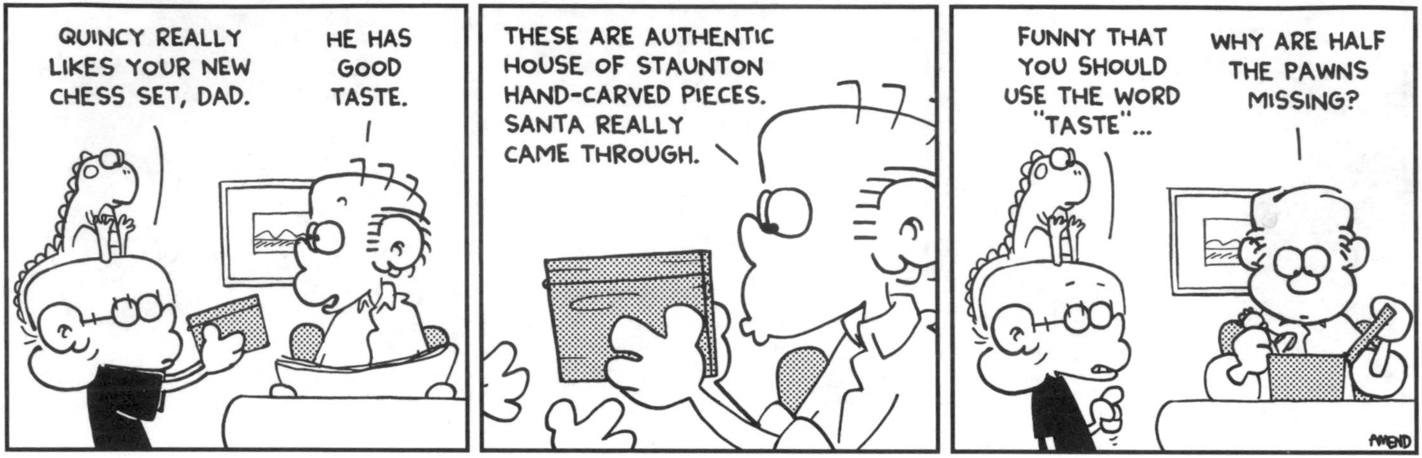
QUINCY REALLY LIKES YOUR NEW CHESS SET, DAD.
HE HAS GOOD TASTE.
THESE ARE AUTHENTIC HOUSE OF STAUNTON HAND-CARVED PIECES. SANTA REALLY CAME THROUGH.
FUNNY THAT YOU SHOULD USE THE WORD "TASTE"...
WHY ARE HALF THE PAWNS MISSING?
AMEND

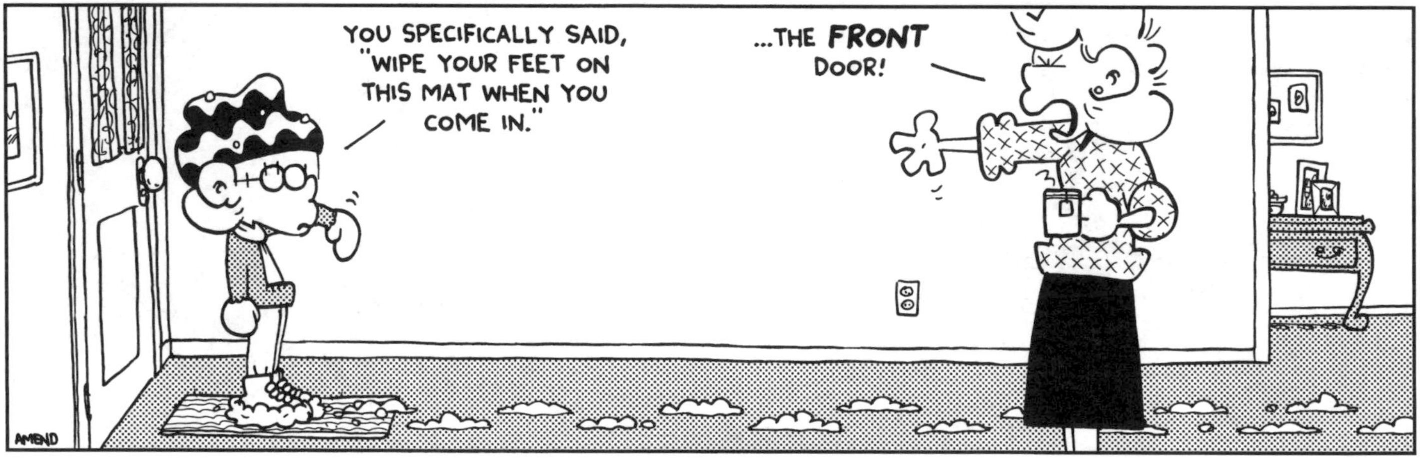
YOU SPECIFICALLY SAID, "WIPE YOUR FEET ON THIS MAT WHEN YOU COME IN."
...THE **FRONT** DOOR!
AMEND

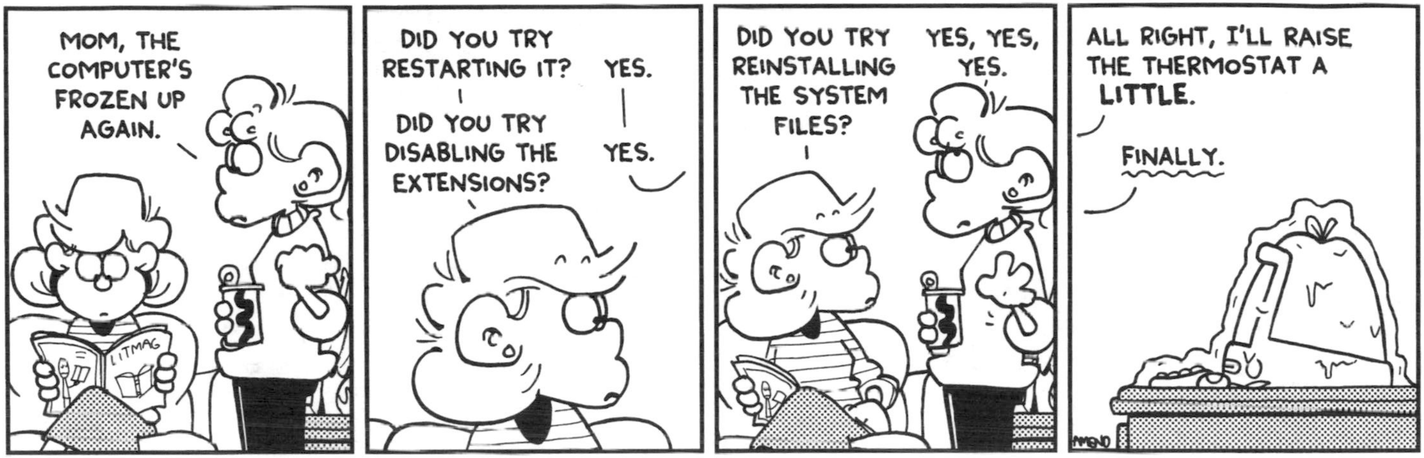
MOM, THE COMPUTER'S FROZEN UP AGAIN.
DID YOU TRY RESTARTING IT?
YES.
DID YOU TRY DISABLING THE EXTENSIONS?
YES.
DID YOU TRY REINSTALLING THE SYSTEM FILES?
YES, YES, YES.
ALL RIGHT, I'LL RAISE THE THERMOSTAT A **LITTLE**.
FINALLY.
LITMAG
AMEND

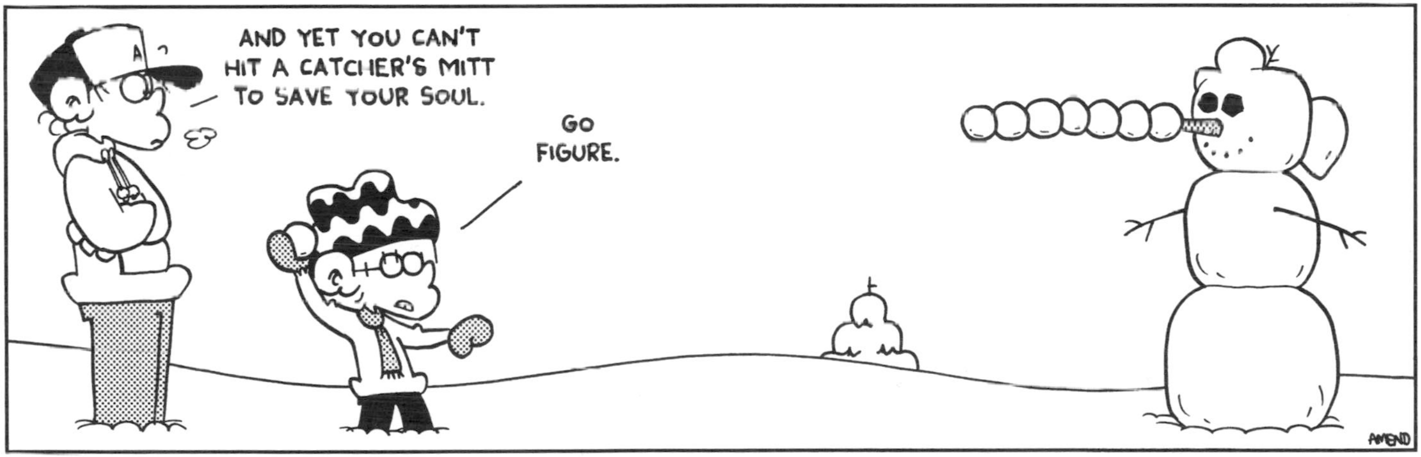
AND YET YOU CAN'T HIT A CATCHER'S MITT TO SAVE YOUR SOUL.
GO FIGURE.
AMEND

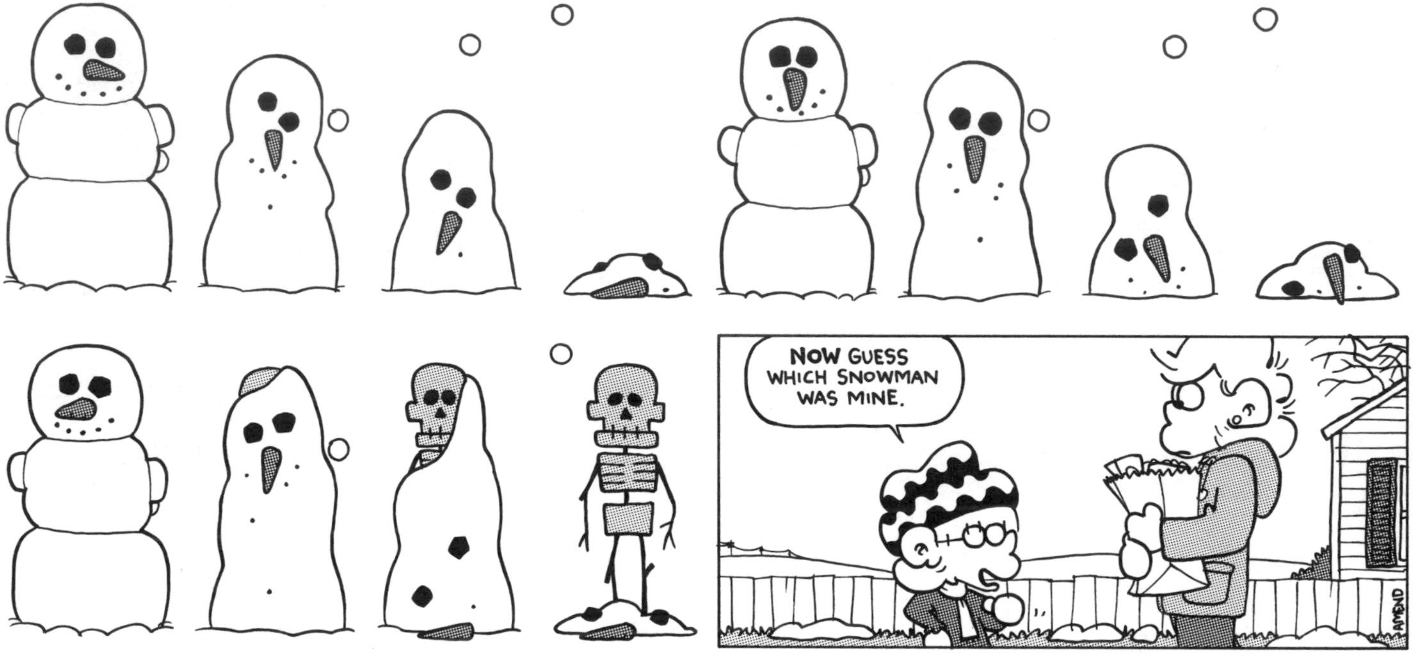
NOW GUESS WHICH SNOWMAN WAS MINE.
AMEND

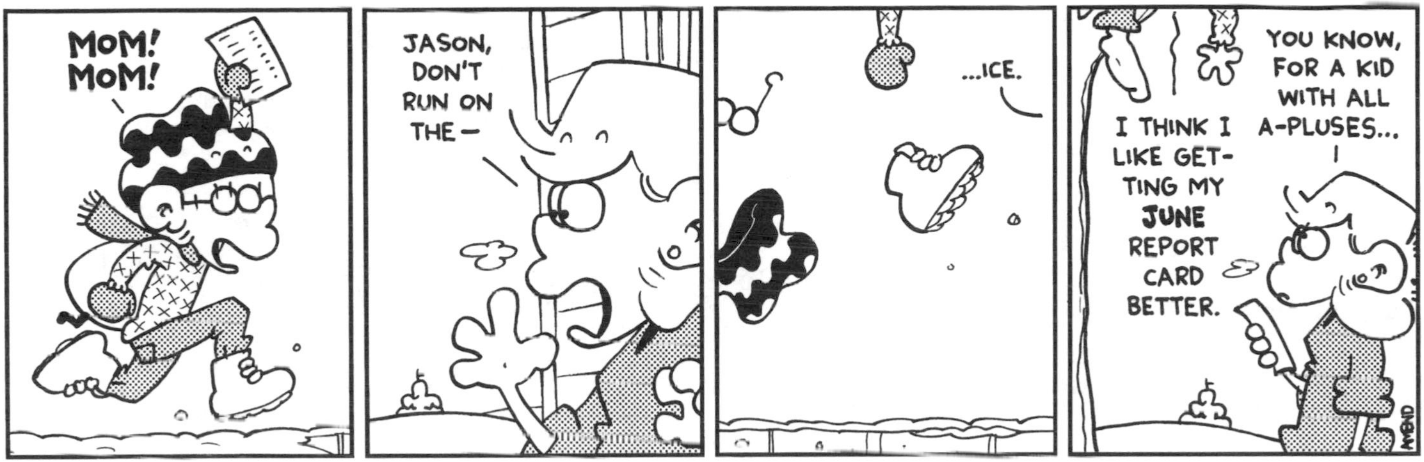
MOM! MOM!
JASON, DON'T RUN ON THE—
...ICE.
YOU KNOW, FOR A KID WITH ALL A-PLUSES...
I THINK I LIKE GETTING MY **JUNE** REPORT CARD BETTER.
AMEND

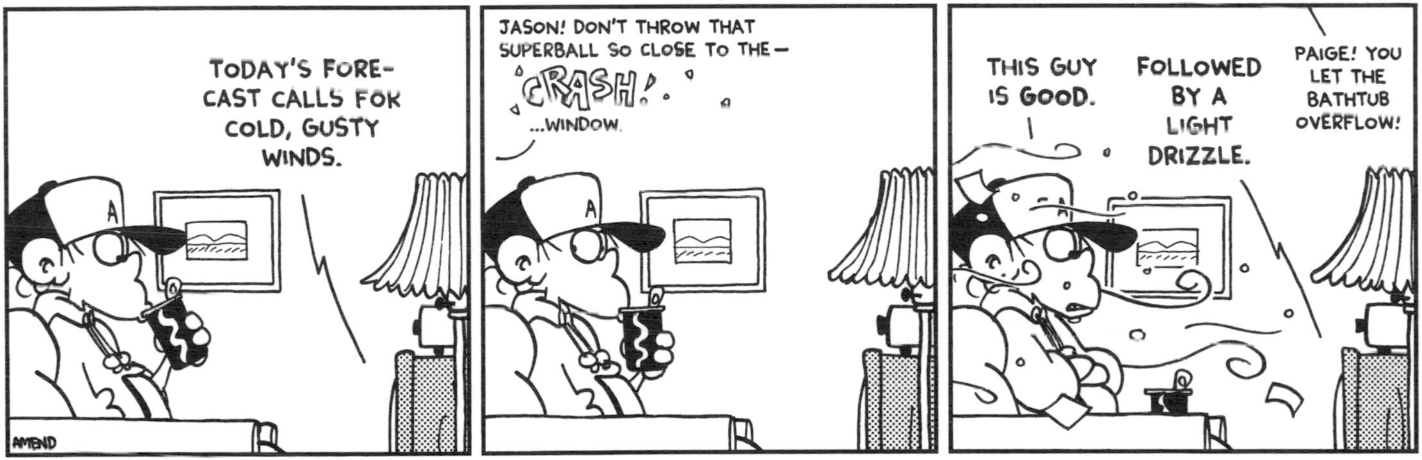
TODAY'S FORECAST CALLS FOR COLD, GUSTY WINDS.
AMEND
JASON! DON'T THROW THAT SUPERBALL SO CLOSE TO THE—
CRASH!
...WINDOW.
THIS GUY IS **GOOD**.
FOLLOWED BY A LIGHT DRIZZLE.
PAIGE! YOU LET THE BATHTUB OVERFLOW!

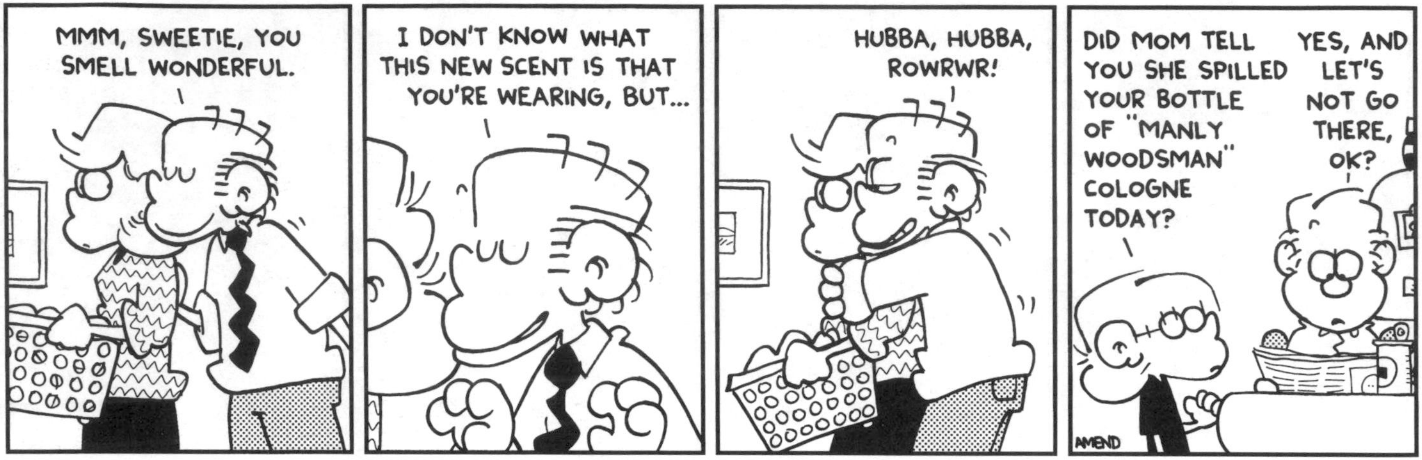
MMM, SWEETIE, YOU SMELL WONDERFUL.
I DON'T KNOW WHAT THIS NEW SCENT IS THAT YOU'RE WEARING, BUT...
HUBBA, HUBBA, ROWRWR!
DID MOM TELL YOU SHE SPILLED YOUR BOTTLE OF "MANLY WOODSMAN" COLOGNE TODAY?
YES, AND LET'S NOT GO THERE, OK?
AMEND

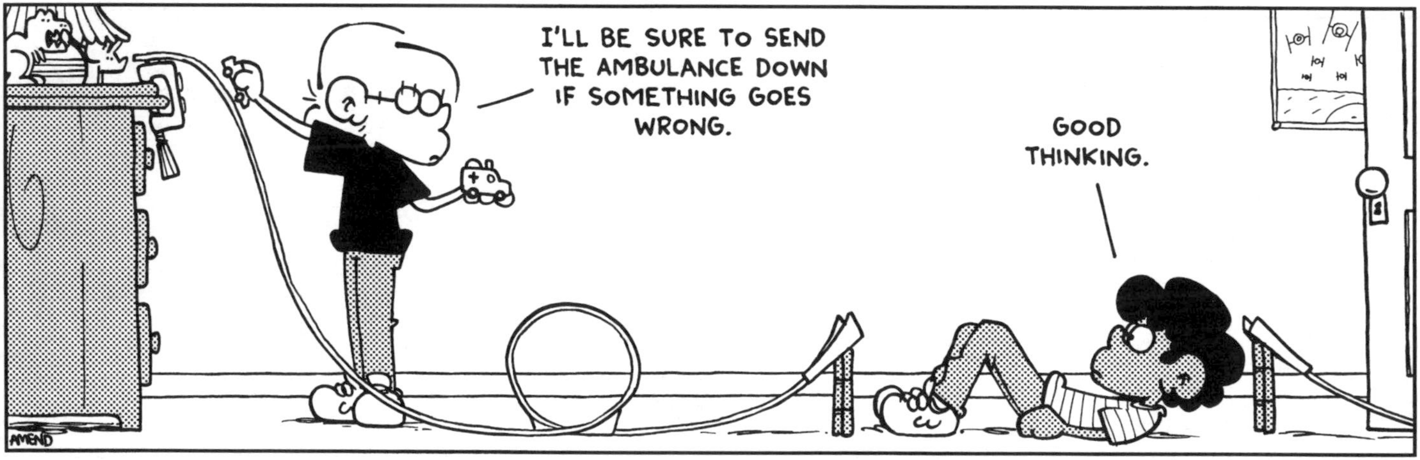
I'LL BE SURE TO SEND THE AMBULANCE DOWN IF SOMETHING GOES WRONG.
GOOD THINKING.
AMEND

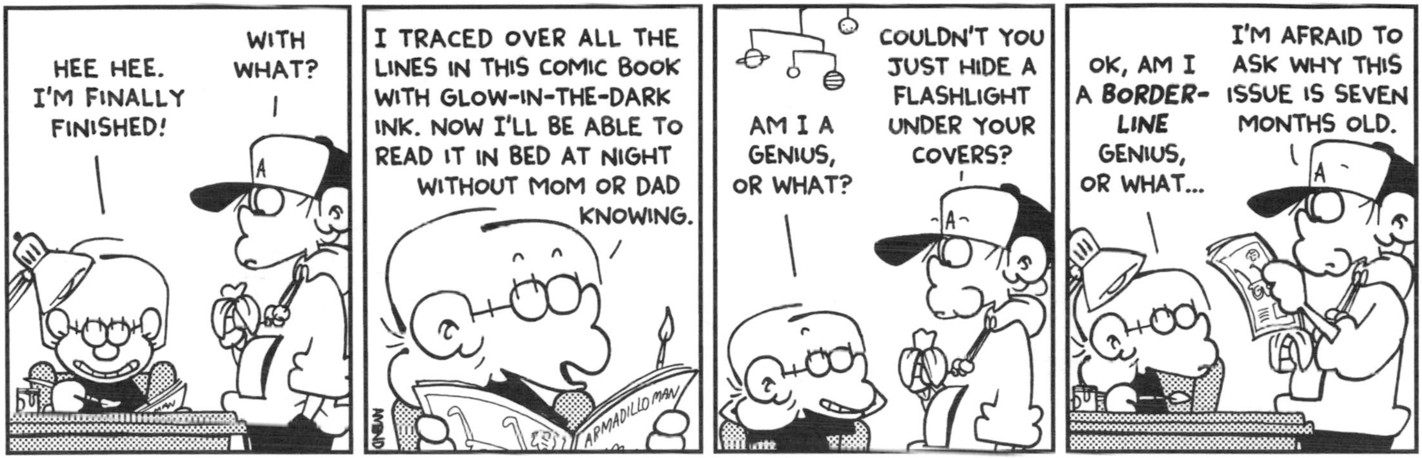
HEE HEE. I'M FINALLY FINISHED!
WITH WHAT?
I TRACED OVER ALL THE LINES IN THIS COMIC BOOK WITH GLOW-IN-THE-DARK INK. NOW I'LL BE ABLE TO READ IT IN BED AT NIGHT WITHOUT MOM OR DAD KNOWING.
ARMADILLO MAN
AM I A GENIUS, OR WHAT?
COULDN'T YOU JUST HIDE A FLASHLIGHT UNDER YOUR COVERS?
OK, AM I A **BORDER-LINE** GENIUS, OR WHAT...
I'M AFRAID TO ASK WHY THIS ISSUE IS SEVEN MONTHS OLD.
AMEND

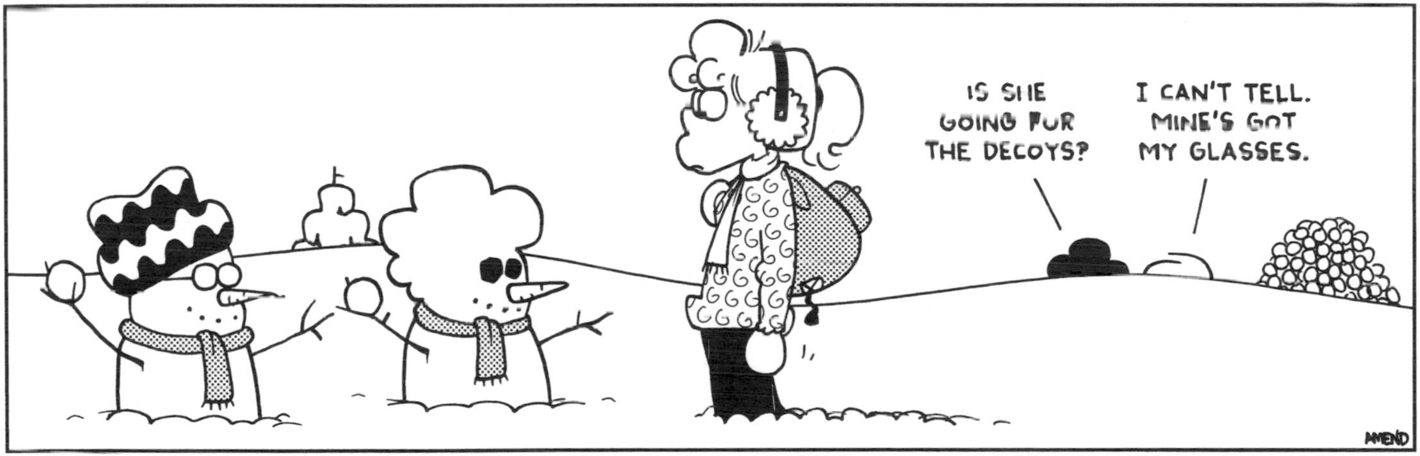
IS SHE GOING FOR THE DECOYS?
I CAN'T TELL. MINE'S GOT MY GLASSES.
AMEND

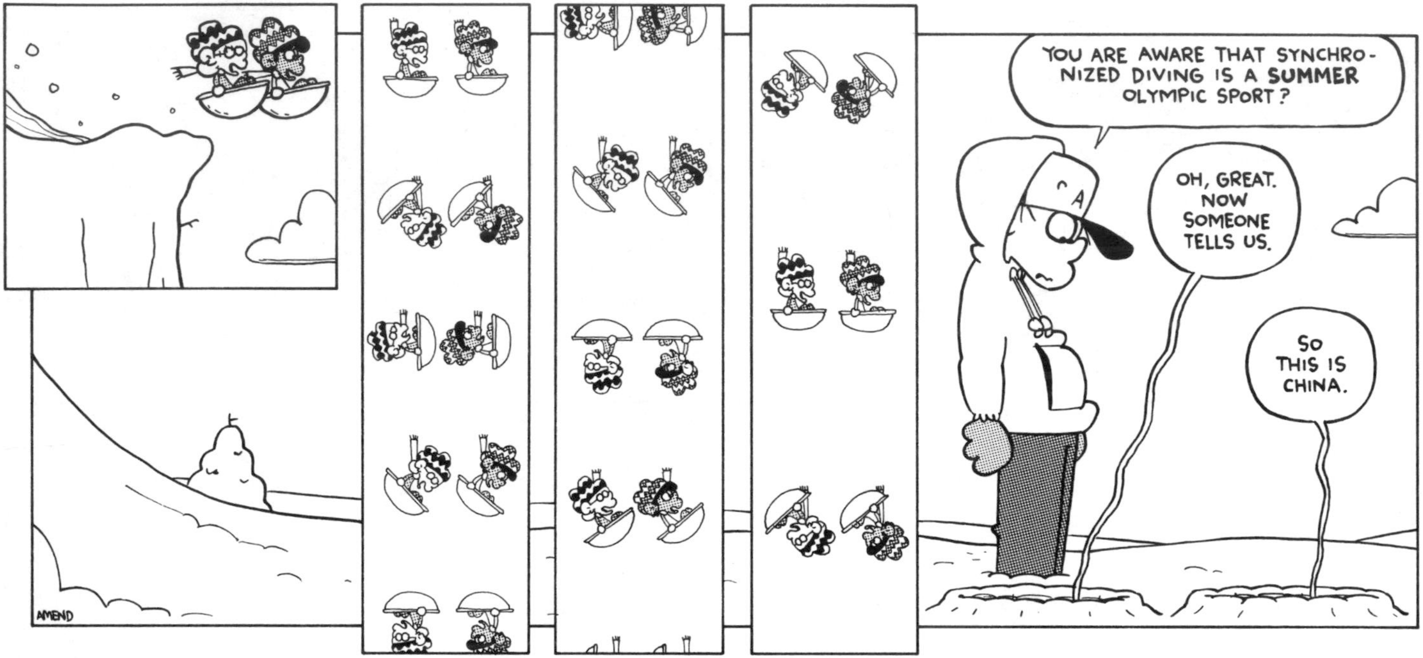
AMEND
YOU ARE AWARE THAT SYNCHRONIZED DIVING IS A **SUMMER** OLYMPIC SPORT?
OH, GREAT. NOW SOMEONE TELLS US.
SO THIS IS CHINA.

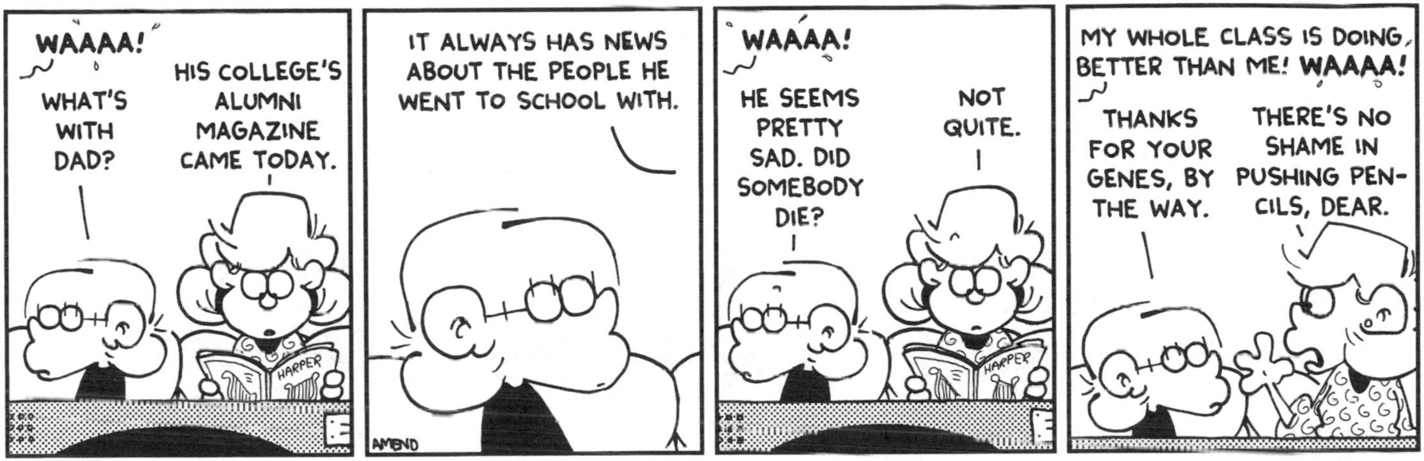
WAAAA!
WHAT'S WITH DAD?
HIS COLLEGE'S ALUMNI MAGAZINE CAME TODAY.
HARPER
IT ALWAYS HAS NEWS ABOUT THE PEOPLE HE WENT TO SCHOOL WITH.
AMEND
WAAAA!
HE SEEMS PRETTY SAD. DID SOMEBODY DIE?
NOT QUITE.
HARPER
MY WHOLE CLASS IS DOING BETTER THAN ME! WAAAA!
THANKS FOR YOUR GENES, BY THE WAY.
THERE'S NO SHAME IN PUSHING PENCILS, DEAR.

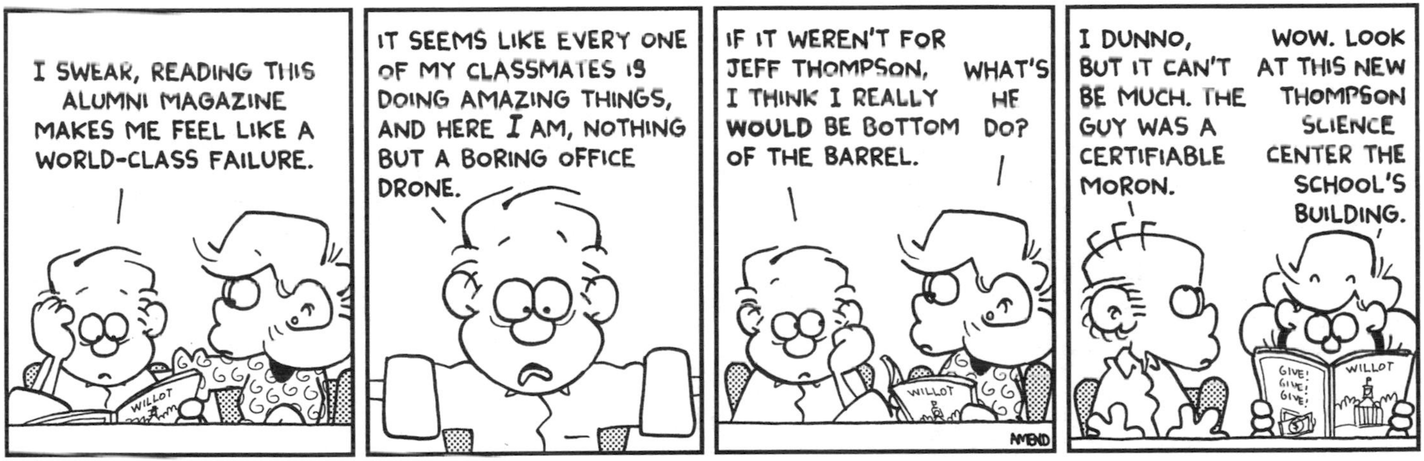
I SWEAR, READING THIS ALUMNI MAGAZINE MAKES ME FEEL LIKE A WORLD-CLASS FAILURE.
WILLOT
IT SEEMS LIKE EVERY ONE OF MY CLASSMATES IS DOING AMAZING THINGS, AND HERE I AM, NOTHING BUT A BORING OFFICE DRONE.
IF IT WEREN'T FOR JEFF THOMPSON, I THINK I REALLY WOULD BE BOTTOM OF THE BARREL.
WHAT'S HE DO?
WILLOT
AMEND
I DUNNO, BUT IT CAN'T BE MUCH. THE GUY WAS A CERTIFIABLE MORON.
WOW. LOOK AT THIS NEW THOMPSON SCIENCE CENTER THE SCHOOL'S BUILDING.
GIVE! GIVE! GIVE!
WILLOT

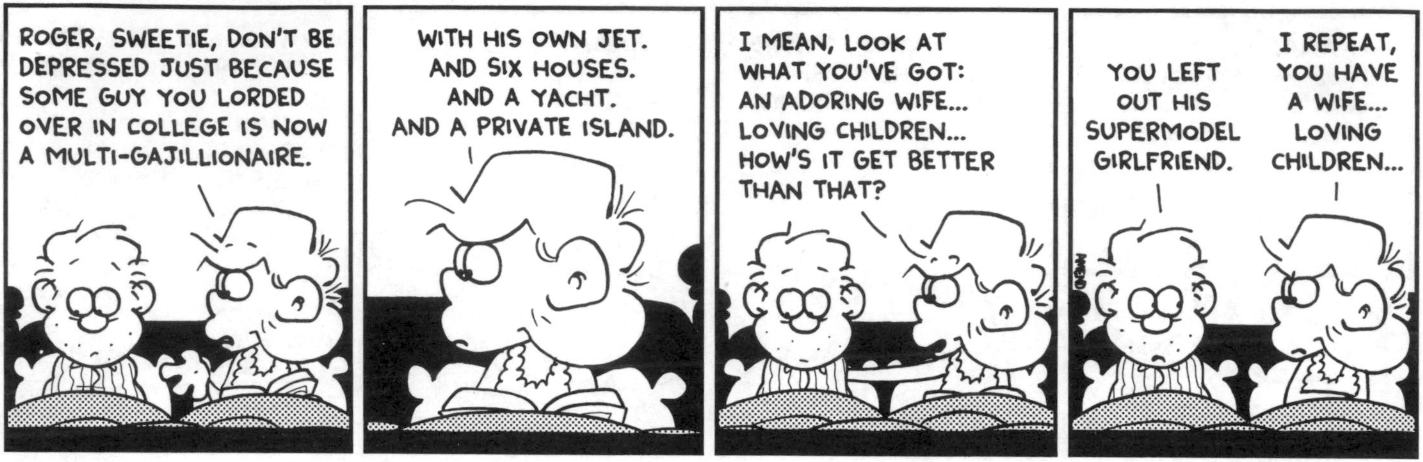
ROGER, SWEETIE, DON'T BE DEPRESSED JUST BECAUSE SOME GUY YOU LORDED OVER IN COLLEGE IS NOW A MULTI-GAJILLIONAIRE.
WITH HIS OWN JET. AND SIX HOUSES. AND A YACHT. AND A PRIVATE ISLAND.
I MEAN, LOOK AT WHAT YOU'VE GOT: AN ADORING WIFE... LOVING CHILDREN... HOW'S IT GET BETTER THAN THAT?
YOU LEFT OUT HIS SUPERMODEL GIRLFRIEND.
I REPEAT, YOU HAVE A WIFE... LOVING CHILDREN...
AMEND

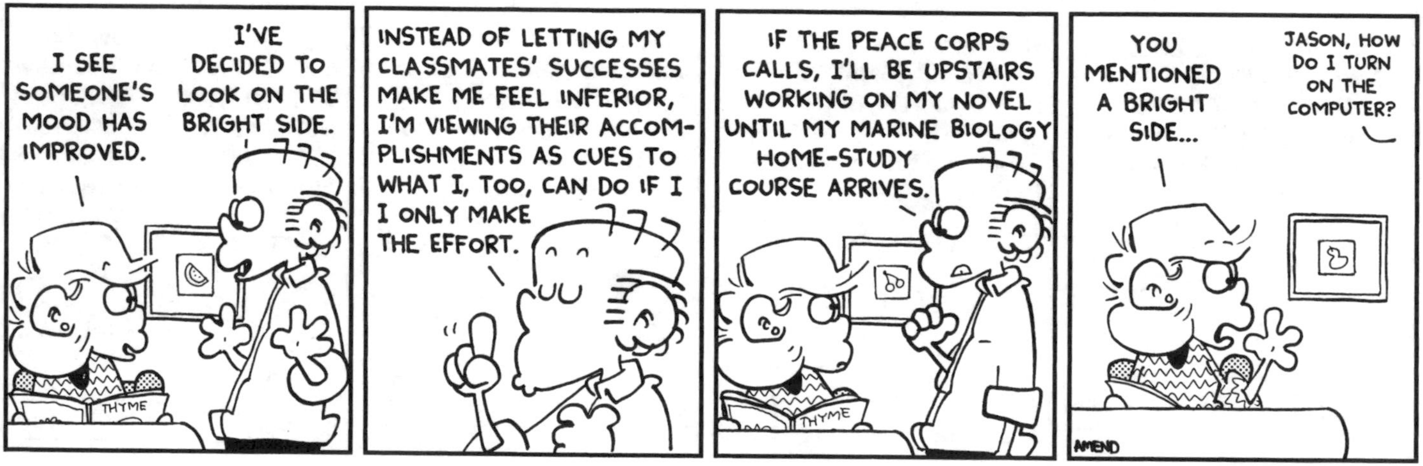
I SEE SOMEONE'S MOOD HAS IMPROVED.
I'VE DECIDED TO LOOK ON THE BRIGHT SIDE.
THYME
INSTEAD OF LETTING MY CLASSMATES' SUCCESSES MAKE ME FEEL INFERIOR, I'M VIEWING THEIR ACCOMPLISHMENTS AS CUES TO WHAT I, TOO, CAN DO IF I I ONLY MAKE THE EFFORT.
IF THE PEACE CORPS CALLS, I'LL BE UPSTAIRS WORKING ON MY NOVEL UNTIL MY MARINE BIOLOGY HOME-STUDY COURSE ARRIVES.
THYME
YOU MENTIONED A BRIGHT SIDE...
JASON, HOW DO I TURN ON THE COMPUTER?
AMEND

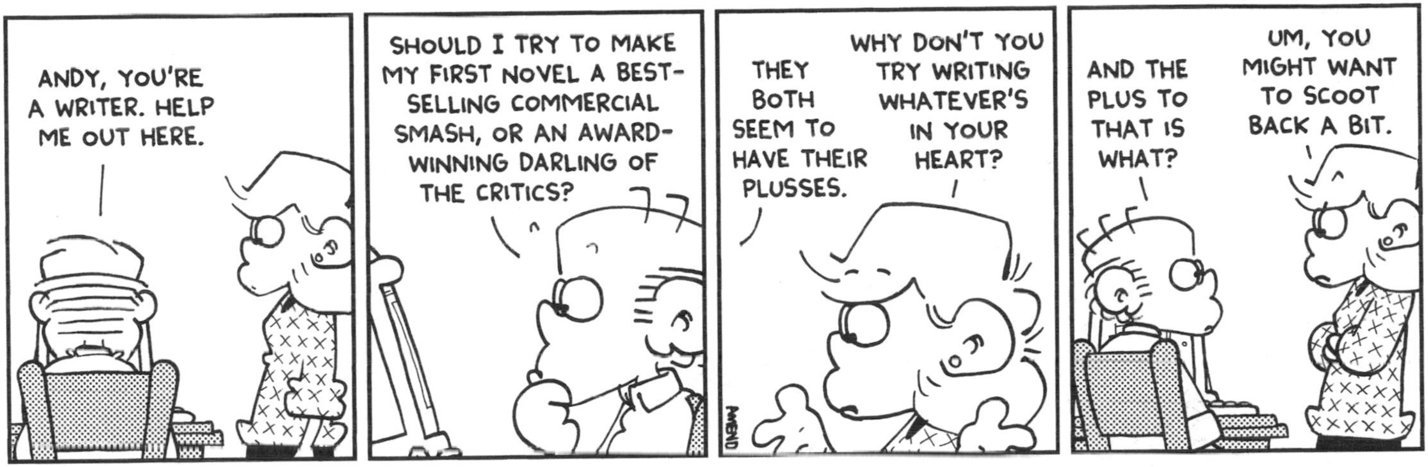
ANDY, YOU'RE A WRITER. HELP ME OUT HERE.
SHOULD I TRY TO MAKE MY FIRST NOVEL A BEST-SELLING COMMERCIAL SMASH, OR AN AWARD-WINNING DARLING OF THE CRITICS?
THEY BOTH SEEM TO HAVE THEIR PLUSSES.
WHY DON'T YOU TRY WRITING WHATEVER'S IN YOUR HEART?
AMEND
AND THE PLUS TO THAT IS WHAT?
UM, YOU MIGHT WANT TO SCOOT BACK A BIT.

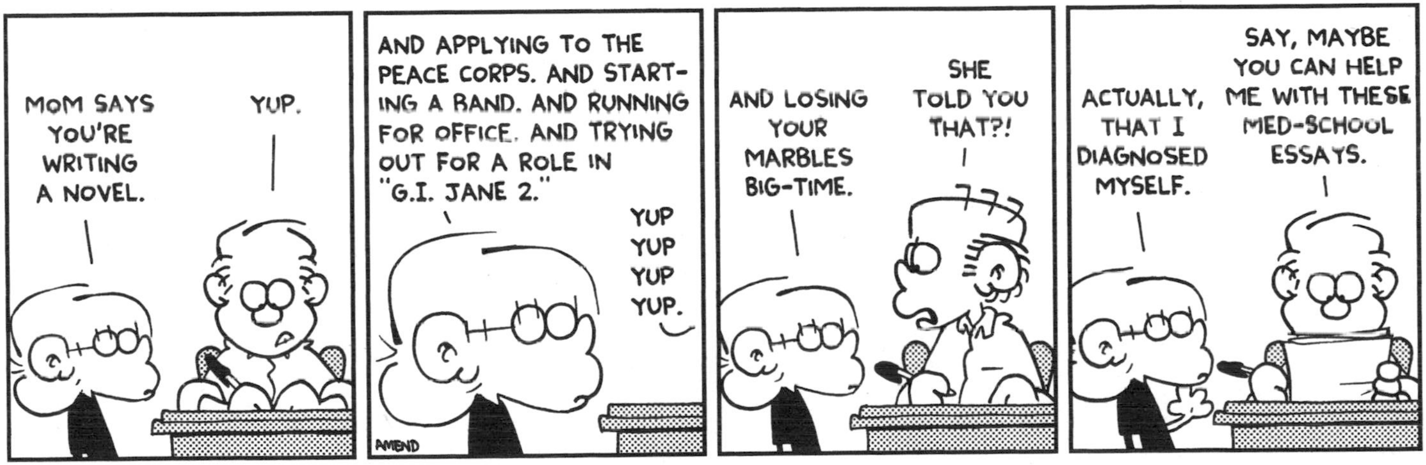
MOM SAYS YOU'RE WRITING A NOVEL.
YUP.
AND APPLYING TO THE PEACE CORPS. AND STARTING A BAND. AND RUNNING FOR OFFICE. AND TRYING OUT FOR A ROLE IN "G.I. JANE 2."
YUP YUP YUP YUP.
AMEND
AND LOSING YOUR MARBLES BIG-TIME.
SHE TOLD YOU THAT?!
ACTUALLY, THAT I DIAGNOSED MYSELF.
SAY, MAYBE YOU CAN HELP ME WITH THESE MED-SCHOOL ESSAYS.

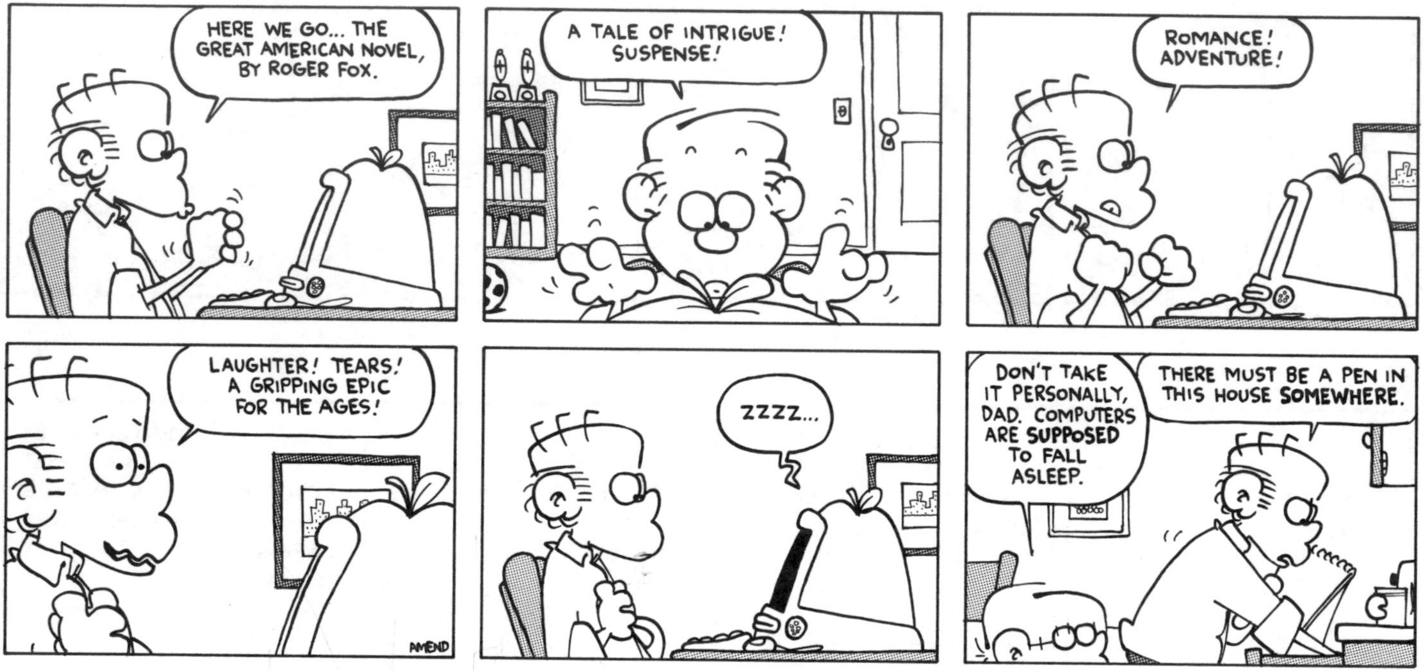
HERE WE GO... THE GREAT AMERICAN NOVEL, BY ROGER FOX.
A TALE OF INTRIGUE! SUSPENSE!
ROMANCE! ADVENTURE!
LAUGHTER! TEARS! A GRIPPING EPIC FOR THE AGES!
AMEND
ZZZZ...
DON'T TAKE IT PERSONALLY, DAD. COMPUTERS ARE SUPPOSED TO FALL ASLEEP.
THERE MUST BE A PEN IN THIS HOUSE SOMEWHERE.

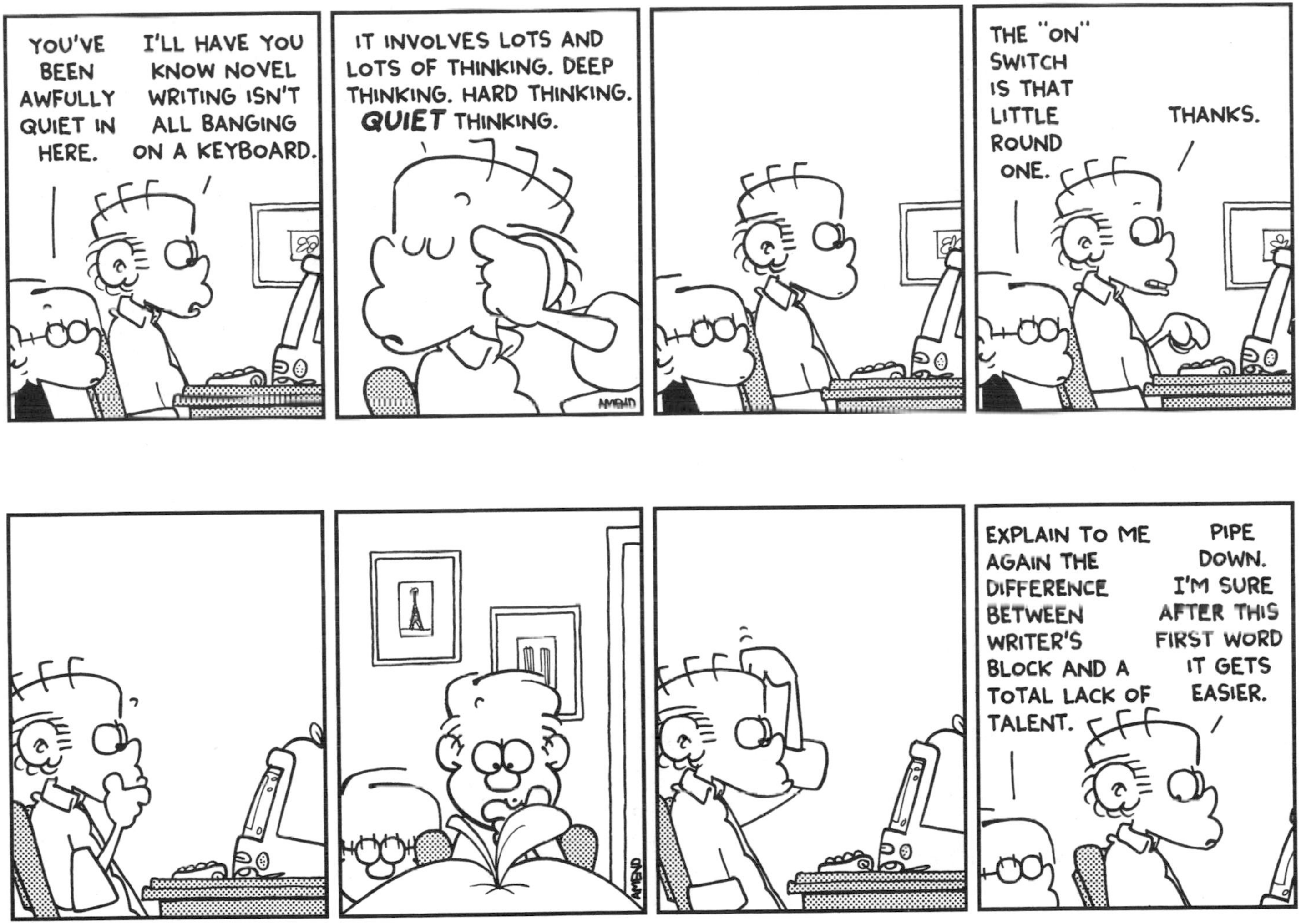
YOU'VE BEEN AWFULLY QUIET IN HERE.
I'LL HAVE YOU KNOW NOVEL WRITING ISN'T ALL BANGING ON A KEYBOARD.
IT INVOLVES LOTS AND LOTS OF THINKING. DEEP THINKING. HARD THINKING. QUIET THINKING.
THE "ON" SWITCH IS THAT LITTLE ROUND ONE.
THANKS.
EXPLAIN TO ME AGAIN THE DIFFERENCE BETWEEN WRITER'S BLOCK AND A TOTAL LACK OF TALENT.
PIPE DOWN. I'M SURE AFTER THIS FIRST WORD IT GETS EASIER.

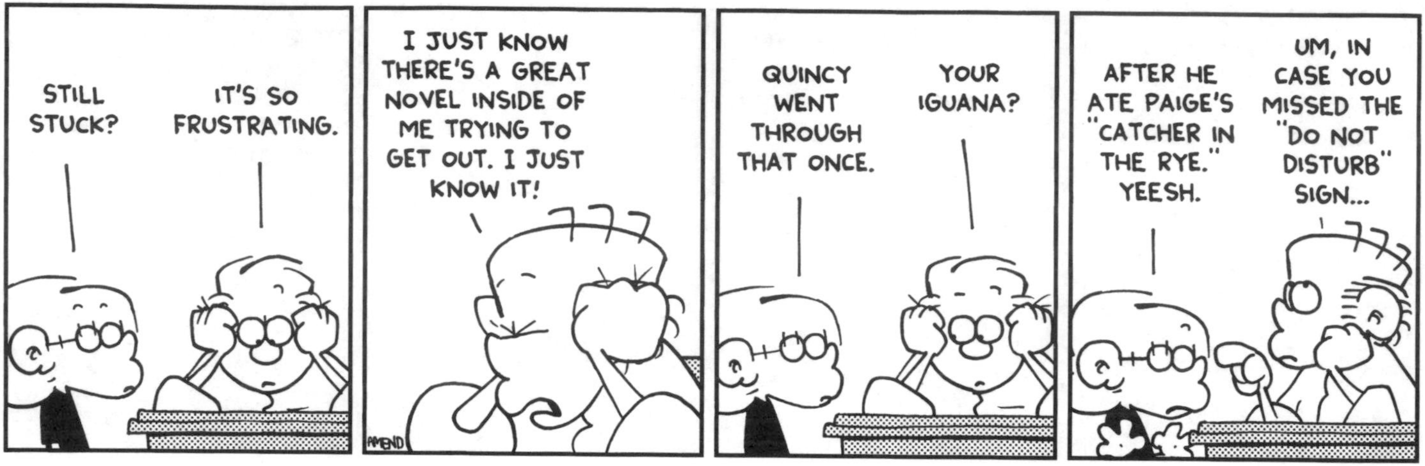
STILL STUCK?
IT'S SO FRUSTRATING.
I JUST KNOW THERE'S A GREAT NOVEL INSIDE OF ME TRYING TO GET OUT. I JUST KNOW IT!
QUINCY WENT THROUGH THAT ONCE.
YOUR IGUANA?
AFTER HE ATE PAIGE'S "CATCHER IN THE RYE." YEESH.
UM, IN CASE YOU MISSED THE "DO NOT DISTURB" SIGN...
AMEND

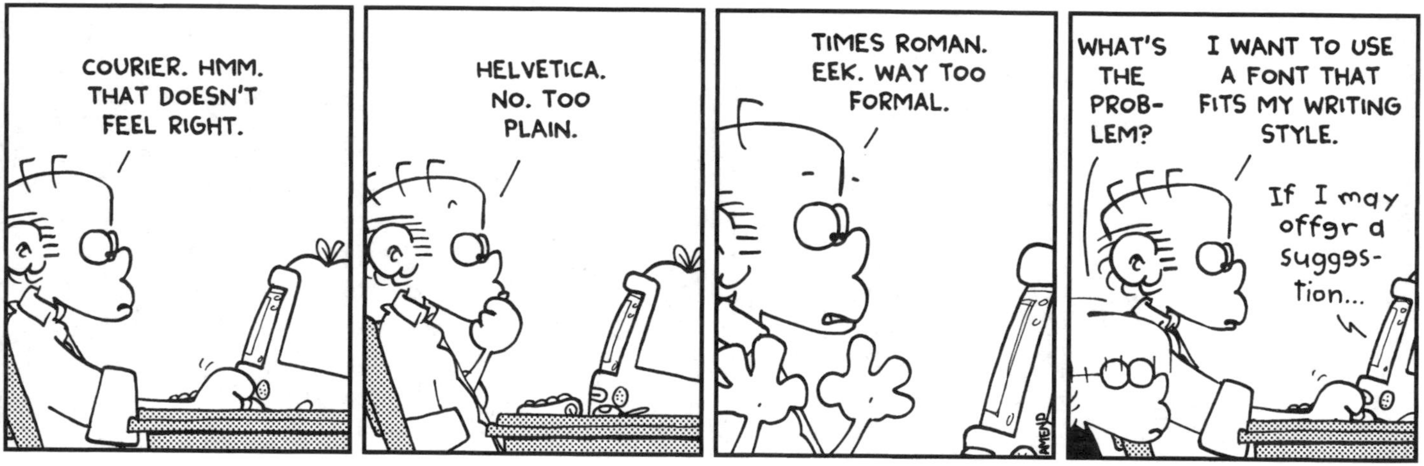
COURIER. HMM. THAT DOESN'T FEEL RIGHT.
HELVETICA. NO. TOO PLAIN.
TIMES ROMAN. EEK. WAY TOO FORMAL.
AMEND
WHAT'S THE PROB-LEM?
I WANT TO USE A FONT THAT FITS MY WRITING STYLE.
If I may offer a sugges-tion...

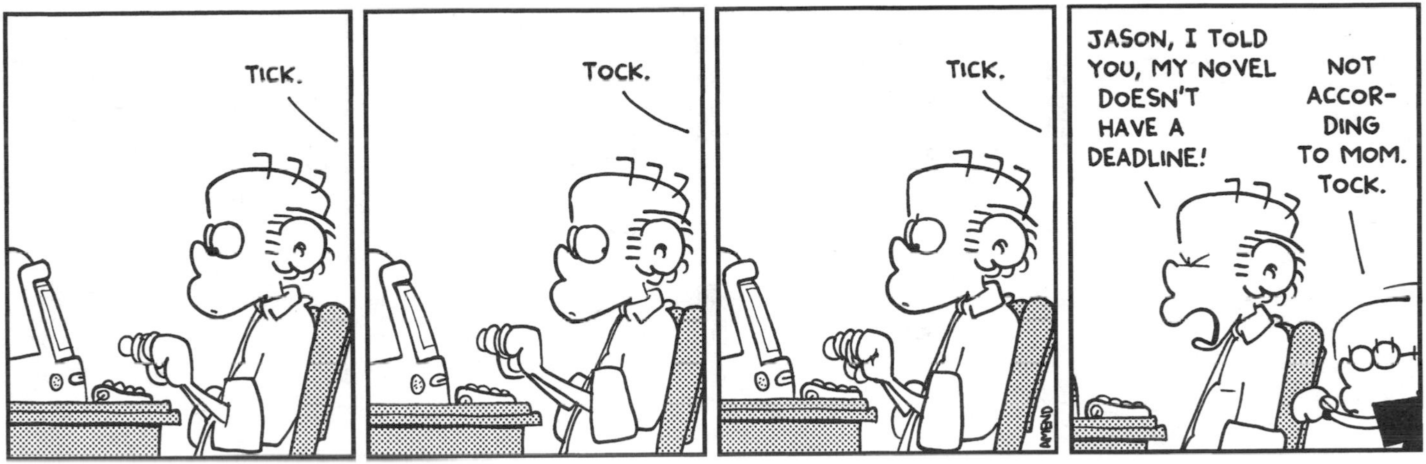
TICK.
TOCK.
TICK.
JASON, I TOLD YOU, MY NOVEL DOESN'T HAVE A DEADLINE!
NOT ACCORDING TO MOM. TOCK.

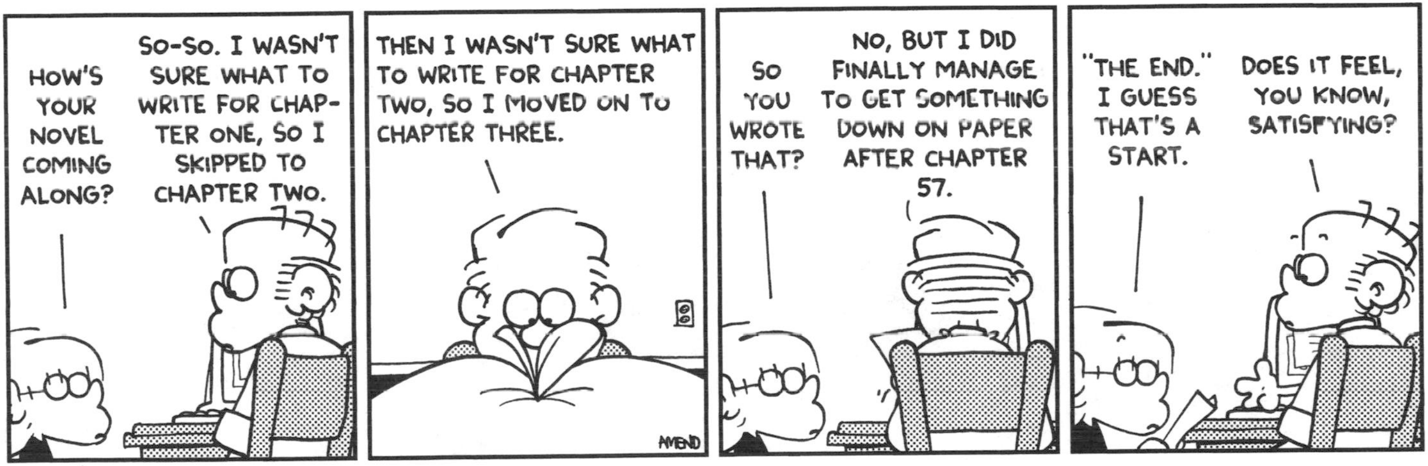
HOW'S YOUR NOVEL COMING ALONG?
SO-SO. I WASN'T SURE WHAT TO WRITE FOR CHAPTER ONE, SO I SKIPPED TO CHAPTER TWO.
THEN I WASN'T SURE WHAT TO WRITE FOR CHAPTER TWO, SO I MOVED ON TO CHAPTER THREE.
SO YOU WROTE THAT?
NO, BUT I DID FINALLY MANAGE TO GET SOMETHING DOWN ON PAPER AFTER CHAPTER 57.
"THE END." I GUESS THAT'S A START.
DOES IT FEEL, YOU KNOW, SATISFYING?

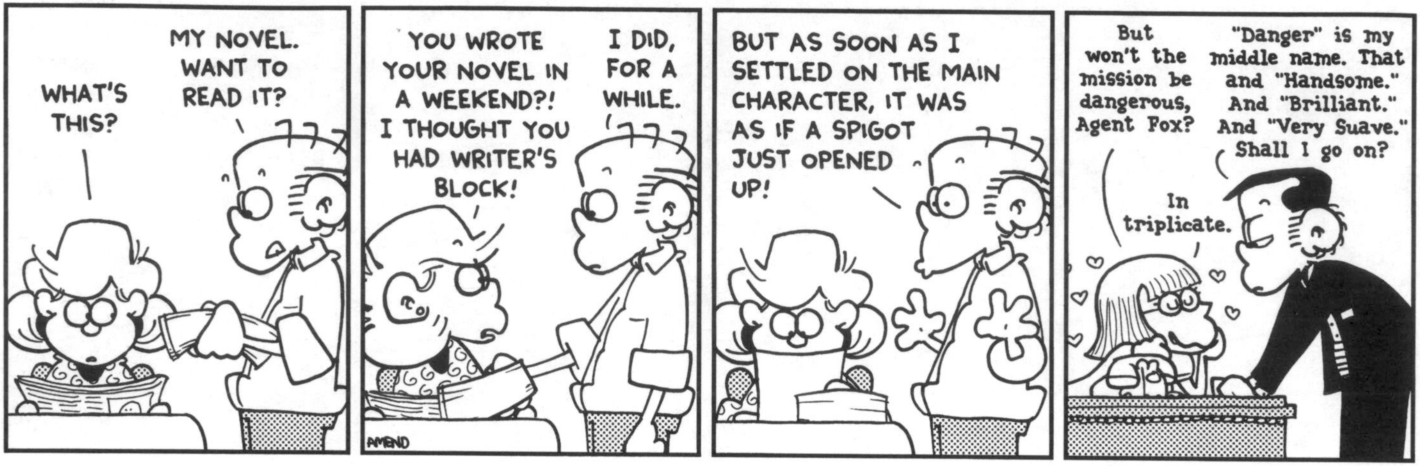
WHAT'S THIS?
MY NOVEL. WANT TO READ IT?
YOU WROTE YOUR NOVEL IN A WEEKEND?! I THOUGHT YOU HAD WRITER'S BLOCK!
I DID, FOR A WHILE.
AMEND
BUT AS SOON AS I SETTLED ON THE MAIN CHARACTER, IT WAS AS IF A SPIGOT JUST OPENED UP!
But won't the mission be dangerous, Agent Fox?
"Danger" is my middle name. That and "Handsome." And "Brilliant." And "Very Suave." Shall I go on?
In triplicate.

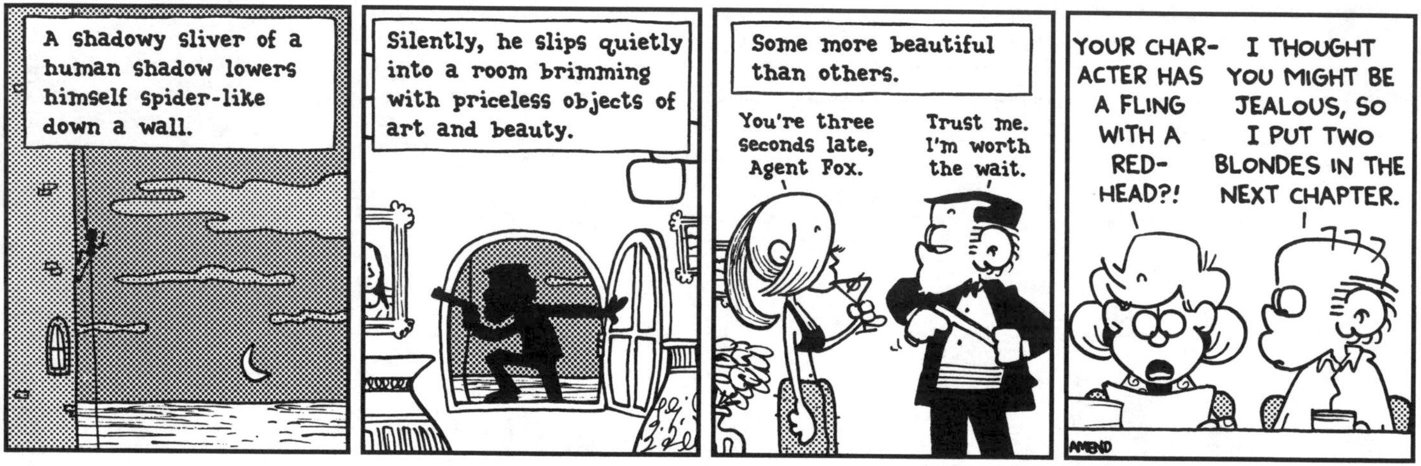
A shadowy sliver of a human shadow lowers himself spider-like down a wall.
Silently, he slips quietly into a room brimming with priceless objects of art and beauty.
Some more beautiful than others.
You're three seconds late, Agent Fox.
Trust me. I'm worth the wait.
YOUR CHARACTER HAS A FLING WITH A RED-HEAD?!
I THOUGHT YOU MIGHT BE JEALOUS, SO I PUT TWO BLONDES IN THE NEXT CHAPTER.
AMEND

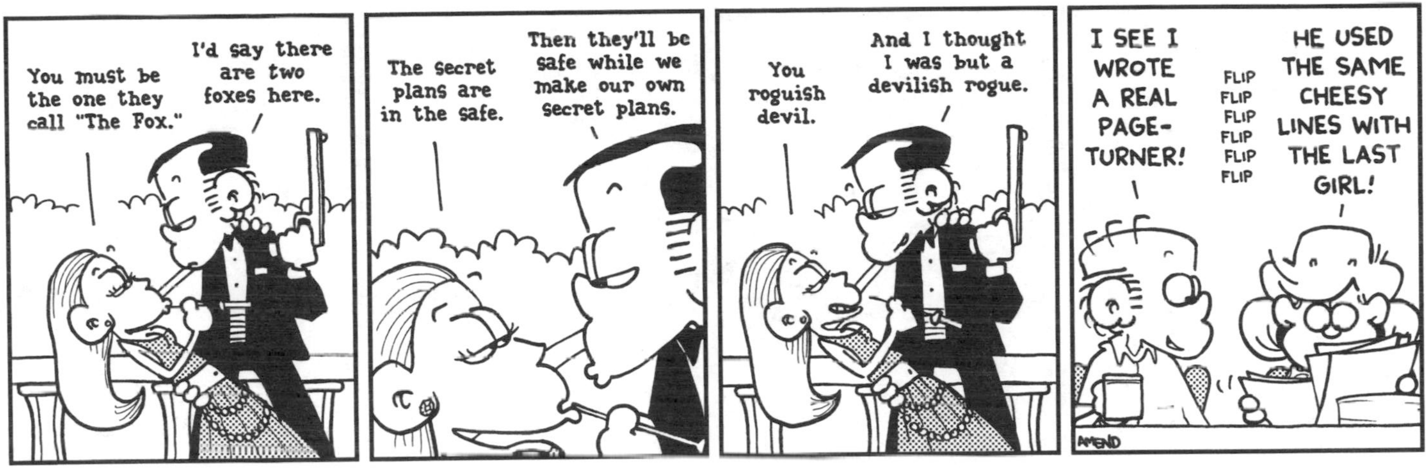
You must be the one they call "The Fox."
I'd say there are two foxes here.
The secret plans are in the safe.
Then they'll be safe while we make our own secret plans.
You roguish devil.
And I thought I was but a devilish rogue.
I SEE I WROTE A REAL PAGE-TURNER!
FLIP FLIP FLIP FLIP FLIP FLIP
HE USED THE SAME CHEESY LINES WITH THE LAST GIRL!
AMEND

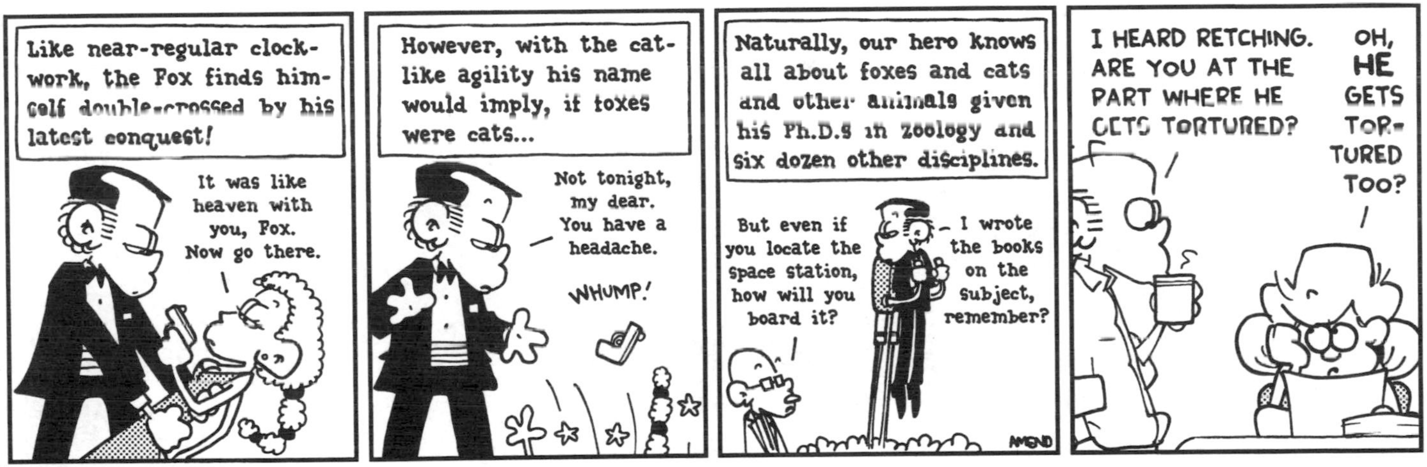
Like near-regular clockwork, the Fox finds himself double-crossed by his latest conquest!
It was like heaven with you, Fox. Now go there.
However, with the cat-like agility his name would imply, if foxes were cats...
Not tonight, my dear. You have a headache.
WHUMP!
Naturally, our hero knows all about foxes and cats and other animals given his Ph.D.s in zoology and six dozen other disciplines.
But even if you locate the space station, how will you board it?
I wrote the books on the subject, remember?
AMEND
I HEARD RETCHING. ARE YOU AT THE PART WHERE HE GETS TORTURED?
OH, HE GETS TOR-TURED TOO?

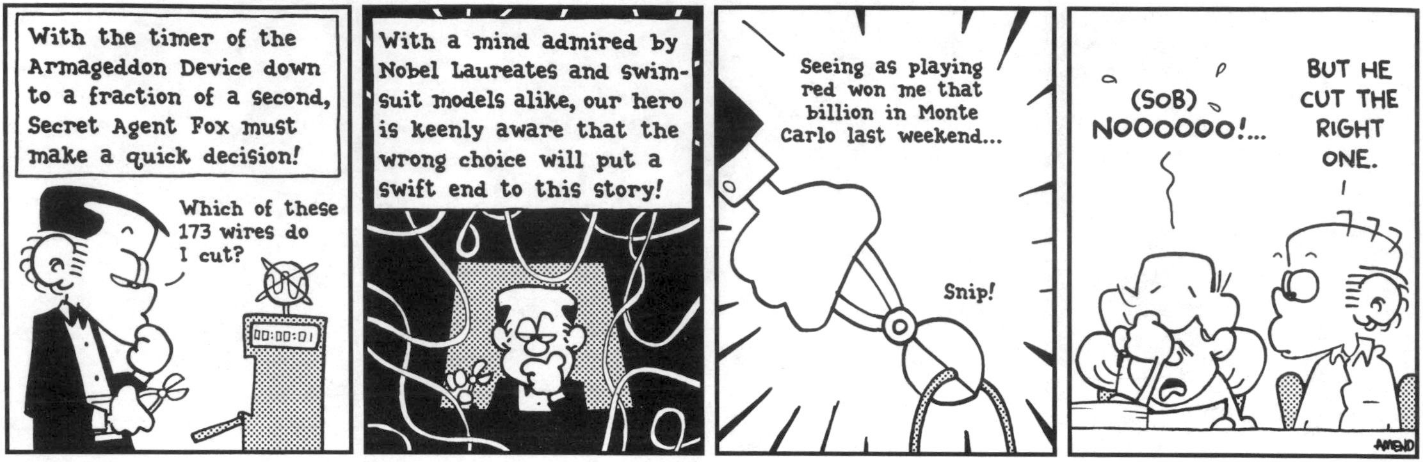
With the timer of the Armageddon Device down to a fraction of a second, Secret Agent Fox must make a quick decision!
Which of these 173 wires do I cut?
00:00:01
With a mind admired by Nobel Laureates and swim-suit models alike, our hero is keenly aware that the wrong choice will put a swift end to this story!
Seeing as playing red won me that billion in Monte Carlo last weekend...
Snip!
(SOB) NOOOOOO!...
BUT HE CUT THE RIGHT ONE.
AMEND

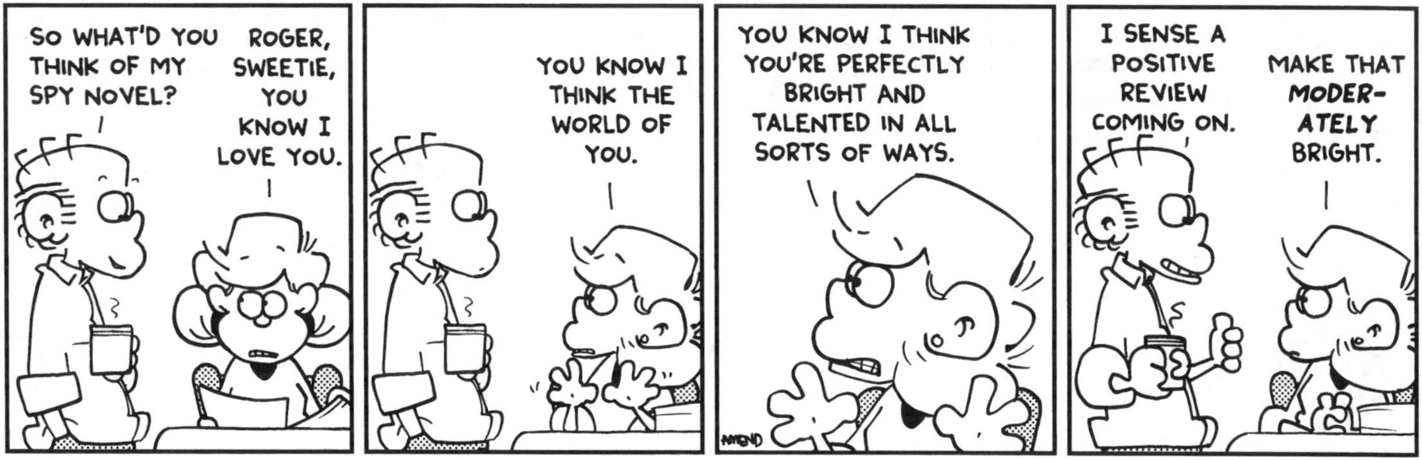
SO WHAT'D YOU THINK OF MY SPY NOVEL?
ROGER, SWEETIE, YOU KNOW I LOVE YOU.
YOU KNOW I THINK THE WORLD OF YOU.
YOU KNOW I THINK YOU'RE PERFECTLY BRIGHT AND TALENTED IN ALL SORTS OF WAYS.
AMEND
I SENSE A POSITIVE REVIEW COMING ON.
MAKE THAT *MODER-ATELY* BRIGHT.

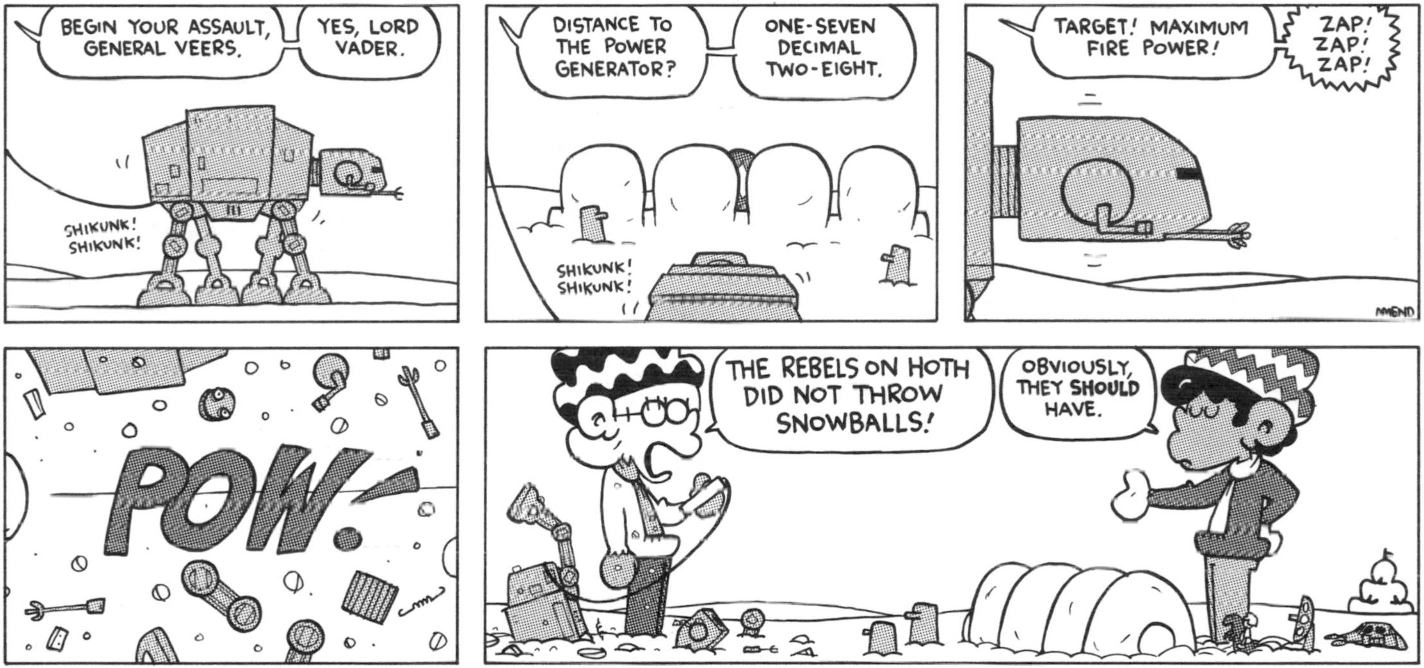
BEGIN YOUR ASSAULT, GENERAL VEERS.
YES, LORD VADER.
SHIKUNK! SHIKUNK!
DISTANCE TO THE POWER GENERATOR?
ONE-SEVEN DECIMAL TWO-EIGHT.
SHIKUNK! SHIKUNK!
TARGET! MAXIMUM FIRE POWER!
ZAP! ZAP! ZAP!
POW!
THE REBELS ON HOTH DID NOT THROW SNOWBALLS!
OBVIOUSLY, THEY SHOULD HAVE.

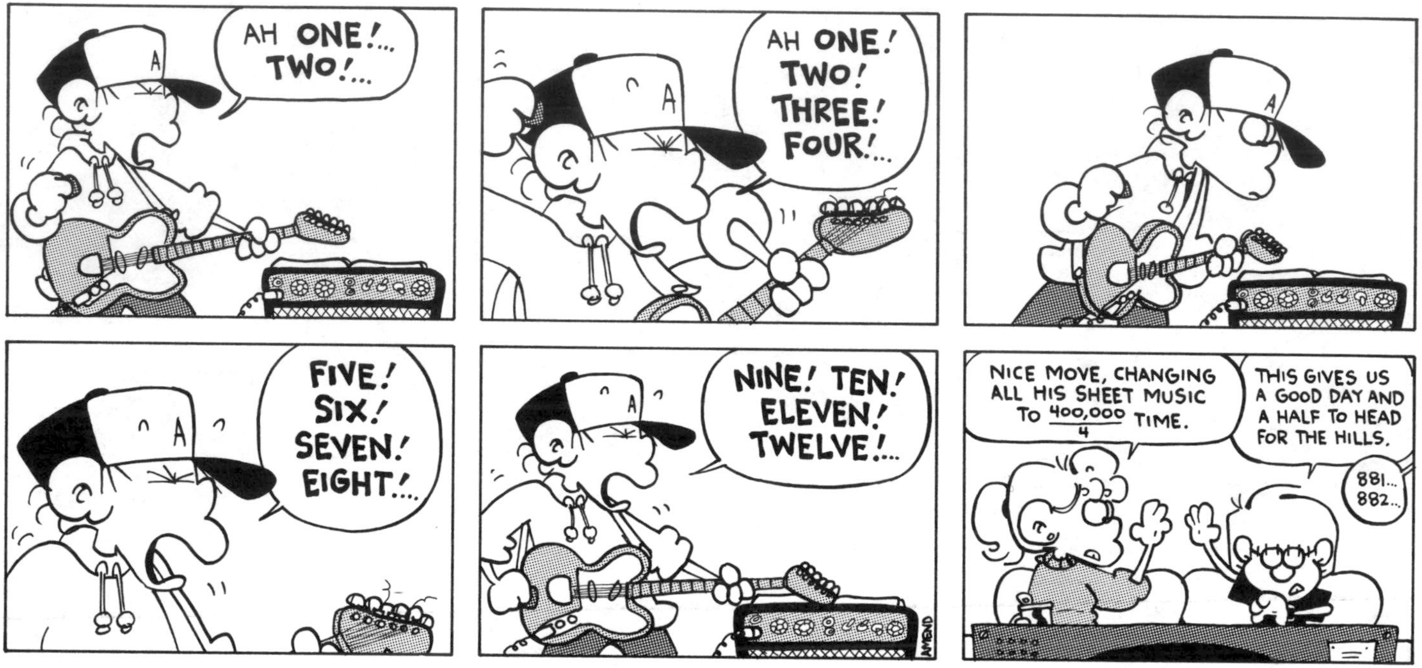

AH ONE!... TWO!...
AH ONE! TWO! THREE! FOUR!...
FIVE! SIX! SEVEN! EIGHT!...
NINE! TEN! ELEVEN! TWELVE!...
NICE MOVE, CHANGING ALL HIS SHEET MUSIC TO 400,000/4 TIME.
THIS GIVES US A GOOD DAY AND A HALF TO HEAD FOR THE HILLS.
881... 882...

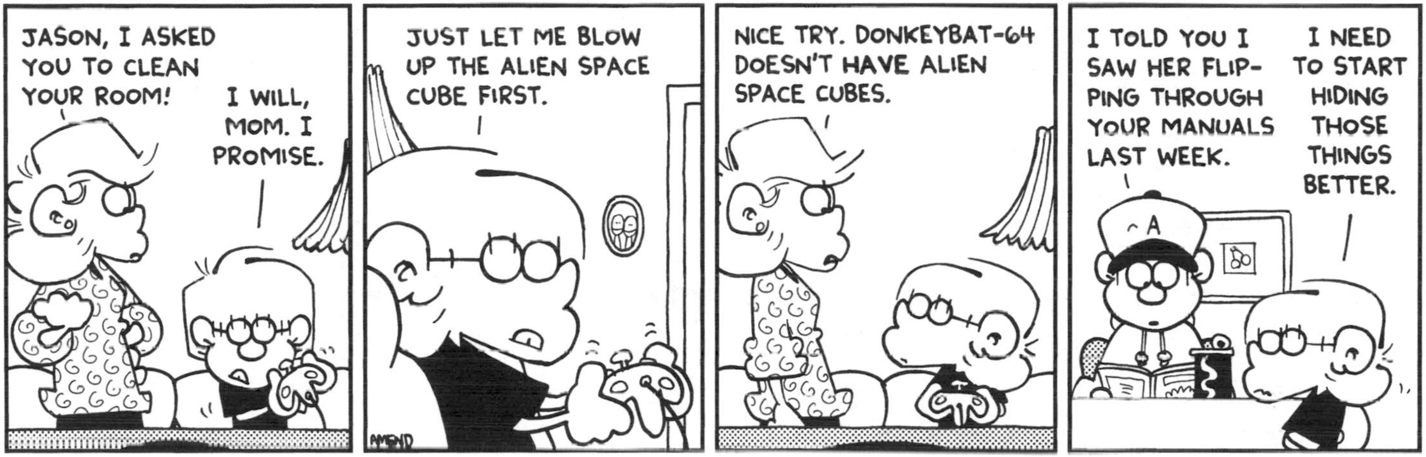
JASON, I ASKED YOU TO CLEAN YOUR ROOM!
I WILL, MOM. I PROMISE.
JUST LET ME BLOW UP THE ALIEN SPACE CUBE FIRST.
NICE TRY. DONKEYBAT-64 DOESN'T HAVE ALIEN SPACE CUBES.
I TOLD YOU I SAW HER FLIP-PING THROUGH YOUR MANUALS LAST WEEK.
I NEED TO START HIDING THOSE THINGS BETTER.

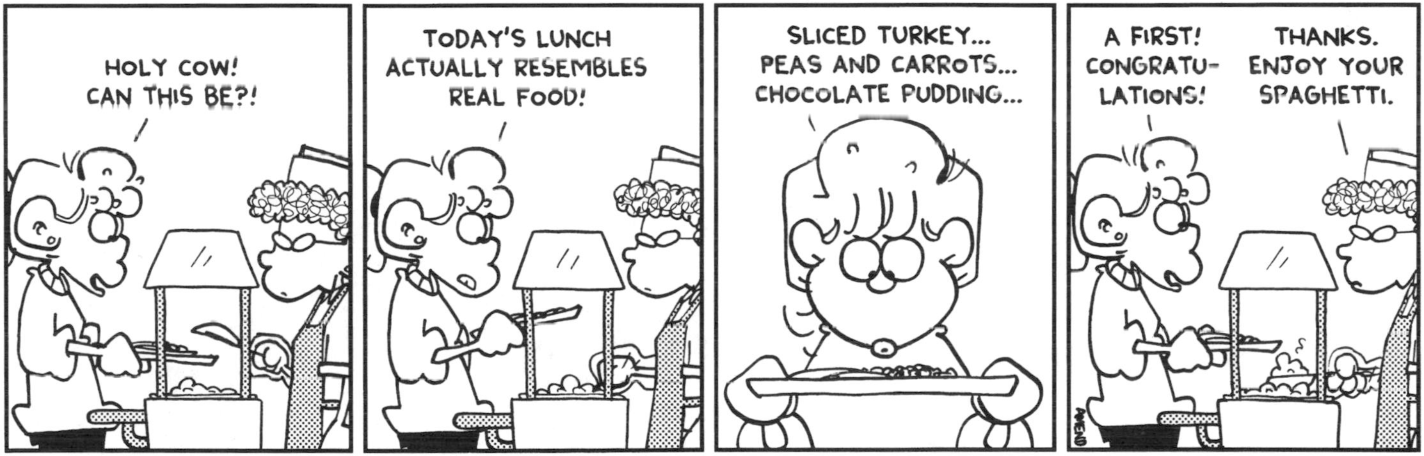
HOLY COW! CAN THIS BE?!
TODAY'S LUNCH ACTUALLY RESEMBLES REAL FOOD!
SLICED TURKEY... PEAS AND CARROTS... CHOCOLATE PUDDING...
A FIRST! CONGRATU-LATIONS!
THANKS. ENJOY YOUR SPAGHETTI.

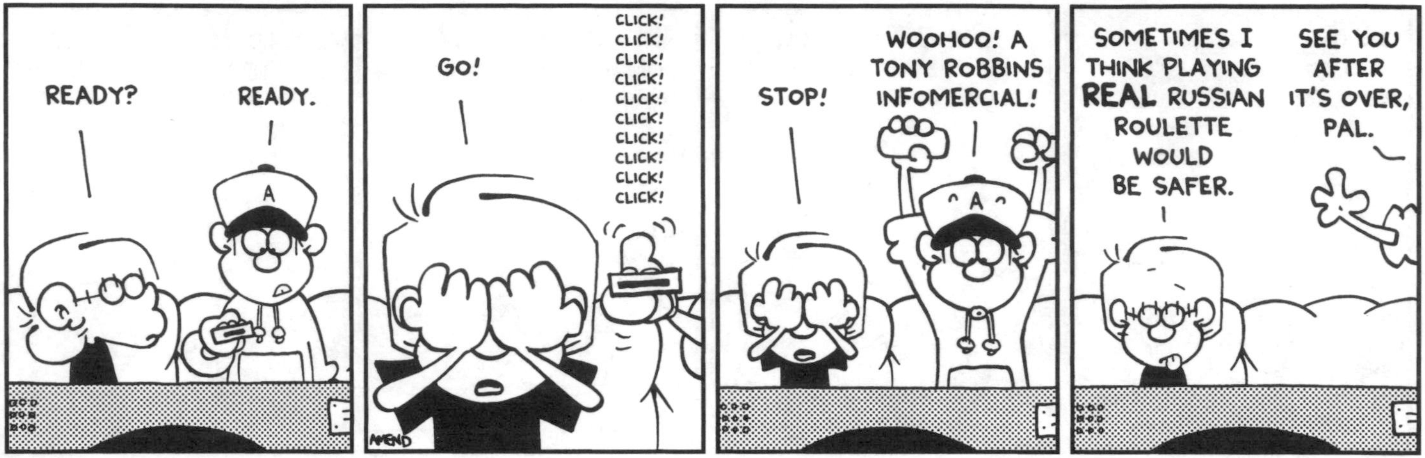
READY?
READY.
GO!
CLICK! CLICK! CLICK! CLICK! CLICK! CLICK! CLICK! CLICK! CLICK! CLICK!
STOP!
WOOHOO! A TONY ROBBINS INFOMERCIAL!
SOMETIMES I THINK PLAYING **REAL** RUSSIAN ROULETTE WOULD BE SAFER.
SEE YOU AFTER IT'S OVER, PAL.
AMEND

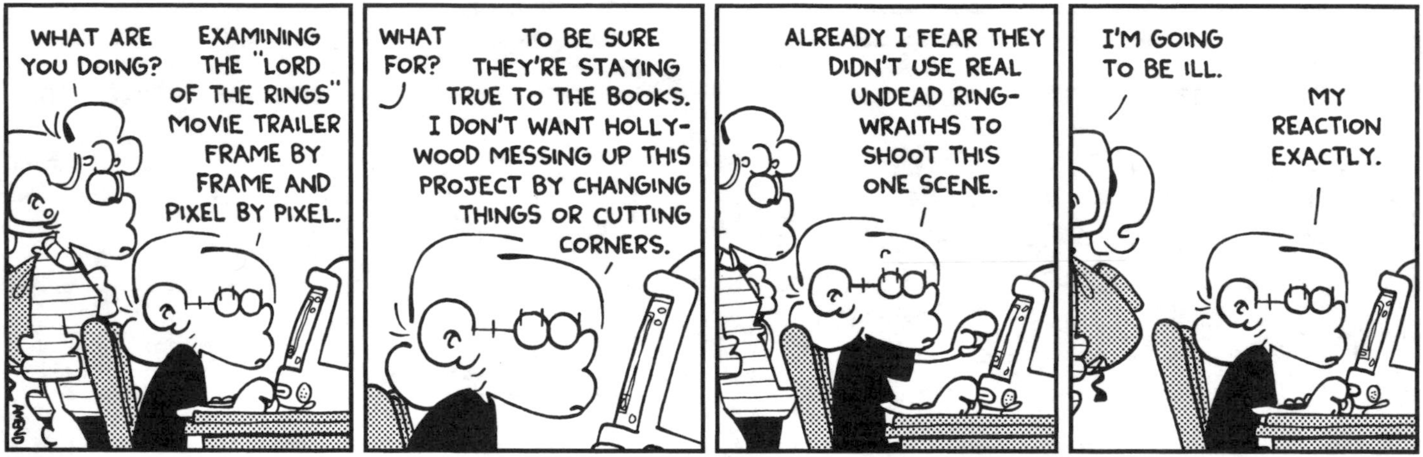
WHAT ARE YOU DOING?
EXAMINING THE "LORD OF THE RINGS" MOVIE TRAILER FRAME BY FRAME AND PIXEL BY PIXEL.
AMEND
WHAT FOR?
TO BE SURE THEY'RE STAYING TRUE TO THE BOOKS. I DON'T WANT HOLLY-WOOD MESSING UP THIS PROJECT BY CHANGING THINGS OR CUTTING CORNERS.
ALREADY I FEAR THEY DIDN'T USE REAL UNDEAD RING-WRAITHS TO SHOOT THIS ONE SCENE.
I'M GOING TO BE ILL.
MY REACTION EXACTLY.

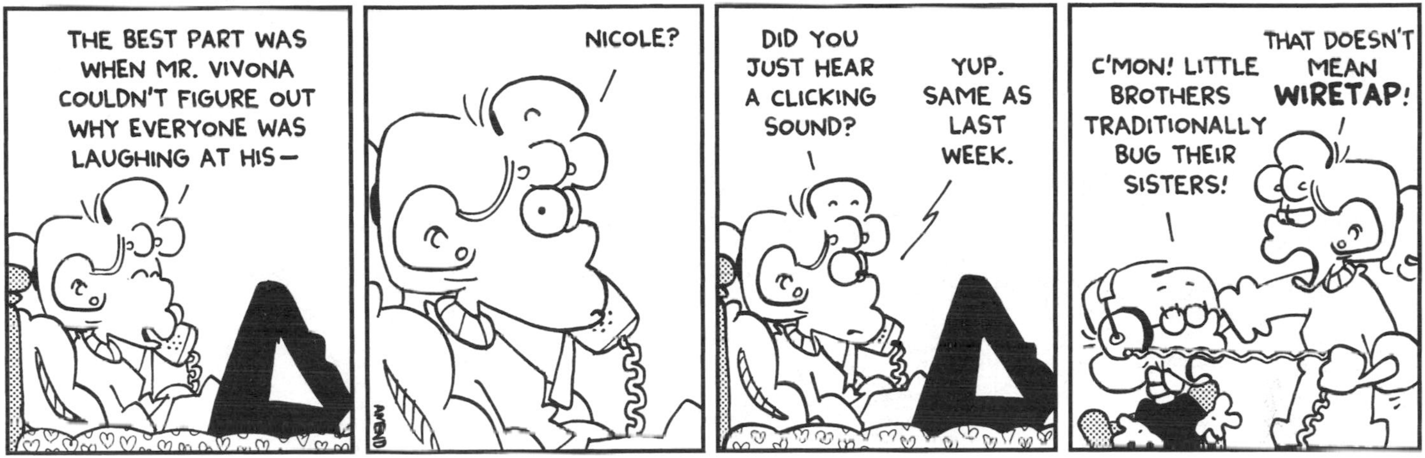
THE BEST PART WAS WHEN MR. VIVONA COULDN'T FIGURE OUT WHY EVERYONE WAS LAUGHING AT HIS—
NICOLE?
AMEND
DID YOU JUST HEAR A CLICKING SOUND?
YUP. SAME AS LAST WEEK.
C'MON! LITTLE BROTHERS TRADITIONALLY BUG THEIR SISTERS!
THAT DOESN'T MEAN WIRETAP!

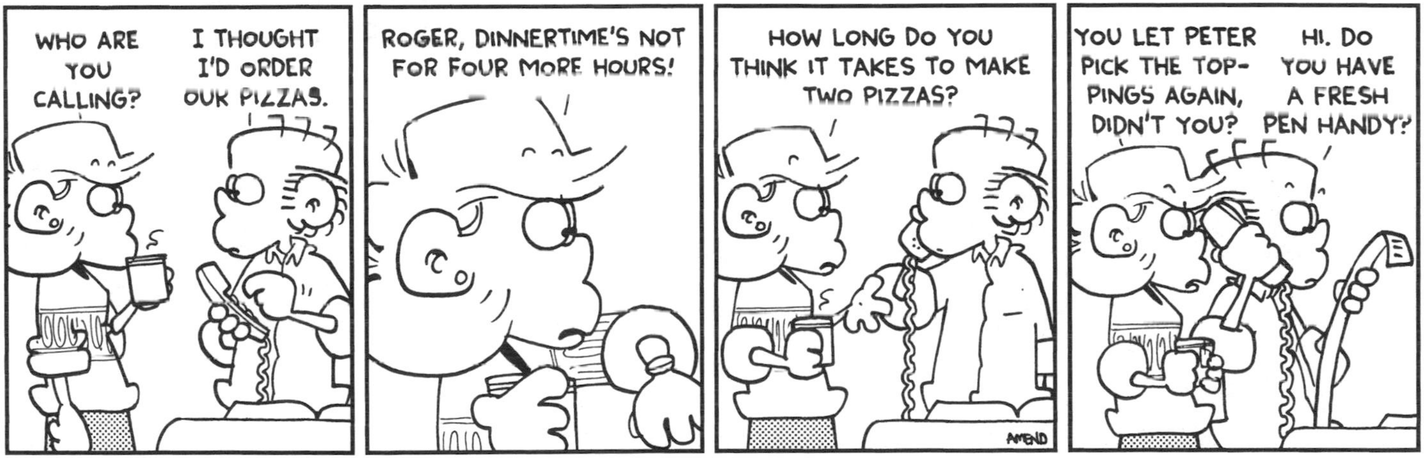
WHO ARE YOU CALLING?
I THOUGHT I'D ORDER OUR PIZZAS.
ROGER, DINNERTIME'S NOT FOR FOUR MORE HOURS!
HOW LONG DO YOU THINK IT TAKES TO MAKE TWO PIZZAS?
AMEND
YOU LET PETER PICK THE TOP-PINGS AGAIN, DIDN'T YOU?
HI. DO YOU HAVE A FRESH PEN HANDY?

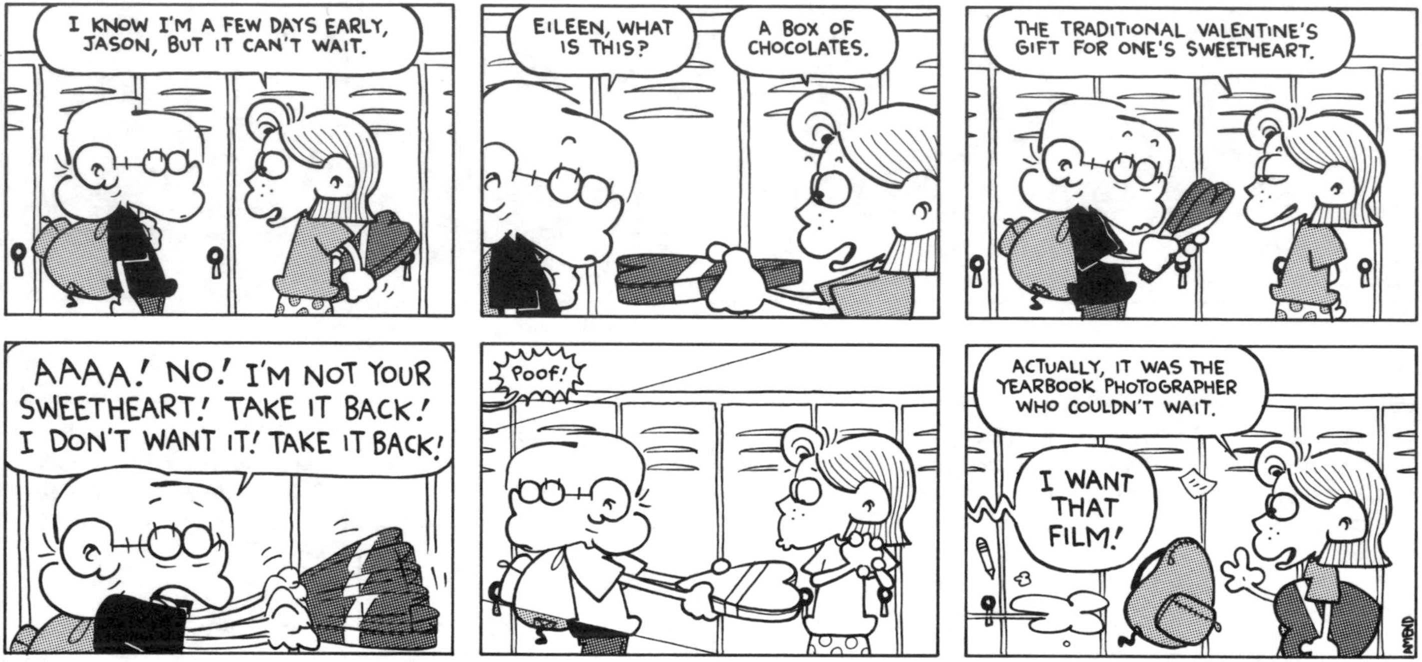
I KNOW I'M A FEW DAYS EARLY, JASON, BUT IT CAN'T WAIT.
EILEEN, WHAT IS THIS?
A BOX OF CHOCOLATES.
THE TRADITIONAL VALENTINE'S GIFT FOR ONE'S SWEETHEART.
AAAA! NO! I'M NOT YOUR SWEETHEART! TAKE IT BACK! I DON'T WANT IT! TAKE IT BACK!
Poof!
ACTUALLY, IT WAS THE YEARBOOK PHOTOGRAPHER WHO COULDN'T WAIT.
I WANT THAT FILM!
AMEND

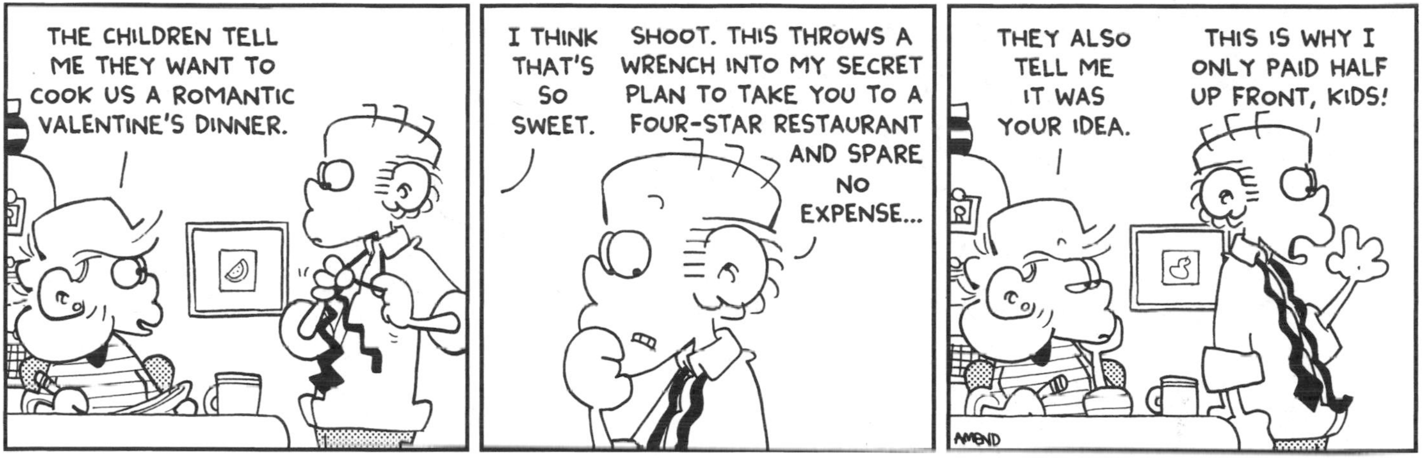
THE CHILDREN TELL ME THEY WANT TO COOK US A ROMANTIC VALENTINE'S DINNER.
I THINK THAT'S SO SWEET.
SHOOT. THIS THROWS A WRENCH INTO MY SECRET PLAN TO TAKE YOU TO A FOUR-STAR RESTAURANT AND SPARE NO EXPENSE...
THEY ALSO TELL ME IT WAS YOUR IDEA.
THIS IS WHY I ONLY PAID HALF UP FRONT, KIDS!
AMEND

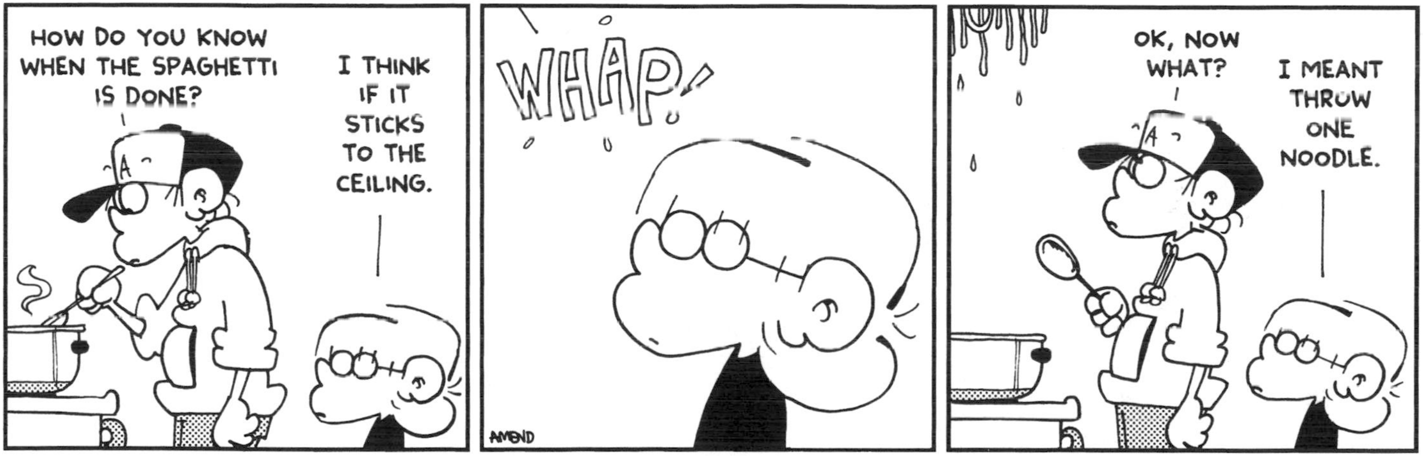
HOW DO YOU KNOW WHEN THE SPAGHETTI IS DONE?
I THINK IF IT STICKS TO THE CEILING.
WHAP!
AMEND
OK, NOW WHAT?
I MEANT THROW ONE NOODLE.

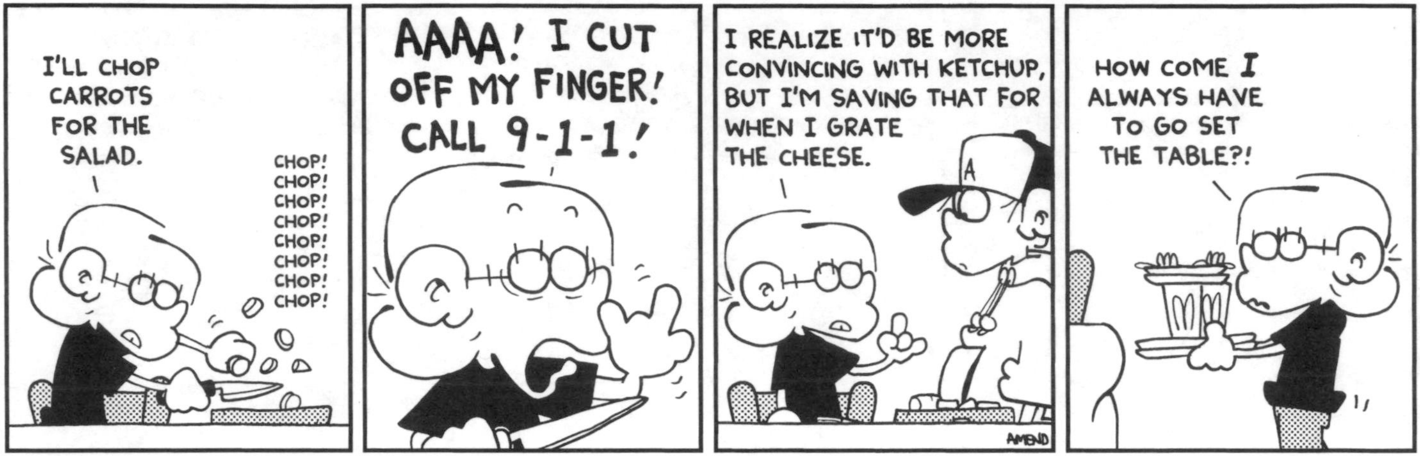
I'LL CHOP CARROTS FOR THE SALAD.
CHOP! CHOP! CHOP! CHOP! CHOP! CHOP! CHOP! CHOP!
AAAA! I CUT OFF MY FINGER! CALL 9-1-1!
I REALIZE IT'D BE MORE CONVINCING WITH KETCHUP, BUT I'M SAVING THAT FOR WHEN I GRATE THE CHEESE.
AMEND
HOW COME *I* ALWAYS HAVE TO GO SET THE TABLE?!

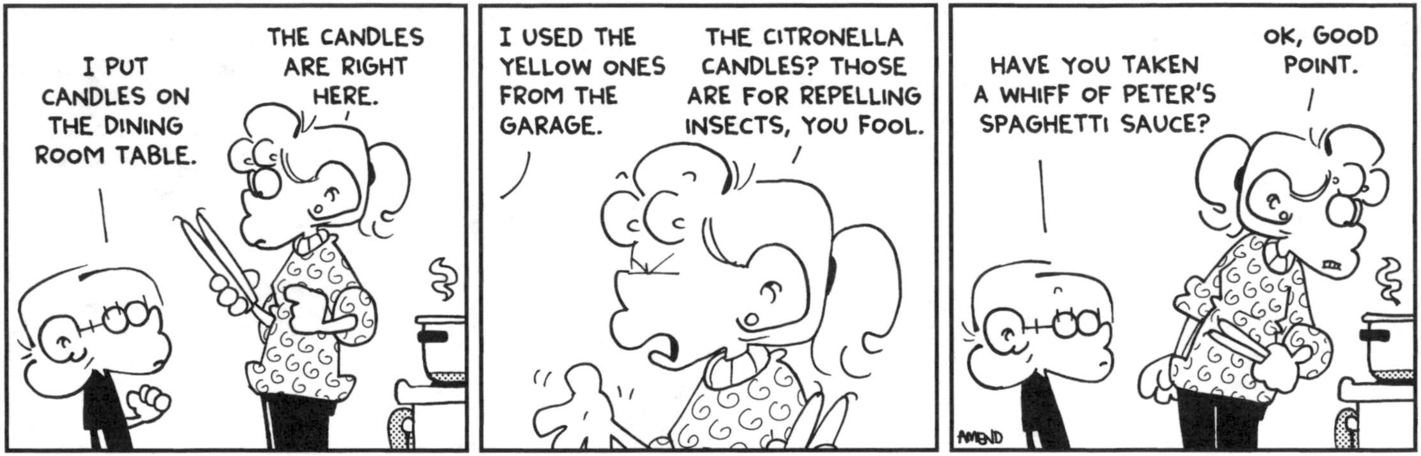
I PUT CANDLES ON THE DINING ROOM TABLE.
THE CANDLES ARE RIGHT HERE.
I USED THE YELLOW ONES FROM THE GARAGE.
THE CITRONELLA CANDLES? THOSE ARE FOR REPELLING INSECTS, YOU FOOL.
HAVE YOU TAKEN A WHIFF OF PETER'S SPAGHETTI SAUCE?
OK, GOOD POINT.
AMEND

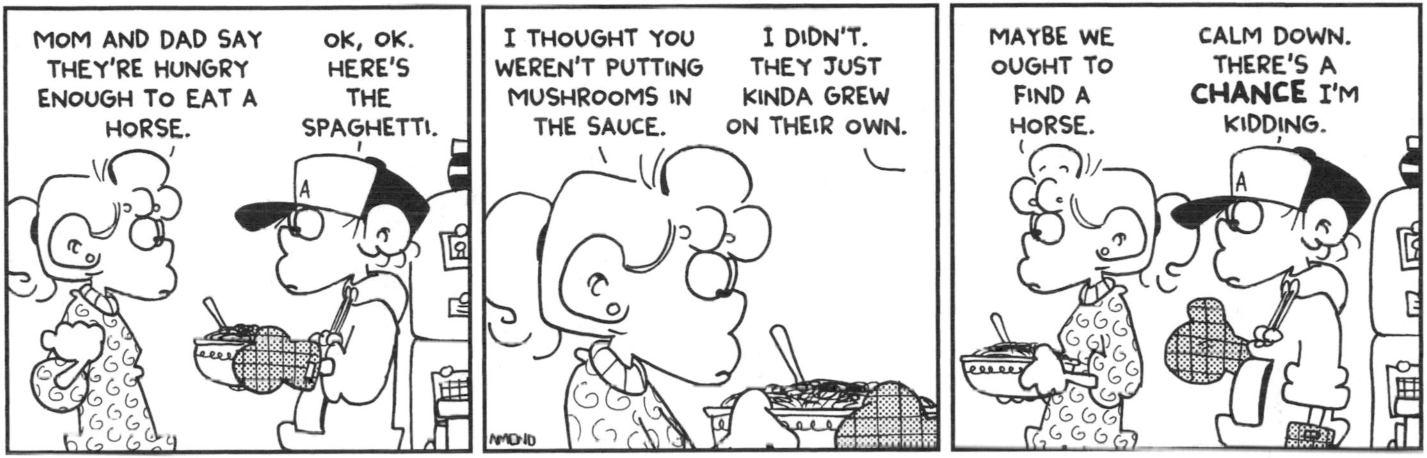
MOM AND DAD SAY THEY'RE HUNGRY ENOUGH TO EAT A HORSE.
OK, OK. HERE'S THE SPAGHETTI.
I THOUGHT YOU WEREN'T PUTTING MUSHROOMS IN THE SAUCE.
I DIDN'T. THEY JUST KINDA GREW ON THEIR OWN.
MAYBE WE OUGHT TO FIND A HORSE.
CALM DOWN. THERE'S A **CHANCE** I'M KIDDING.
AMEND

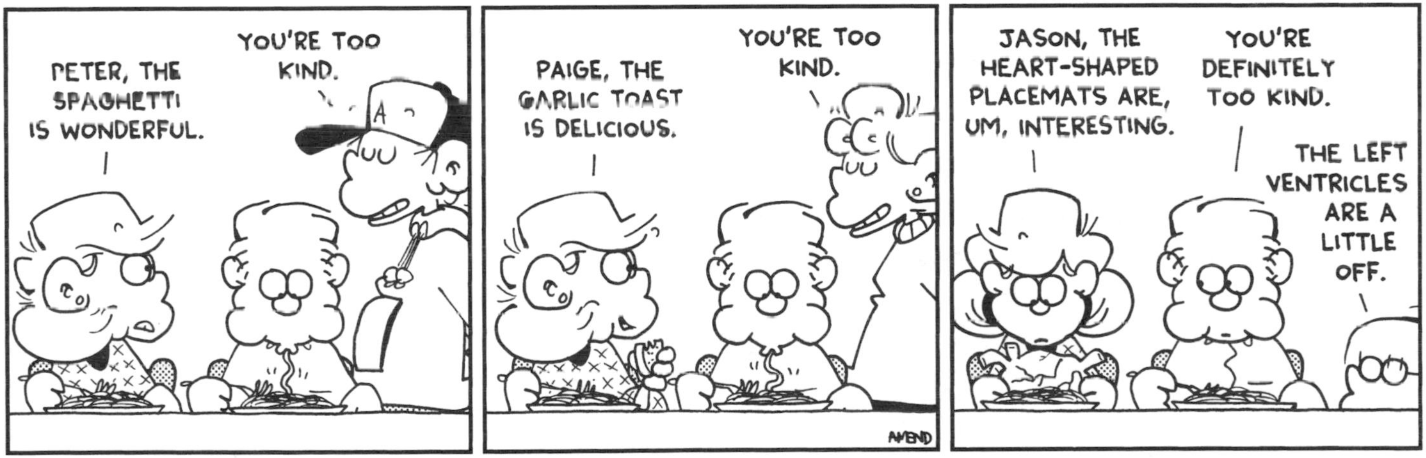
PETER, THE SPAGHETTI IS WONDERFUL.
YOU'RE TOO KIND.
PAIGE, THE GARLIC TOAST IS DELICIOUS.
YOU'RE TOO KIND.
JASON, THE HEART-SHAPED PLACEMATS ARE, UM, INTERESTING.
YOU'RE DEFINITELY TOO KIND.
THE LEFT VENTRICLES ARE A LITTLE OFF.
AMEND

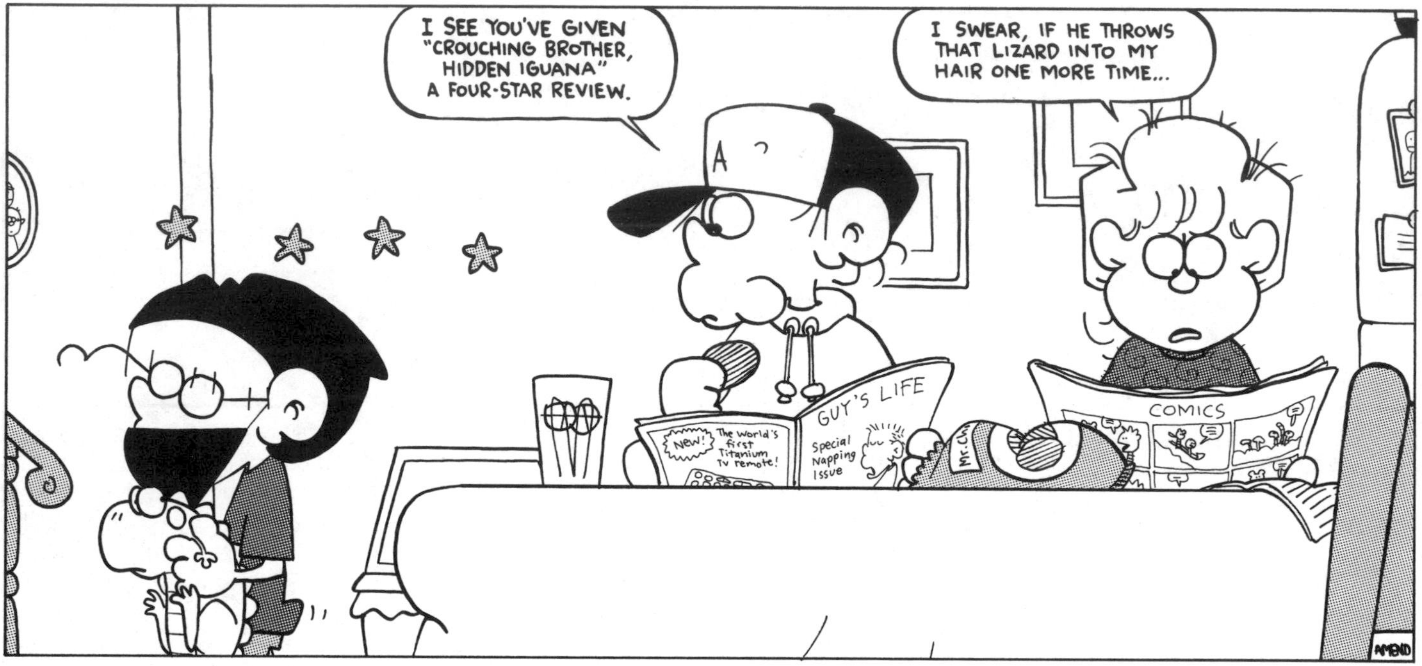
I SEE YOU'VE GIVEN "CROUCHING BROTHER, HIDDEN IGUANA" A FOUR-STAR REVIEW.
I SWEAR, IF HE THROWS THAT LIZARD INTO MY HAIR ONE MORE TIME...
GUY'S LIFE
New!
The world's first Titanium TV remote!
Special Napping Issue
COMICS
AMEND

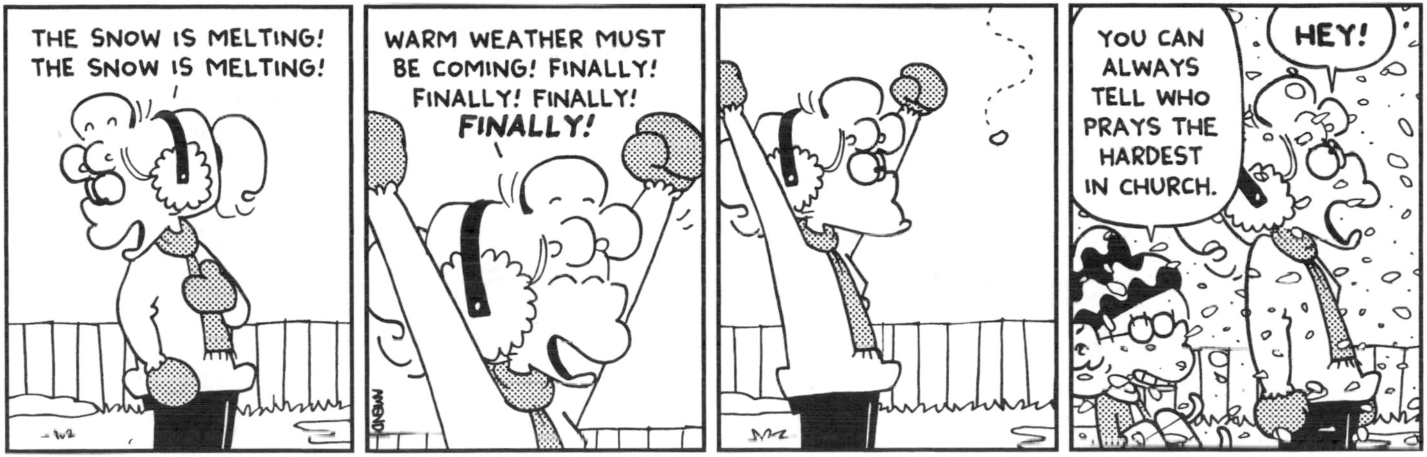
THE SNOW IS MELTING! THE SNOW IS MELTING!
WARM WEATHER MUST BE COMING! FINALLY! FINALLY! FINALLY! FINALLY!
YOU CAN ALWAYS TELL WHO PRAYS THE HARDEST IN CHURCH.
HEY!

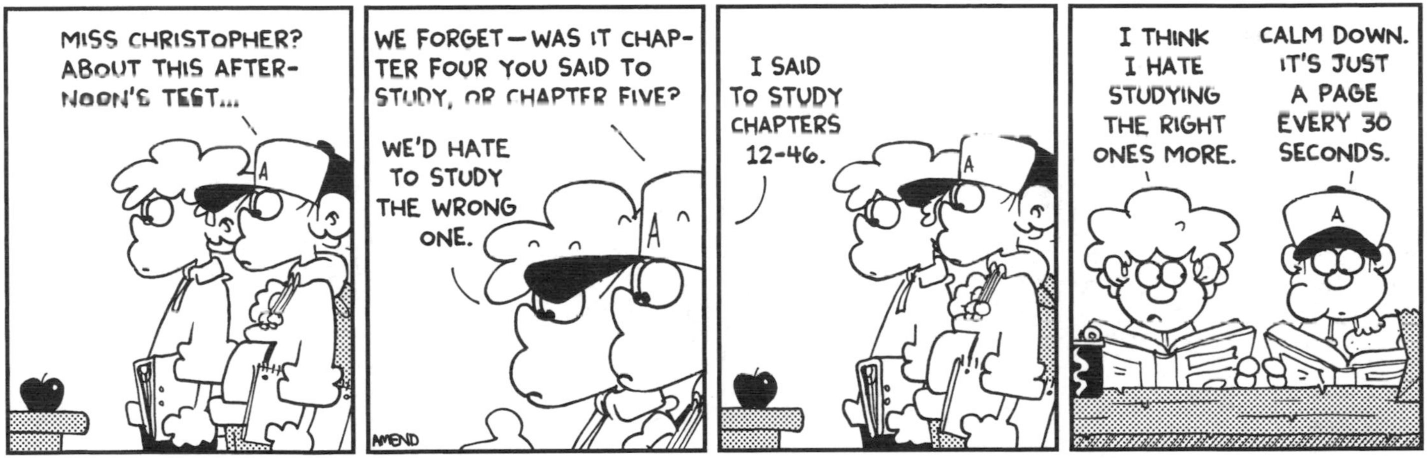
MISS CHRISTOPHER? ABOUT THIS AFTER-NOON'S TEST...
WE FORGET—WAS IT CHAP-TER FOUR YOU SAID TO STUDY, OR CHAPTER FIVE?
WE'D HATE TO STUDY THE WRONG ONE.
AMEND
I SAID TO STUDY CHAPTERS 12-46.
I THINK I HATE STUDYING THE RIGHT ONES MORE.
CALM DOWN. IT'S JUST A PAGE EVERY 30 SECONDS.

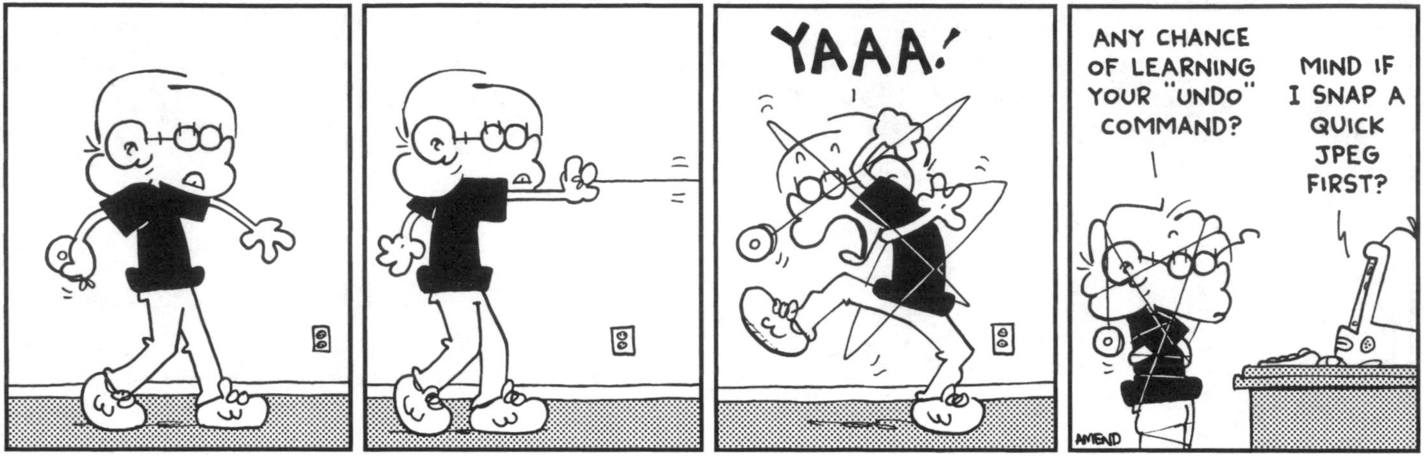
YAAA!
ANY CHANCE OF LEARNING YOUR "UNDO" COMMAND?
MIND IF I SNAP A QUICK JPEG FIRST?
AMEND

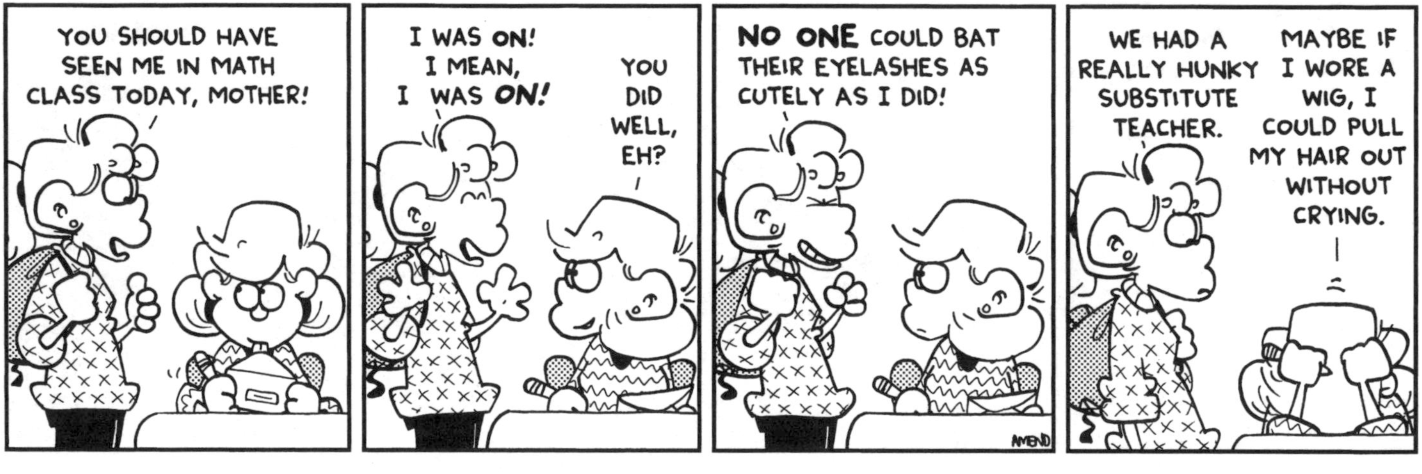
YOU SHOULD HAVE SEEN ME IN MATH CLASS TODAY, MOTHER!
I WAS ON! I MEAN, I WAS **ON!**
YOU DID WELL, EH?
NO ONE COULD BAT THEIR EYELASHES AS CUTELY AS I DID!
AMEND
WE HAD A REALLY HUNKY SUBSTITUTE TEACHER.
MAYBE IF I WORE A WIG, I COULD PULL MY HAIR OUT WITHOUT CRYING.

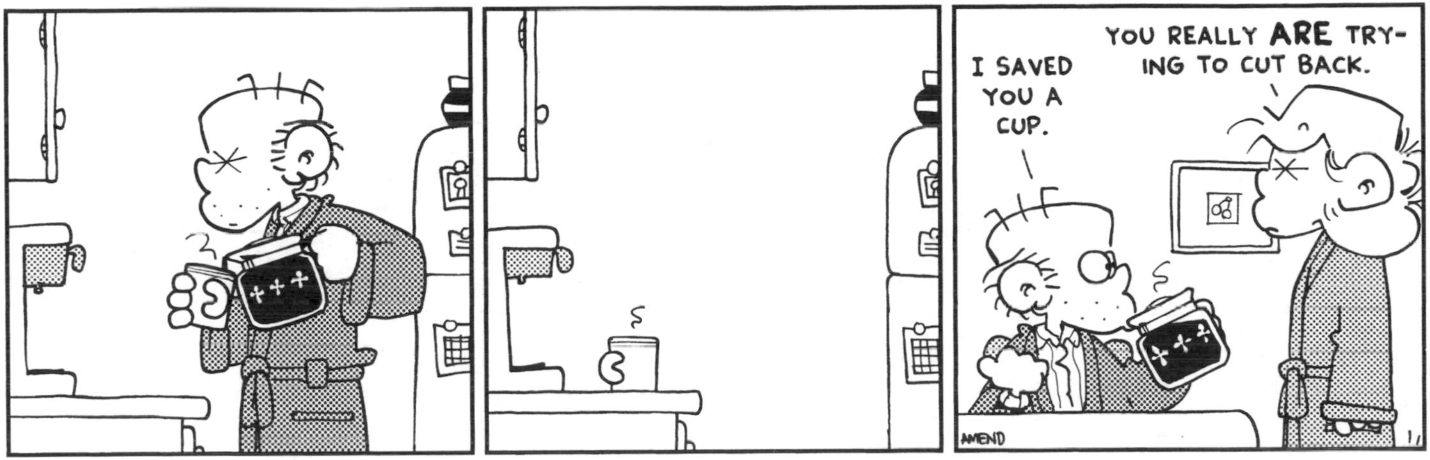
I SAVED YOU A CUP.
YOU REALLY **ARE** TRYING TO CUT BACK.
AMEND

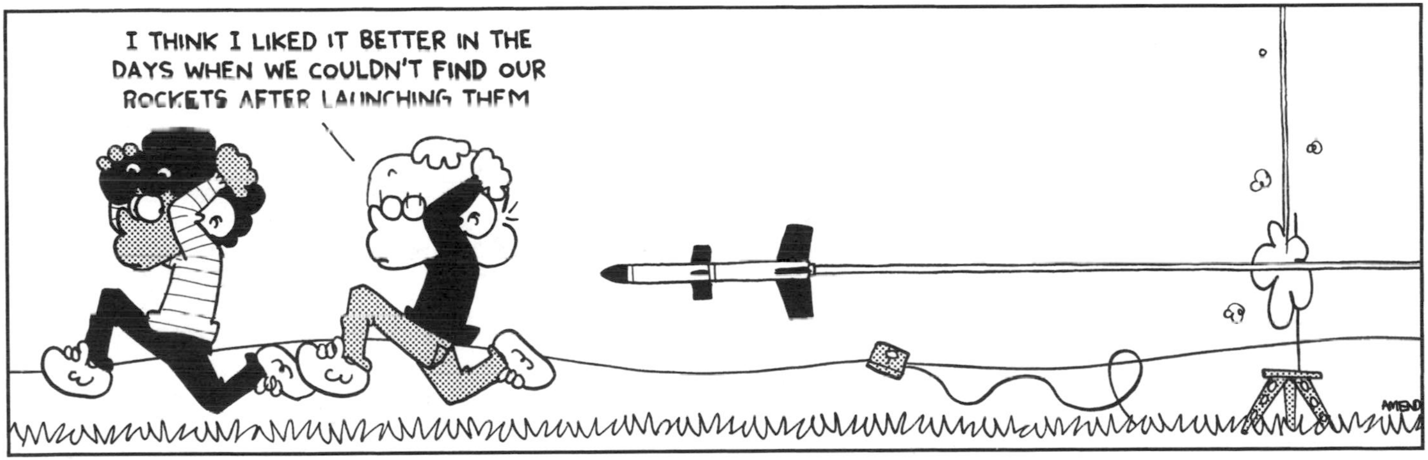
I THINK I LIKED IT BETTER IN THE DAYS WHEN WE COULDN'T FIND OUR ROCKETS AFTER LAUNCHING THEM
AMEND

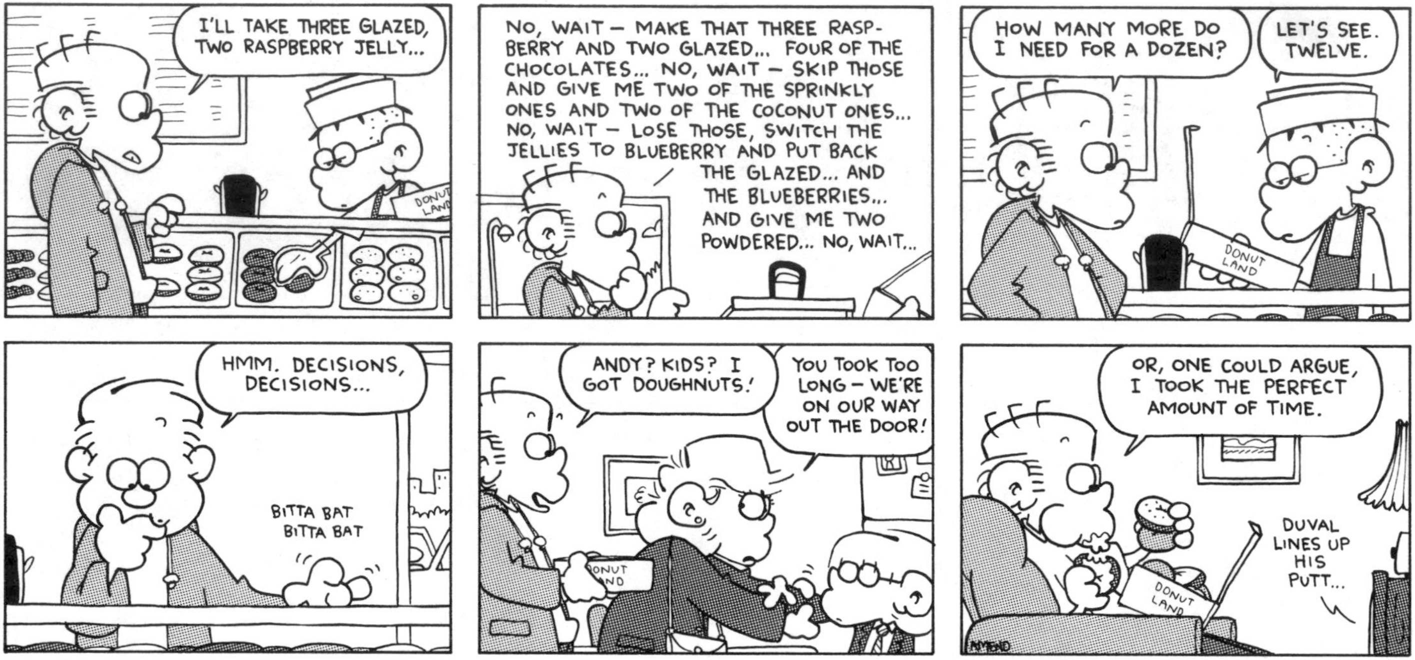
I'LL TAKE THREE GLAZED, TWO RASPBERRY JELLY...
DONUT LAND
NO, WAIT – MAKE THAT THREE RASPBERRY AND TWO GLAZED... FOUR OF THE CHOCOLATES... NO, WAIT – SKIP THOSE AND GIVE ME TWO OF THE SPRINKLY ONES AND TWO OF THE COCONUT ONES... NO, WAIT – LOSE THOSE, SWITCH THE JELLIES TO BLUEBERRY AND PUT BACK THE GLAZED... AND THE BLUEBERRIES... AND GIVE ME TWO POWDERED... NO, WAIT...
HOW MANY MORE DO I NEED FOR A DOZEN?
LET'S SEE. TWELVE.
DONUT LAND
HMM. DECISIONS, DECISIONS...
BITTA BAT BITTA BAT
ANDY? KIDS? I GOT DOUGHNUTS!
YOU TOOK TOO LONG – WE'RE ON OUR WAY OUT THE DOOR!
OR, ONE COULD ARGUE, I TOOK THE PERFECT AMOUNT OF TIME.
DUVAL LINES UP HIS PUTT...
DONUT LAND
AMEND

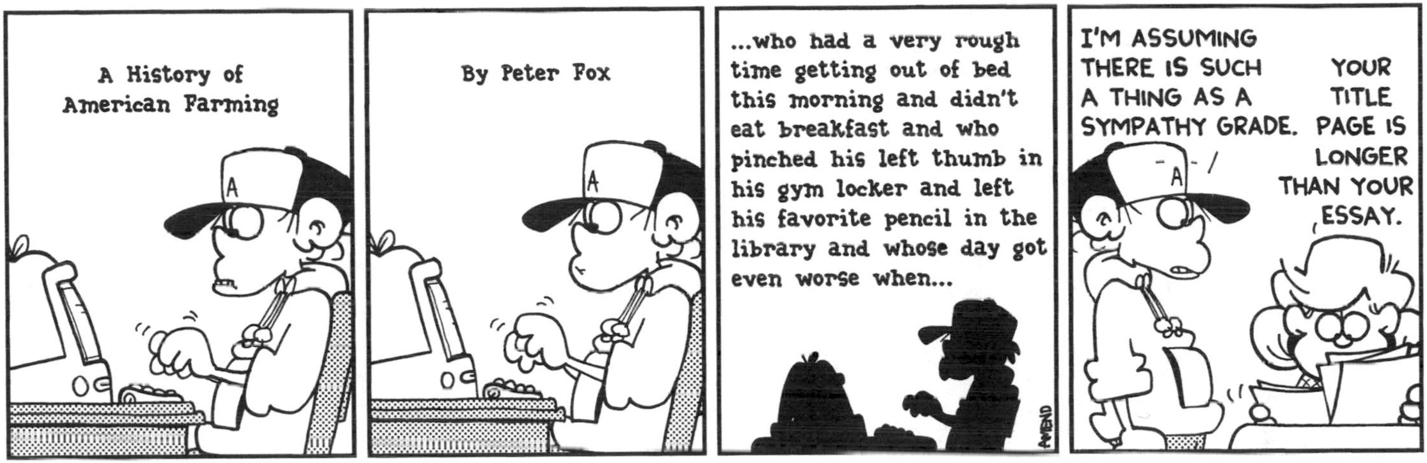
A History of American Farming
By Peter Fox
...who had a very rough time getting out of bed this morning and didn't eat breakfast and who pinched his left thumb in his gym locker and left his favorite pencil in the library and whose day got even worse when...
AMEND
I'M ASSUMING THERE IS SUCH A THING AS A SYMPATHY GRADE.
YOUR TITLE PAGE IS LONGER THAN YOUR ESSAY.

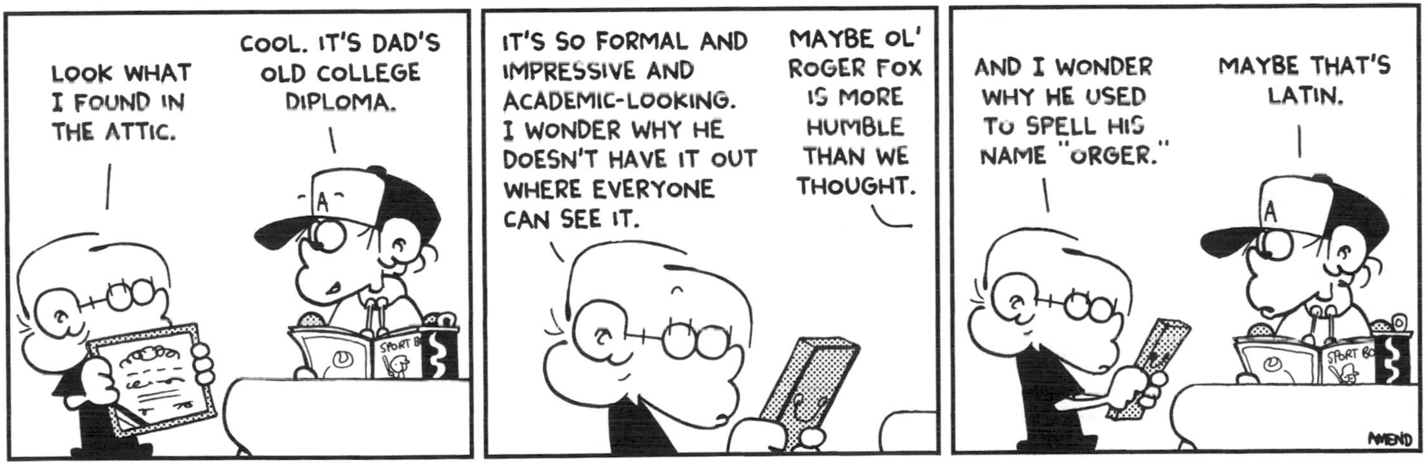
LOOK WHAT I FOUND IN THE ATTIC.
COOL. IT'S DAD'S OLD COLLEGE DIPLOMA.
IT'S SO FORMAL AND IMPRESSIVE AND ACADEMIC-LOOKING. I WONDER WHY HE DOESN'T HAVE IT OUT WHERE EVERYONE CAN SEE IT.
MAYBE OL' ROGER FOX IS MORE HUMBLE THAN WE THOUGHT.
AND I WONDER WHY HE USED TO SPELL HIS NAME "ORGER."
MAYBE THAT'S LATIN.
AMEND

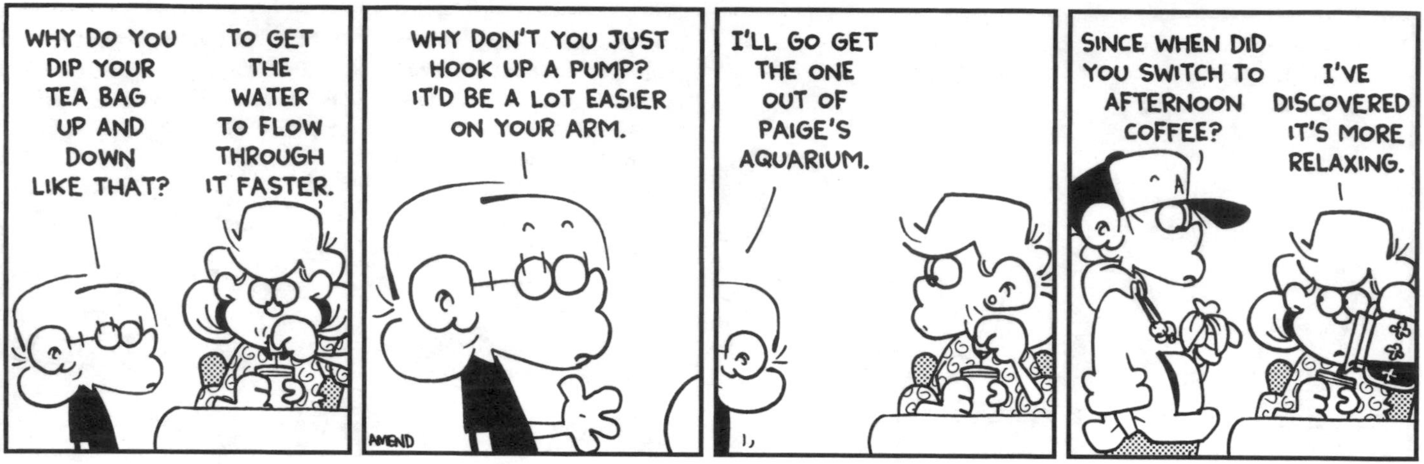
WHY DO YOU DIP YOUR TEA BAG UP AND DOWN LIKE THAT?
TO GET THE WATER TO FLOW THROUGH IT FASTER.
WHY DON'T YOU JUST HOOK UP A PUMP? IT'D BE A LOT EASIER ON YOUR ARM.
AMEND
I'LL GO GET THE ONE OUT OF PAIGE'S AQUARIUM.
SINCE WHEN DID YOU SWITCH TO AFTERNOON COFFEE?
I'VE DISCOVERED IT'S MORE RELAXING.

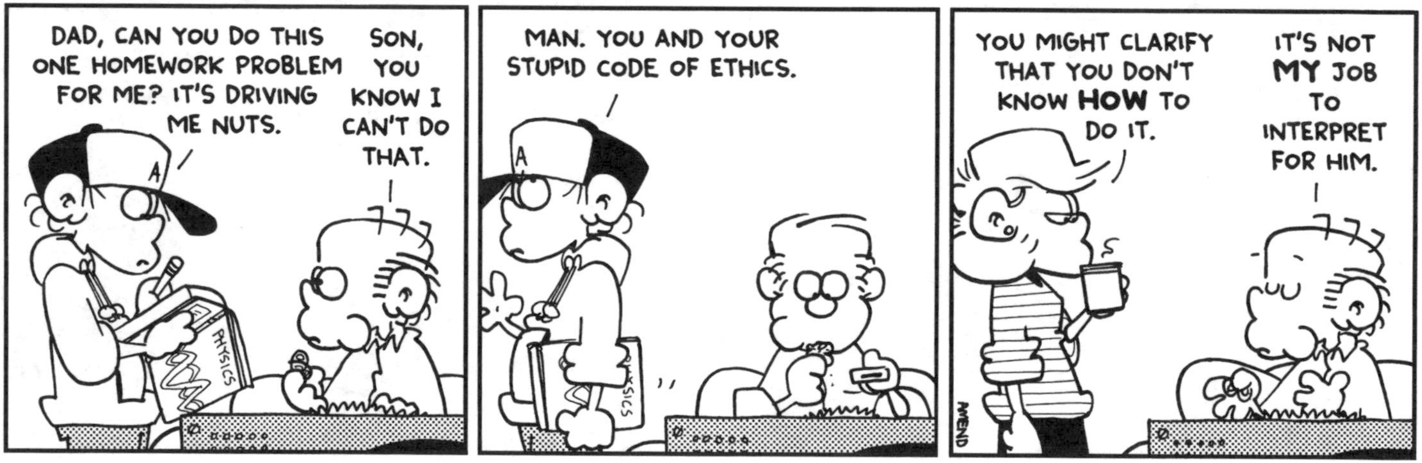
DAD, CAN YOU DO THIS ONE HOMEWORK PROBLEM FOR ME? IT'S DRIVING ME NUTS.
SON, YOU KNOW I CAN'T DO THAT.
PHYSICS
MAN. YOU AND YOUR STUPID CODE OF ETHICS.
YOU MIGHT CLARIFY THAT YOU DON'T KNOW HOW TO DO IT.
IT'S NOT MY JOB TO INTERPRET FOR HIM.
AMEND

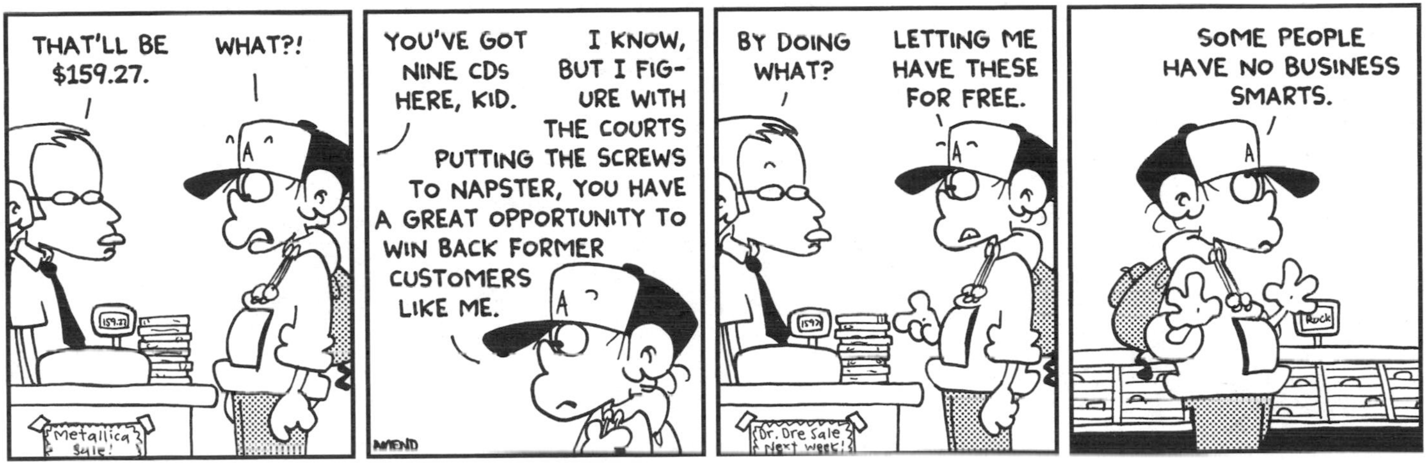
THAT'LL BE $159.27.
WHAT?!
YOU'VE GOT NINE CDs HERE, KID.
I KNOW, BUT I FIGURE WITH THE COURTS PUTTING THE SCREWS TO NAPSTER, YOU HAVE A GREAT OPPORTUNITY TO WIN BACK FORMER CUSTOMERS LIKE ME.
BY DOING WHAT?
LETTING ME HAVE THESE FOR FREE.
SOME PEOPLE HAVE NO BUSINESS SMARTS.
Metallica Sale!
Dr. Dre Sale Next week!
Rock
AMEND

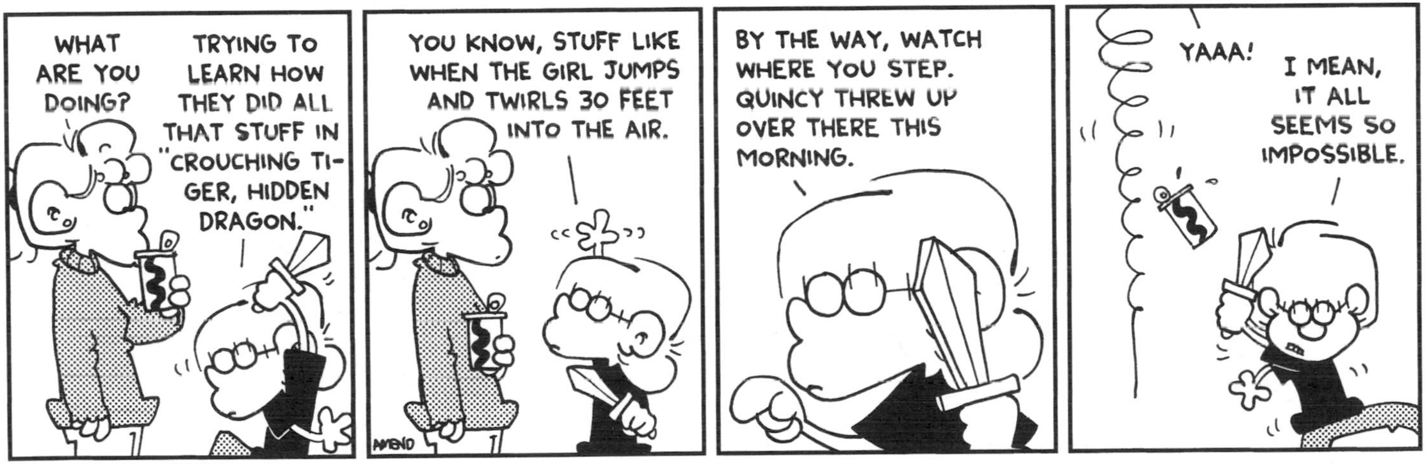
WHAT ARE YOU DOING?
TRYING TO LEARN HOW THEY DID ALL THAT STUFF IN "CROUCHING TIGER, HIDDEN DRAGON."
YOU KNOW, STUFF LIKE WHEN THE GIRL JUMPS AND TWIRLS 30 FEET INTO THE AIR.
BY THE WAY, WATCH WHERE YOU STEP. QUINCY THREW UP OVER THERE THIS MORNING.
YAAA!
I MEAN, IT ALL SEEMS SO IMPOSSIBLE.
AMEND

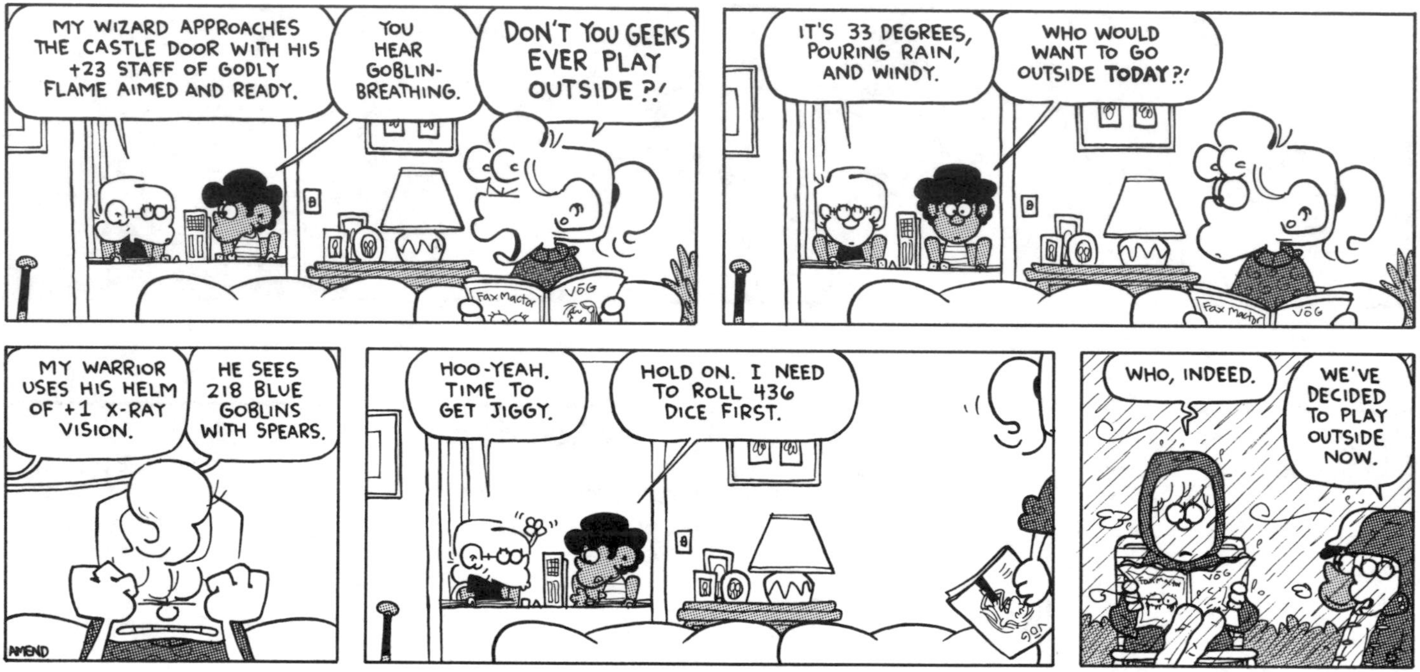
MY WIZARD APPROACHES THE CASTLE DOOR WITH HIS +23 STAFF OF GODLY FLAME AIMED AND READY.
YOU HEAR GOBLIN-BREATHING.
DON'T YOU GEEKS EVER PLAY OUTSIDE ?!
IT'S 33 DEGREES, POURING RAIN, AND WINDY.
WHO WOULD WANT TO GO OUTSIDE **TODAY** ?!
MY WARRIOR USES HIS HELM OF +1 X-RAY VISION.
HE SEES 218 BLUE GOBLINS WITH SPEARS.
AMEND
HOO-YEAH. TIME TO GET JIGGY.
HOLD ON. I NEED TO ROLL 436 DICE FIRST.
WHO, INDEED.
WE'VE DECIDED TO PLAY OUTSIDE NOW.

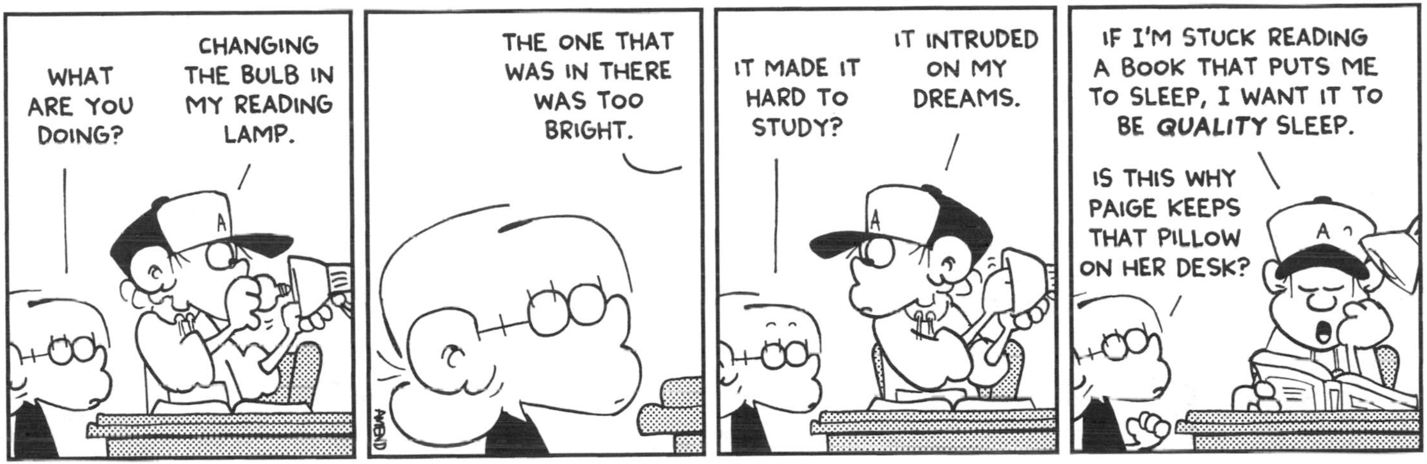
WHAT ARE YOU DOING?
CHANGING THE BULB IN MY READING LAMP.
THE ONE THAT WAS IN THERE WAS TOO BRIGHT.
IT MADE IT HARD TO STUDY?
IT INTRUDED ON MY DREAMS.
IF I'M STUCK READING A BOOK THAT PUTS ME TO SLEEP, I WANT IT TO BE **QUALITY** SLEEP.
IS THIS WHY PAIGE KEEPS THAT PILLOW ON HER DESK?

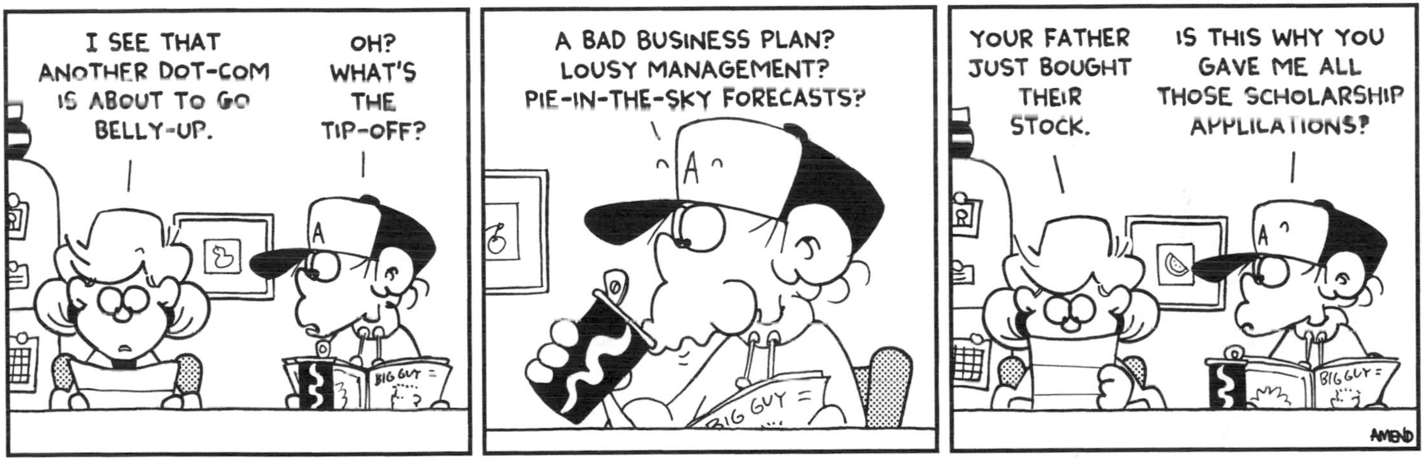
I SEE THAT ANOTHER DOT-COM IS ABOUT TO GO BELLY-UP.
OH? WHAT'S THE TIP-OFF?
A BAD BUSINESS PLAN? LOUSY MANAGEMENT? PIE-IN-THE-SKY FORECASTS?
YOUR FATHER JUST BOUGHT THEIR STOCK.
IS THIS WHY YOU GAVE ME ALL THOSE SCHOLARSHIP APPLICATIONS?
BIG GUY
AMEND

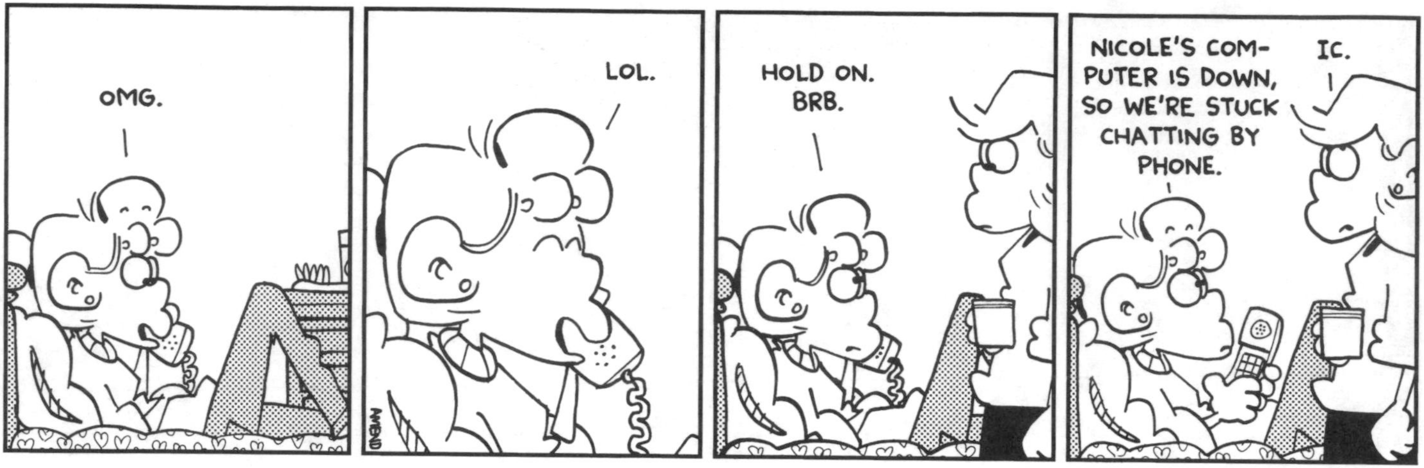
OMG.
LOL.
AMEND
HOLD ON. BRB.
NICOLE'S COMPUTER IS DOWN, SO WE'RE STUCK CHATTING BY PHONE.
IC.

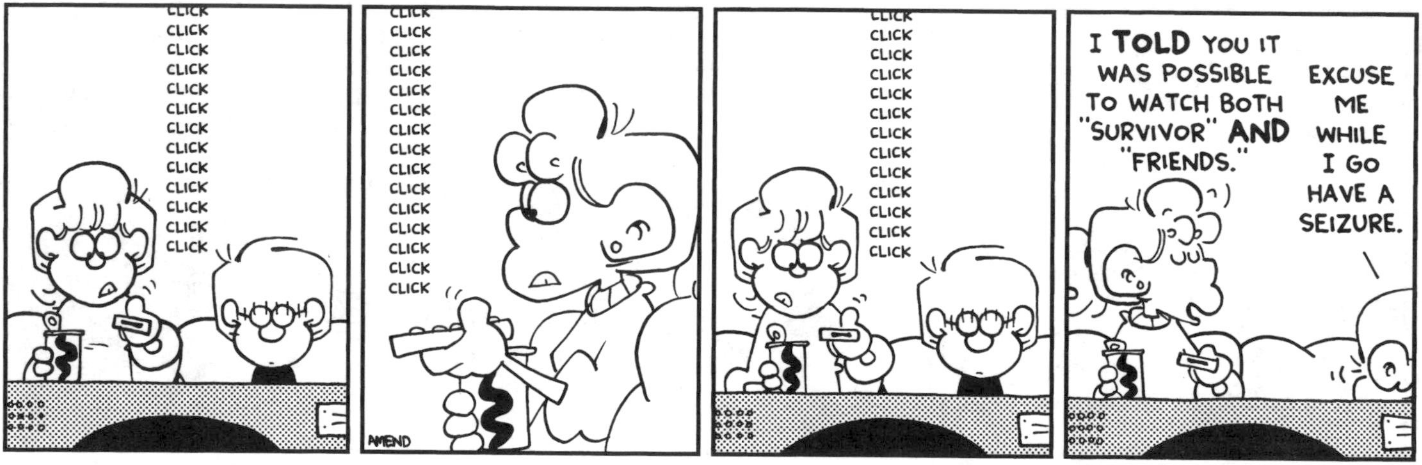
CLICK CLICK CLICK CLICK CLICK CLICK CLICK CLICK CLICK CLICK CLICK CLICK
CLICK CLICK CLICK CLICK CLICK CLICK CLICK CLICK CLICK CLICK CLICK CLICK CLICK CLICK
AMEND
CLICK CLICK CLICK CLICK CLICK CLICK CLICK CLICK CLICK CLICK CLICK CLICK
I **TOLD** YOU IT WAS POSSIBLE TO WATCH BOTH "SURVIVOR" **AND** "FRIENDS."
EXCUSE ME WHILE I GO HAVE A SEIZURE.

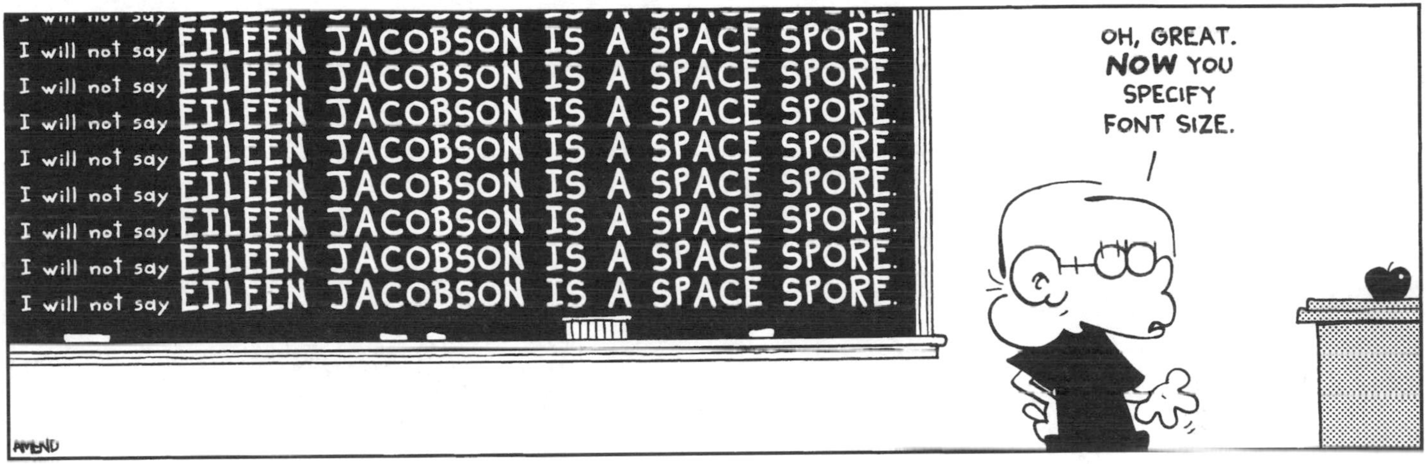
I will not say EILEEN JACOBSON IS A SPACE SPORE.
I will not say EILEEN JACOBSON IS A SPACE SPORE.
I will not say EILEEN JACOBSON IS A SPACE SPORE.
I will not say EILEEN JACOBSON IS A SPACE SPORE.
I will not say EILEEN JACOBSON IS A SPACE SPORE.
I will not say EILEEN JACOBSON IS A SPACE SPORE.
I will not say EILEEN JACOBSON IS A SPACE SPORE.
I will not say EILEEN JACOBSON IS A SPACE SPORE.
OH, GREAT. **NOW** YOU SPECIFY FONT SIZE.
AMEND

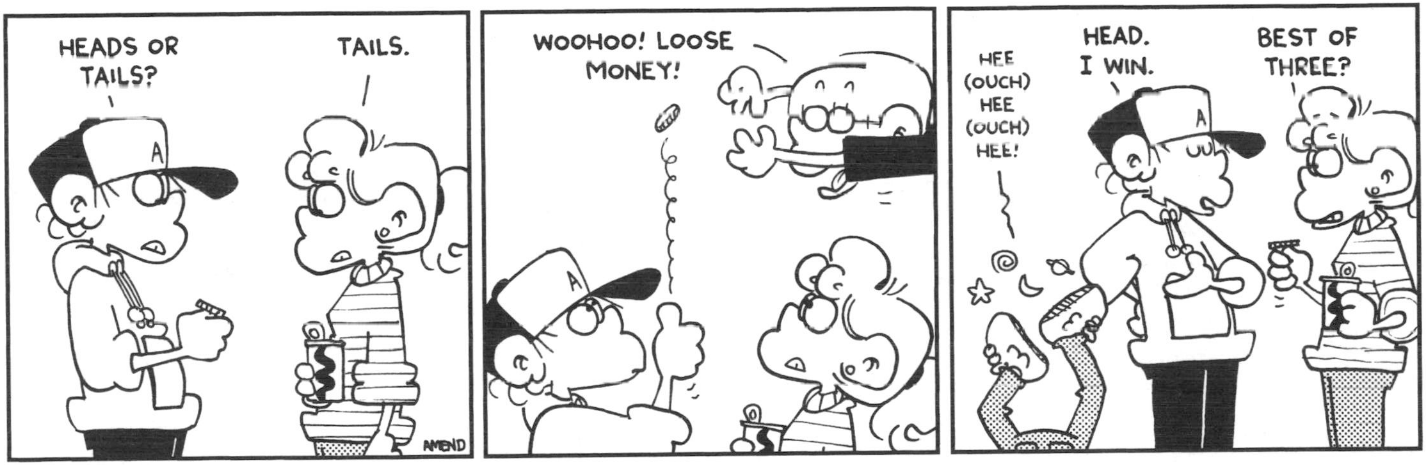
HEADS OR TAILS?
TAILS.
AMEND
WOOHOO! LOOSE MONEY!
HEE (OUCH) HEE (OUCH) HEE!
HEAD. I WIN.
BEST OF THREE?

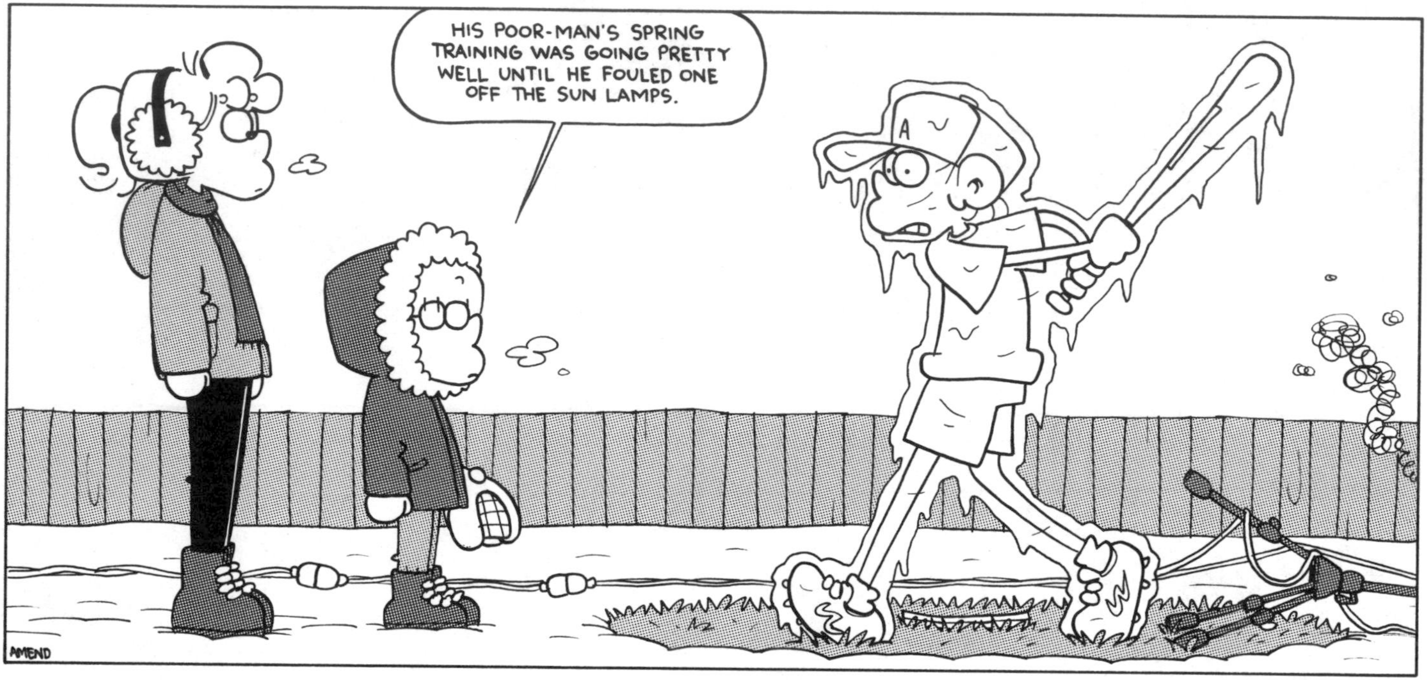
HIS POOR-MAN'S SPRING TRAINING WAS GOING PRETTY WELL UNTIL HE FOULED ONE OFF THE SUN LAMPS.
AMEND

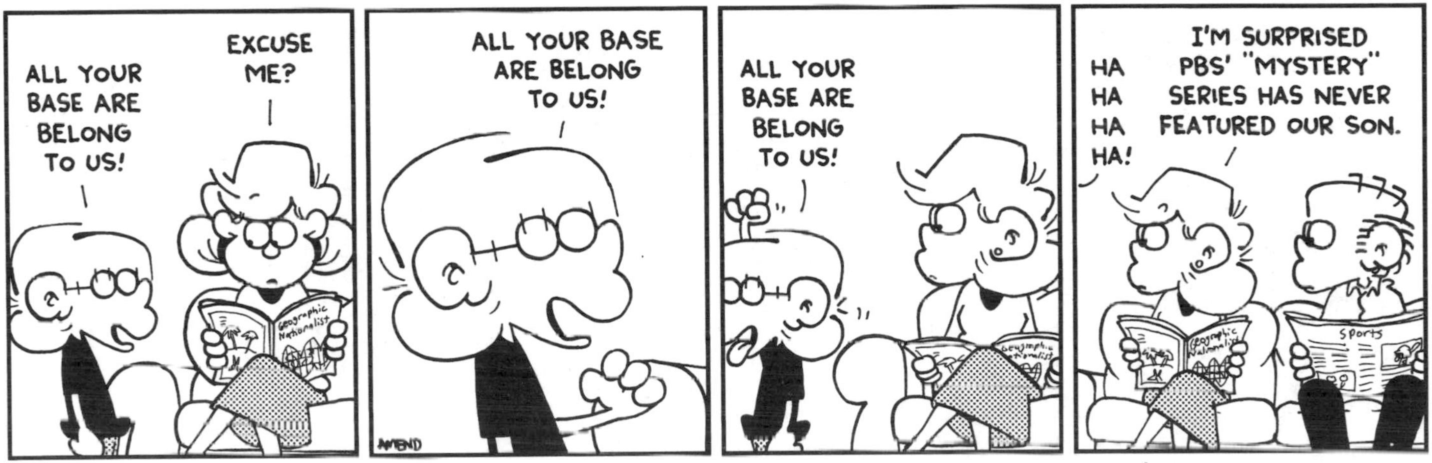
ALL YOUR BASE ARE BELONG TO US!
EXCUSE ME?
ALL YOUR BASE ARE BELONG TO US!
ALL YOUR BASE ARE BELONG TO US!
HA HA HA HA!
I'M SURPRISED PBS' "MYSTERY" SERIES HAS NEVER FEATURED OUR SON.
AMEND

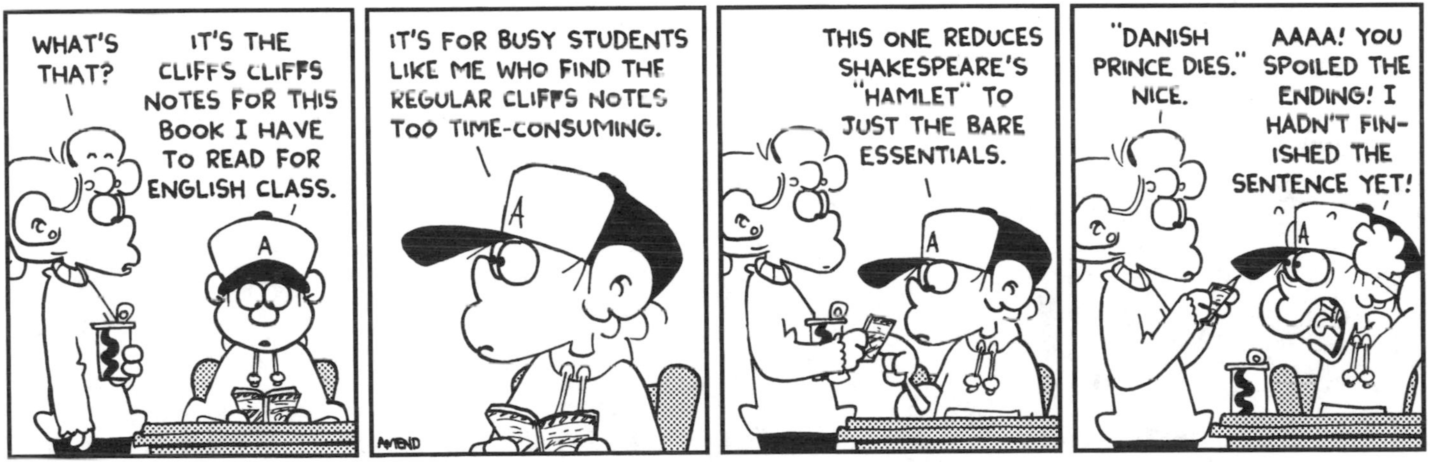
WHAT'S THAT?
IT'S THE CLIFFS CLIFFS NOTES FOR THIS BOOK I HAVE TO READ FOR ENGLISH CLASS.
IT'S FOR BUSY STUDENTS LIKE ME WHO FIND THE REGULAR CLIFFS NOTES TOO TIME-CONSUMING.
THIS ONE REDUCES SHAKESPEARE'S "HAMLET" TO JUST THE BARE ESSENTIALS.
"DANISH PRINCE DIES." NICE.
AAAA! YOU SPOILED THE ENDING! I HADN'T FIN-ISHED THE SENTENCE YET!
AMEND

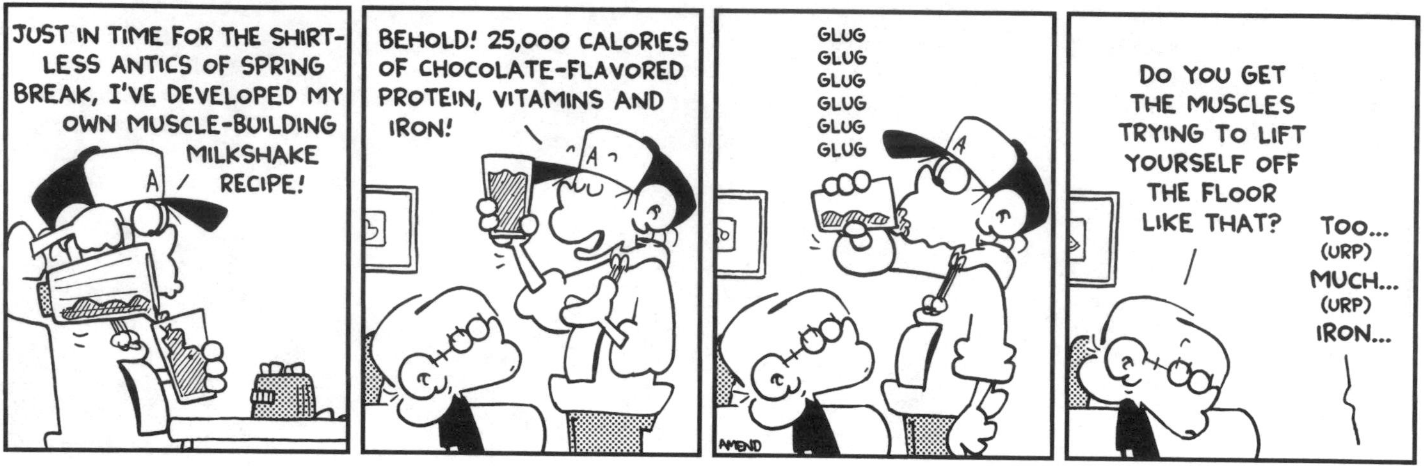
JUST IN TIME FOR THE SHIRTLESS ANTICS OF SPRING BREAK, I'VE DEVELOPED MY OWN MUSCLE-BUILDING MILKSHAKE RECIPE!
BEHOLD! 25,000 CALORIES OF CHOCOLATE-FLAVORED PROTEIN, VITAMINS AND IRON!
GLUG GLUG GLUG GLUG GLUG GLUG
AMEND
DO YOU GET THE MUSCLES TRYING TO LIFT YOURSELF OFF THE FLOOR LIKE THAT?
TOO... (URP) MUCH... (URP) IRON...

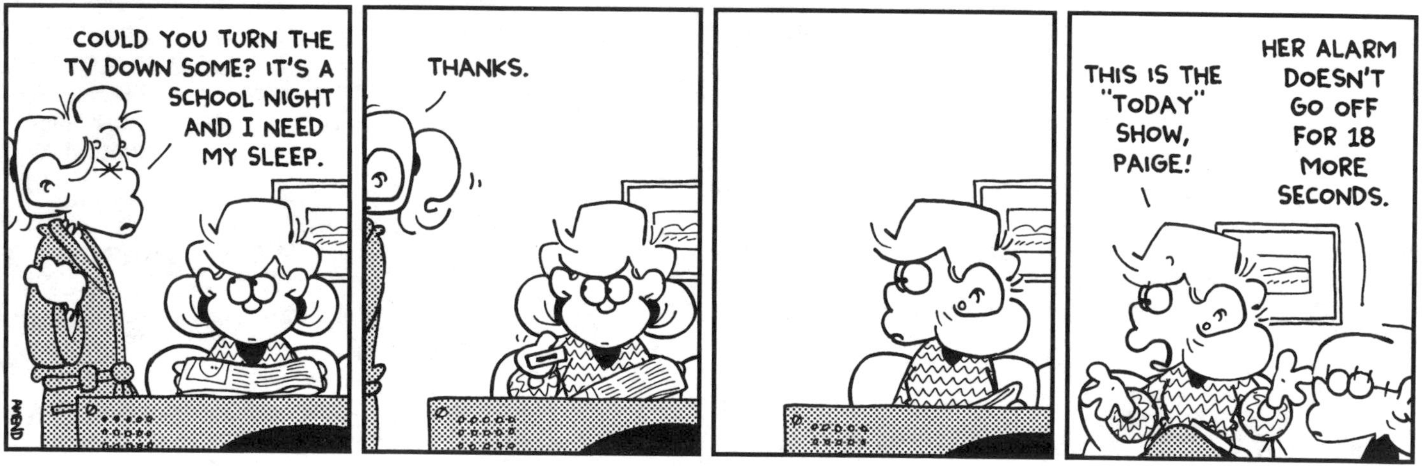
COULD YOU TURN THE TV DOWN SOME? IT'S A SCHOOL NIGHT AND I NEED MY SLEEP.
AMEND
THANKS.
THIS IS THE "TODAY" SHOW, PAIGE!
HER ALARM DOESN'T GO OFF FOR 18 MORE SECONDS.

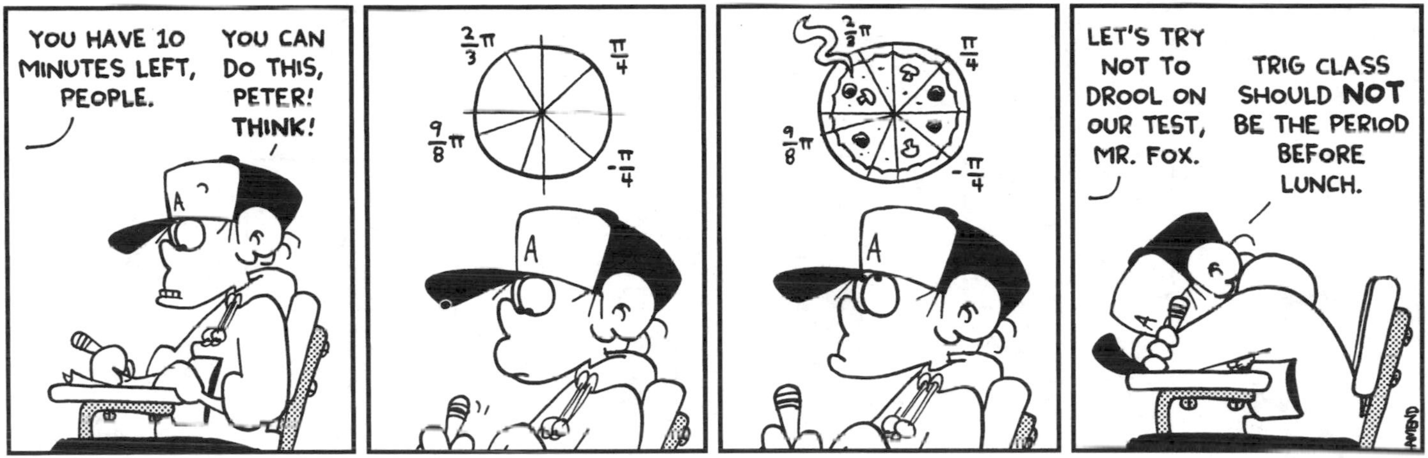
YOU HAVE 10 MINUTES LEFT, PEOPLE.
YOU CAN DO THIS, PETER! THINK!
$\frac{2}{3}\pi$
$\frac{\pi}{4}$
$\frac{9}{8}\pi$
$-\frac{\pi}{4}$
LET'S TRY NOT TO DROOL ON OUR TEST, MR. FOX.
TRIG CLASS SHOULD **NOT** BE THE PERIOD BEFORE LUNCH.
AMEND

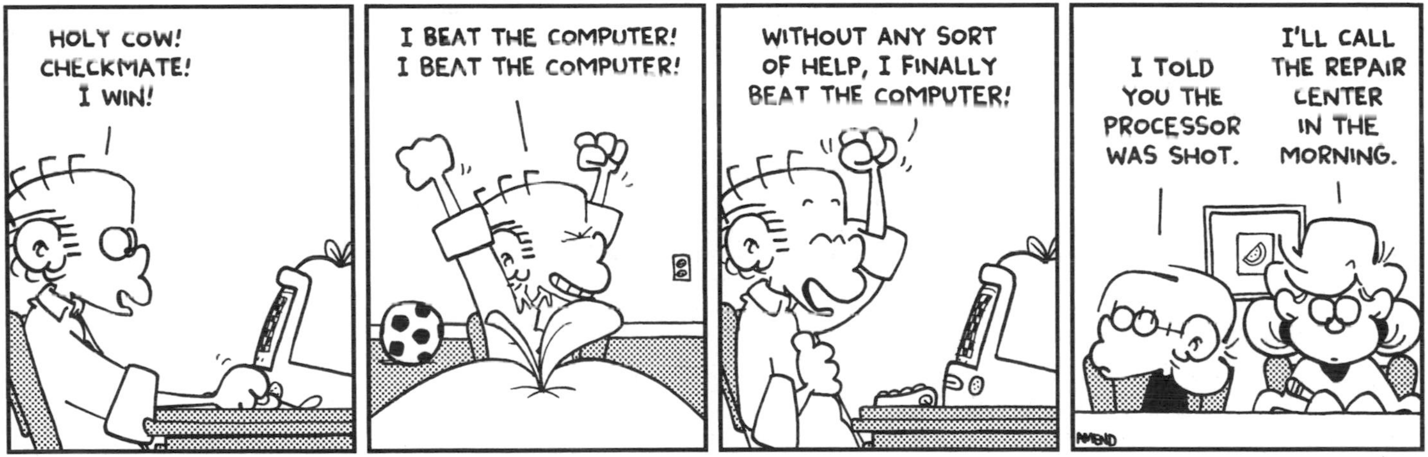
HOLY COW! CHECKMATE! I WIN!
I BEAT THE COMPUTER! I BEAT THE COMPUTER!
WITHOUT ANY SORT OF HELP, I FINALLY BEAT THE COMPUTER!
I TOLD YOU THE PROCESSOR WAS SHOT.
I'LL CALL THE REPAIR CENTER IN THE MORNING.
AMEND

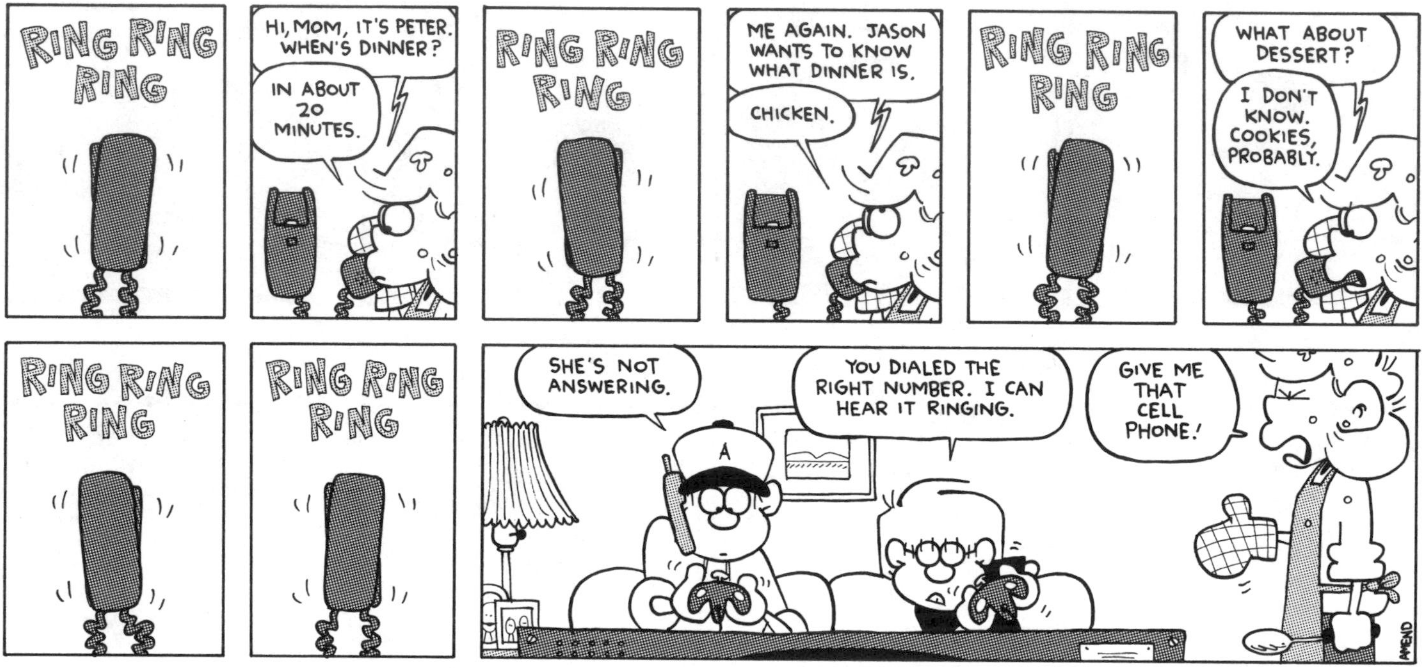
RING RING RING
HI, MOM, IT'S PETER. WHEN'S DINNER?
IN ABOUT 20 MINUTES.
RING RING RING
ME AGAIN. JASON WANTS TO KNOW WHAT DINNER IS.
CHICKEN.
RING RING RING
WHAT ABOUT DESSERT?
I DON'T KNOW. COOKIES, PROBABLY.
RING RING RING
RING RING RING
SHE'S NOT ANSWERING.
YOU DIALED THE RIGHT NUMBER. I CAN HEAR IT RINGING.
GIVE ME THAT CELL PHONE!
AMEND

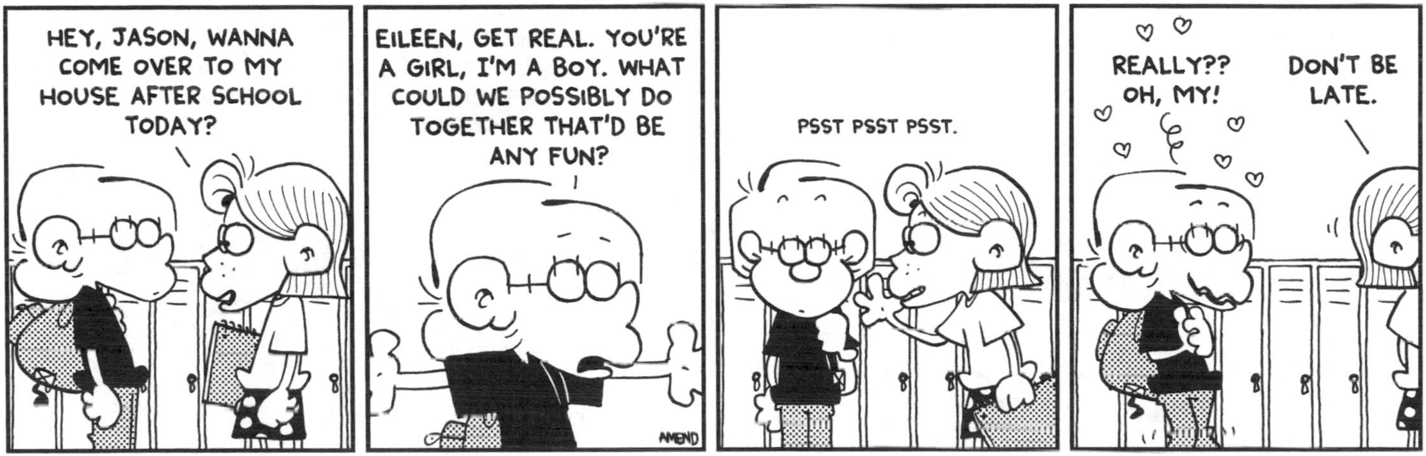
HEY, JASON, WANNA COME OVER TO MY HOUSE AFTER SCHOOL TODAY?
EILEEN, GET REAL. YOU'RE A GIRL, I'M A BOY. WHAT COULD WE POSSIBLY DO TOGETHER THAT'D BE ANY FUN?
AMEND
PSST PSST PSST.
REALLY?? OH, MY!
DON'T BE LATE.

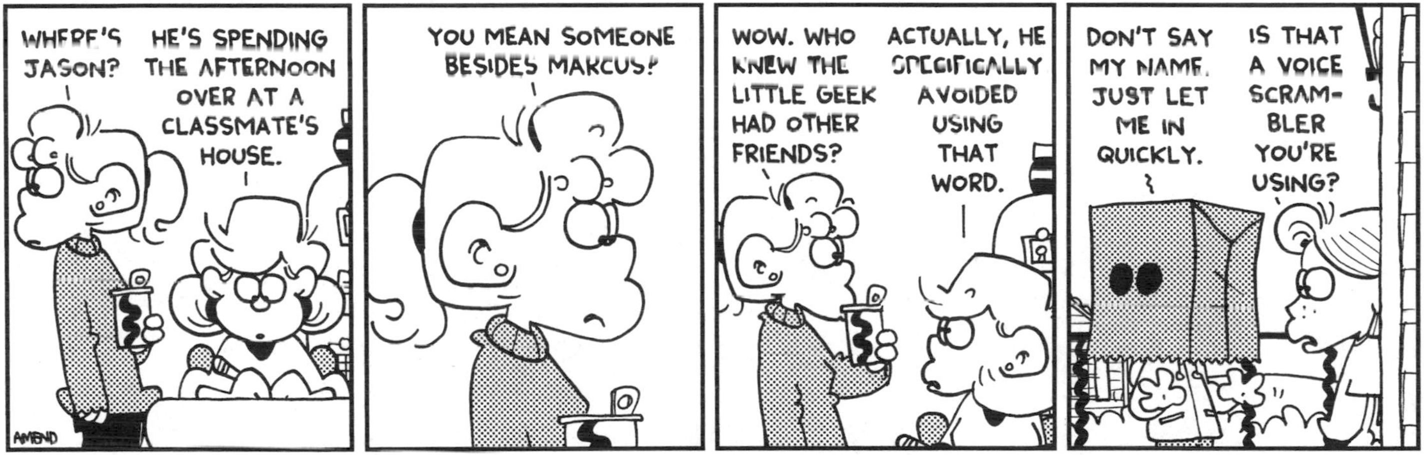
WHERE'S JASON?
HE'S SPENDING THE AFTERNOON OVER AT A CLASSMATE'S HOUSE.
AMEND
YOU MEAN SOMEONE BESIDES MARCUS?
WOW. WHO KNEW THE LITTLE GEEK HAD OTHER FRIENDS?
ACTUALLY, HE SPECIFICALLY AVOIDED USING THAT WORD.
DON'T SAY MY NAME. JUST LET ME IN QUICKLY.
IS THAT A VOICE SCRAMBLER YOU'RE USING?

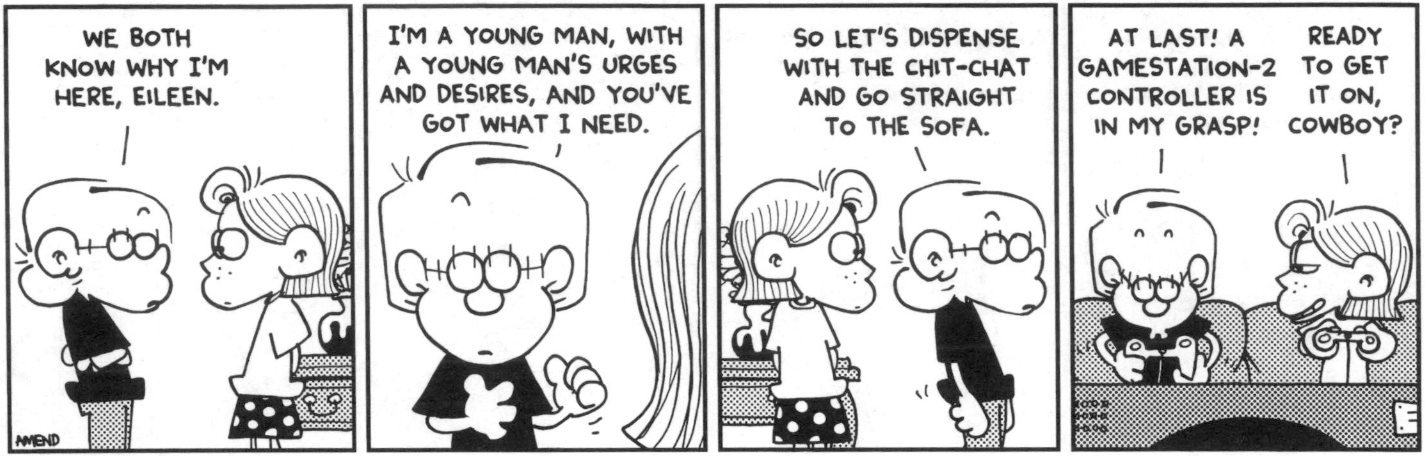
WE BOTH KNOW WHY I'M HERE, EILEEN.
AMEND
I'M A YOUNG MAN, WITH A YOUNG MAN'S URGES AND DESIRES, AND YOU'VE GOT WHAT I NEED.
SO LET'S DISPENSE WITH THE CHIT-CHAT AND GO STRAIGHT TO THE SOFA.
AT LAST! A GAMESTATION-2 CONTROLLER IS IN MY GRASP!
READY TO GET IT ON, COWBOY?

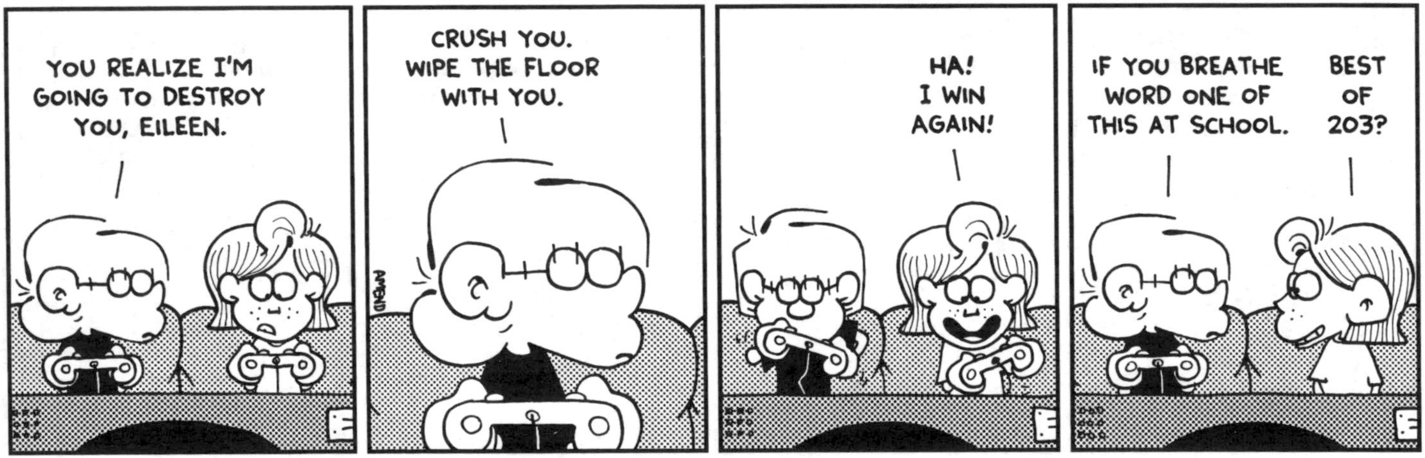
YOU REALIZE I'M GOING TO DESTROY YOU, EILEEN.
CRUSH YOU. WIPE THE FLOOR WITH YOU.
AMEND
HA! I WIN AGAIN!
IF YOU BREATHE WORD ONE OF THIS AT SCHOOL.
BEST OF 203?

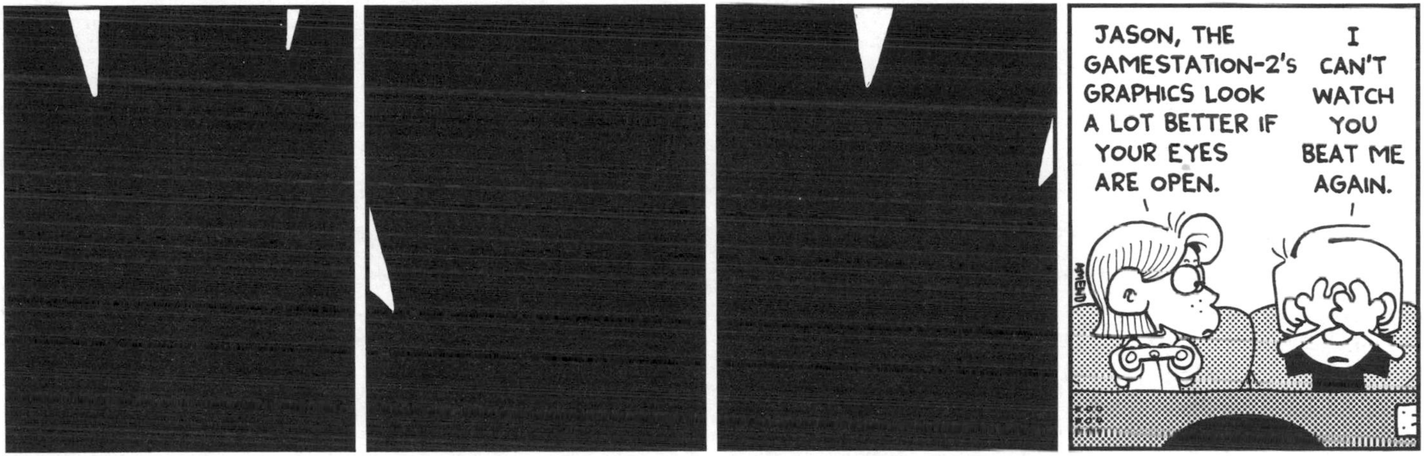
JASON, THE GAMESTATION-2's GRAPHICS LOOK A LOT BETTER IF YOUR EYES ARE OPEN.
I CAN'T WATCH YOU BEAT ME AGAIN.
AMEND

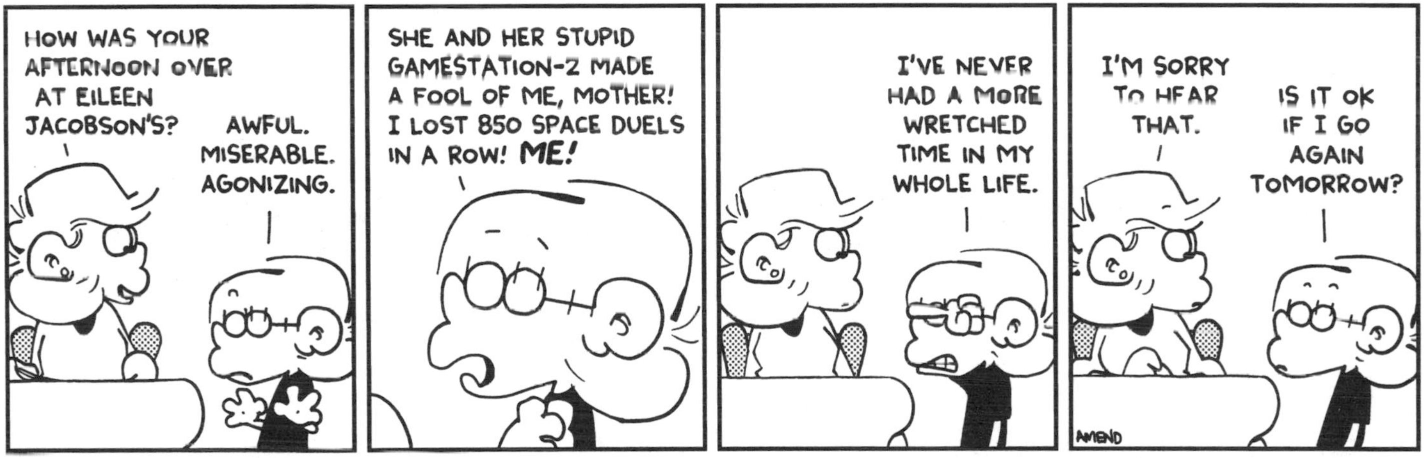
HOW WAS YOUR AFTERNOON OVER AT EILEEN JACOBSON'S?
AWFUL. MISERABLE. AGONIZING.
SHE AND HER STUPID GAMESTATION-2 MADE A FOOL OF ME, MOTHER! I LOST 850 SPACE DUELS IN A ROW! ME!
I'VE NEVER HAD A MORE WRETCHED TIME IN MY WHOLE LIFE.
I'M SORRY TO HEAR THAT.
IS IT OK IF I GO AGAIN TOMORROW?
AMEND

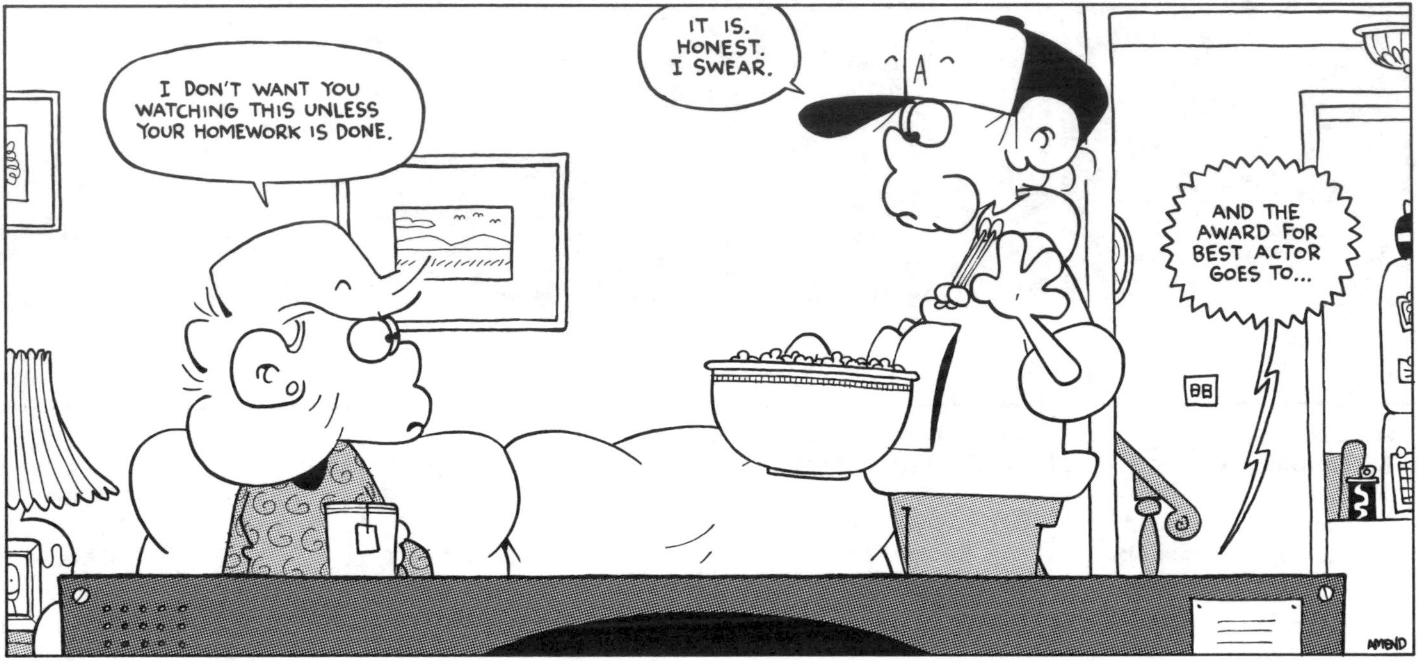
I DON'T WANT YOU WATCHING THIS UNLESS YOUR HOMEWORK IS DONE.
IT IS. HONEST. I SWEAR.
AND THE AWARD FOR BEST ACTOR GOES TO...
AMEND

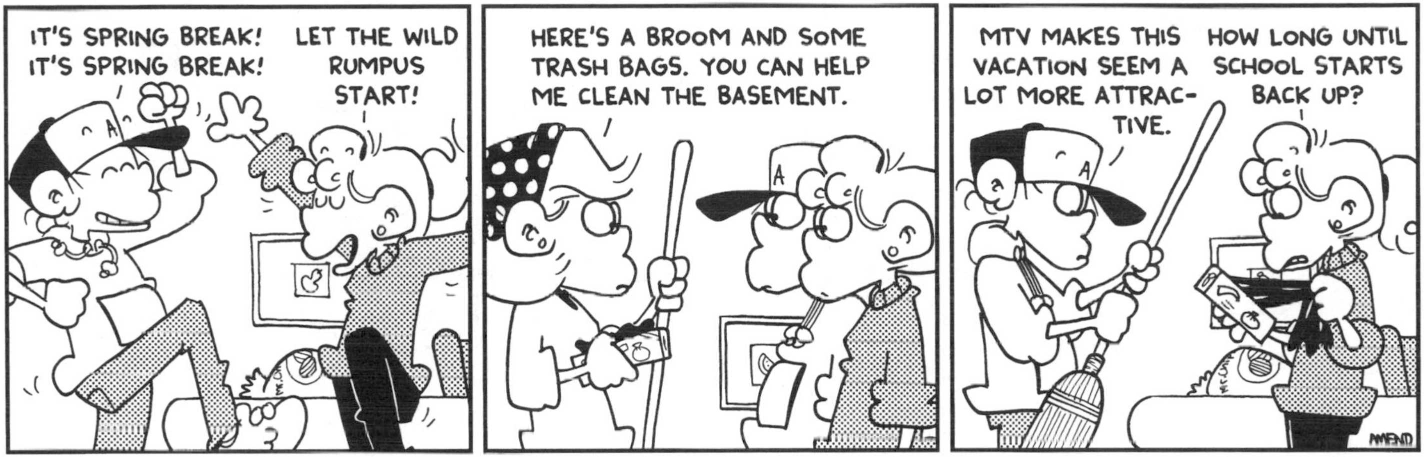
IT'S SPRING BREAK! IT'S SPRING BREAK!
LET THE WILD RUMPUS START!
HERE'S A BROOM AND SOME TRASH BAGS. YOU CAN HELP ME CLEAN THE BASEMENT.
MTV MAKES THIS VACATION SEEM A LOT MORE ATTRAC-TIVE.
HOW LONG UNTIL SCHOOL STARTS BACK UP?
AMEND

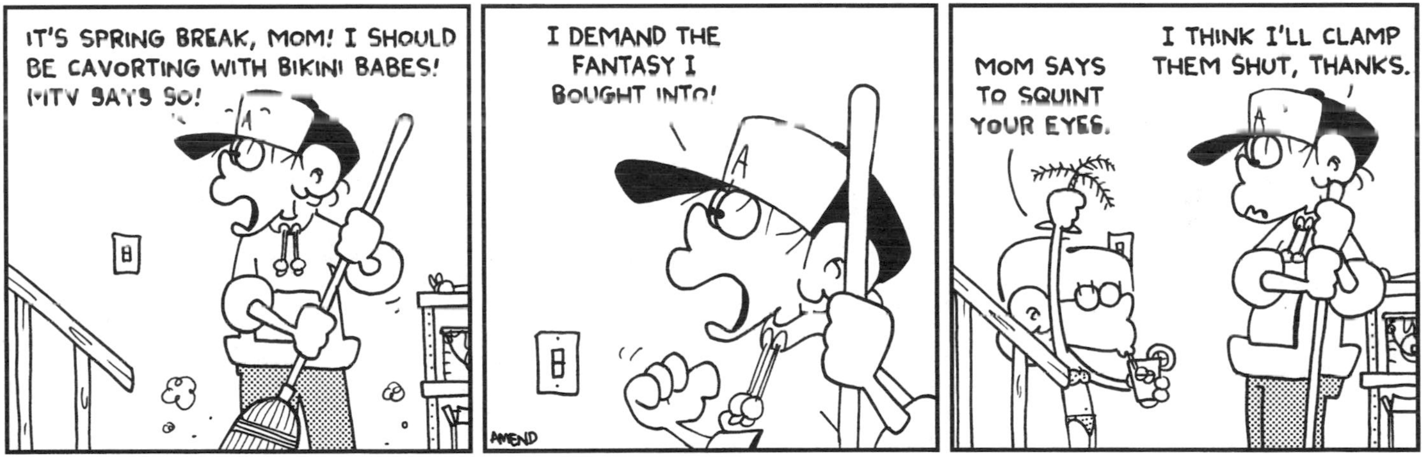
IT'S SPRING BREAK, MOM! I SHOULD BE CAVORTING WITH BIKINI BABES! MTV SAYS SO!
I DEMAND THE FANTASY I BOUGHT INTO!
AMEND
MOM SAYS TO SQUINT YOUR EYES.
I THINK I'LL CLAMP THEM SHUT, THANKS.

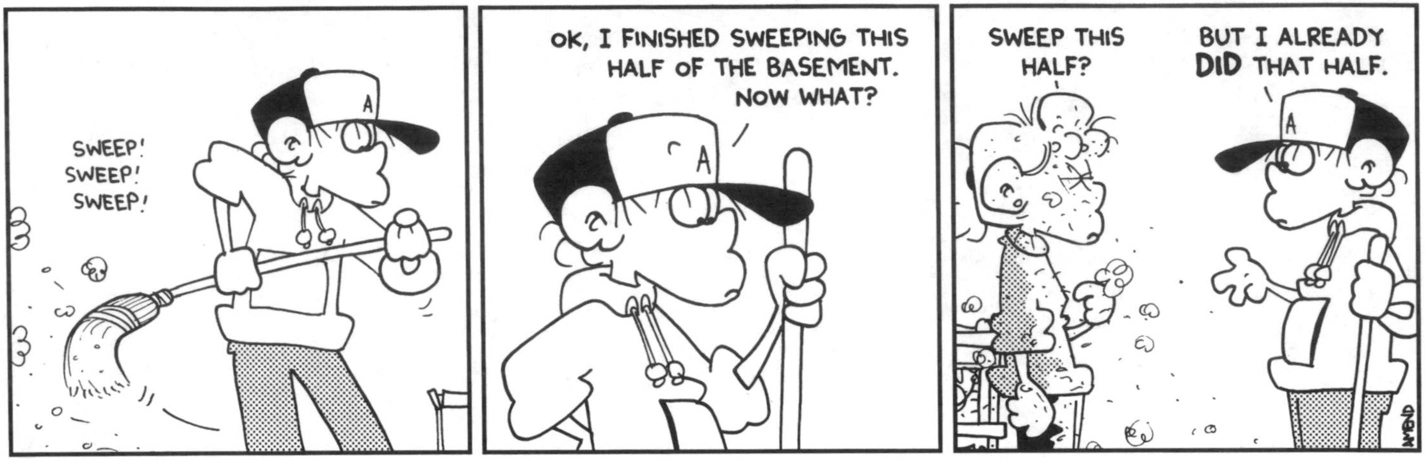
SWEEP! SWEEP! SWEEP!
OK, I FINISHED SWEEPING THIS HALF OF THE BASEMENT. NOW WHAT?
SWEEP THIS HALF?
BUT I ALREADY **DID** THAT HALF.
AMEND

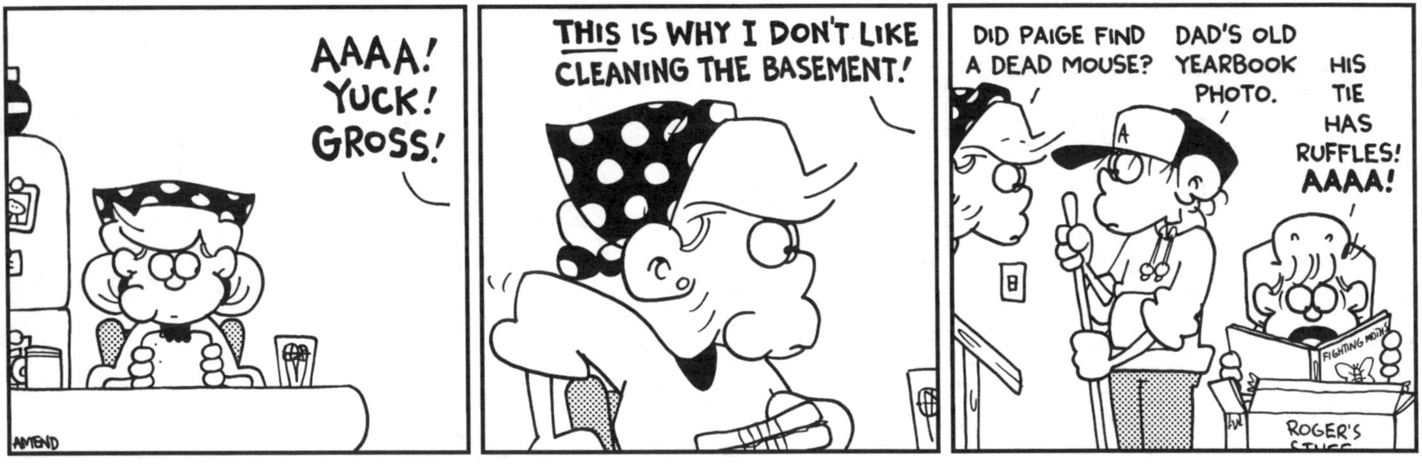
AAAA! YUCK! GROSS!
AMEND
THIS IS WHY I DON'T LIKE CLEANING THE BASEMENT!
DID PAIGE FIND A DEAD MOUSE?
DAD'S OLD YEARBOOK PHOTO.
HIS TIE HAS RUFFLES! AAAA!
FIGHTING MOTHS
ROGER'S

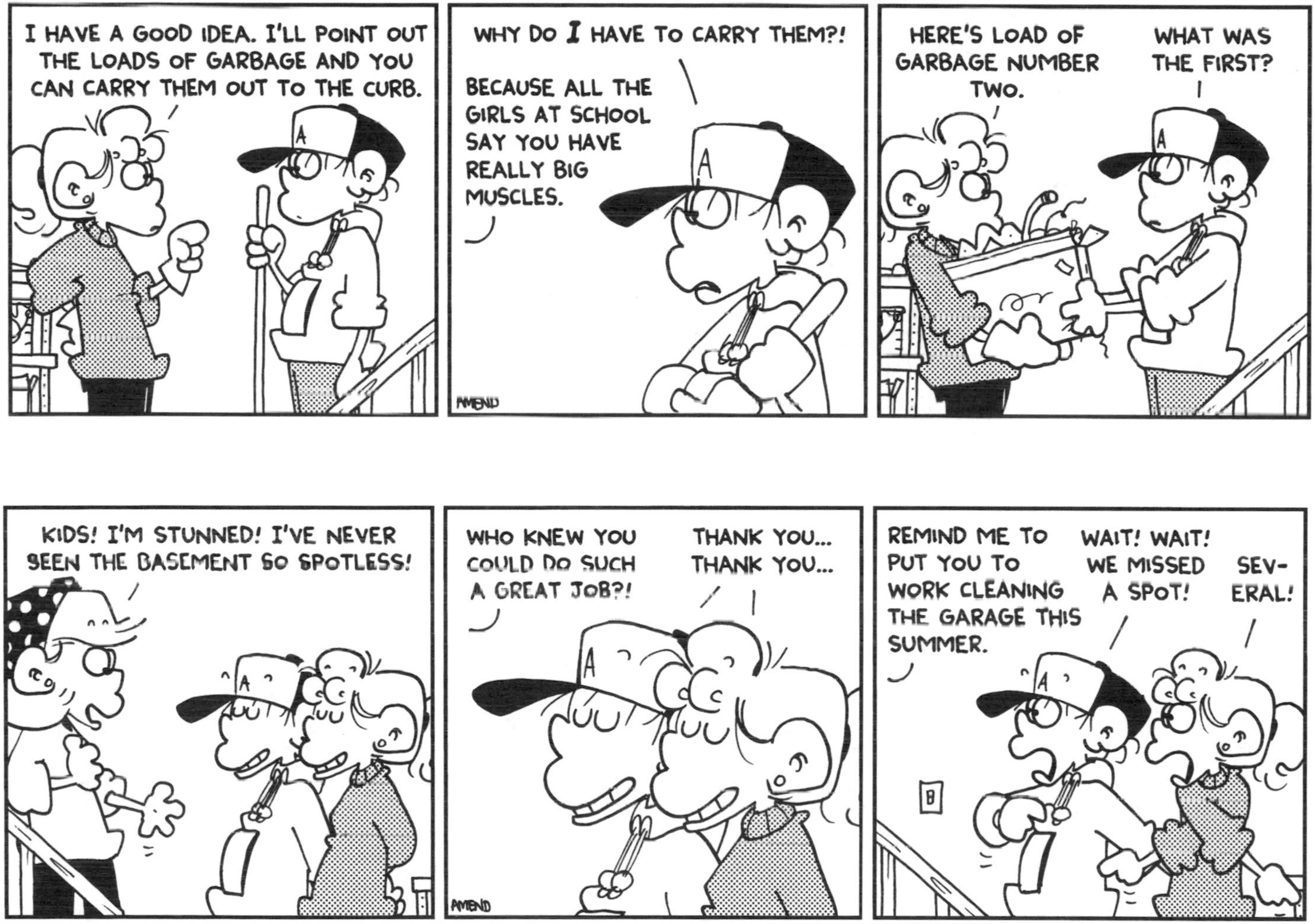
I HAVE A GOOD IDEA. I'LL POINT OUT THE LOADS OF GARBAGE AND YOU CAN CARRY THEM OUT TO THE CURB.
WHY DO I HAVE TO CARRY THEM?!
BECAUSE ALL THE GIRLS AT SCHOOL SAY YOU HAVE REALLY BIG MUSCLES.
AMEND
HERE'S LOAD OF GARBAGE NUMBER TWO.
WHAT WAS THE FIRST?
KIDS! I'M STUNNED! I'VE NEVER SEEN THE BASEMENT SO SPOTLESS!
WHO KNEW YOU COULD DO SUCH A GREAT JOB?!
THANK YOU... THANK YOU...
AMEND
REMIND ME TO PUT YOU TO WORK CLEANING THE GARAGE THIS SUMMER.
WAIT! WAIT! WE MISSED A SPOT!
SEV-ERAL!

REMEMBER A COUPLE OF YEARS AGO WHEN A BUNCH OF CARTOONISTS DREW EACH OTHER'S CHARACTERS ON APRIL FOOLS' DAY?

I THOUGHT IT WAS PRETTY FUNNY.

I WONDER WHY THEY DON'T DO IT AGAIN?

I GUESS IT WOULD GET OLD PRETTY FAST.

AND THERE'S NOTHING WORSE THAN GIMMICKRY FOR GIMMICKRY'S SAKE.

STILL, YOU'D THINK AT LEAST **ONE** OF THEM WOULD BE CLUELESS ENOUGH TO TRY.

PAIGE, PLEASE. THESE PEOPLE ARE PROFESSIONALS.

AMEND (with apologies to CG, CB, SA, AM, GT, LJ, RK, JS and BW)(phew!)

56

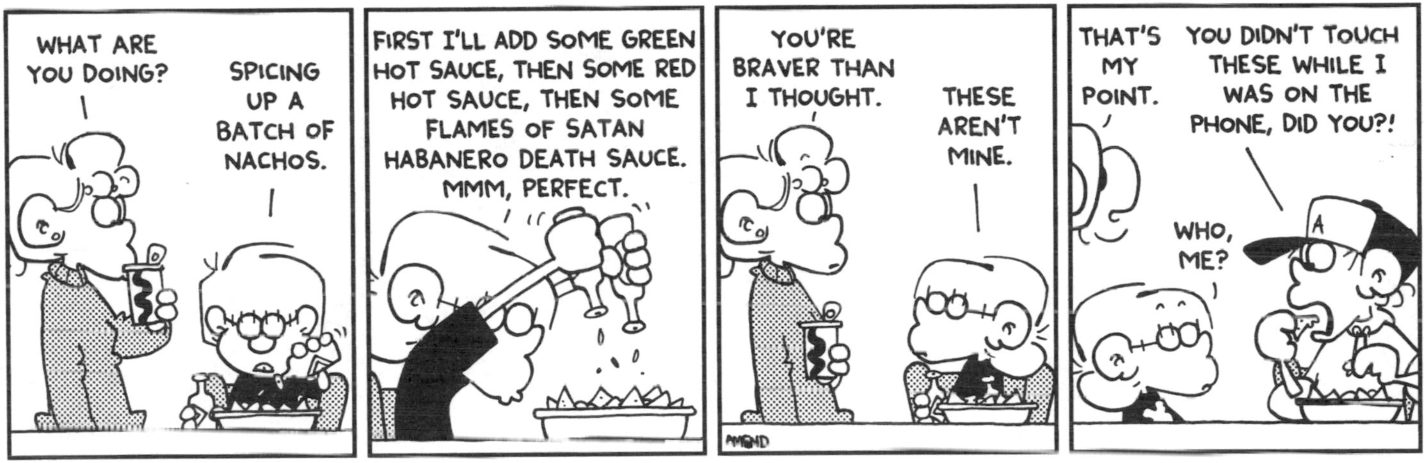
WHAT ARE YOU DOING?
SPICING UP A BATCH OF NACHOS.
FIRST I'LL ADD SOME GREEN HOT SAUCE, THEN SOME RED HOT SAUCE, THEN SOME FLAMES OF SATAN HABANERO DEATH SAUCE. MMM, PERFECT.
YOU'RE BRAVER THAN I THOUGHT.
THESE AREN'T MINE.
AMEND
THAT'S MY POINT.
YOU DIDN'T TOUCH THESE WHILE I WAS ON THE PHONE, DID YOU?!
WHO, ME?

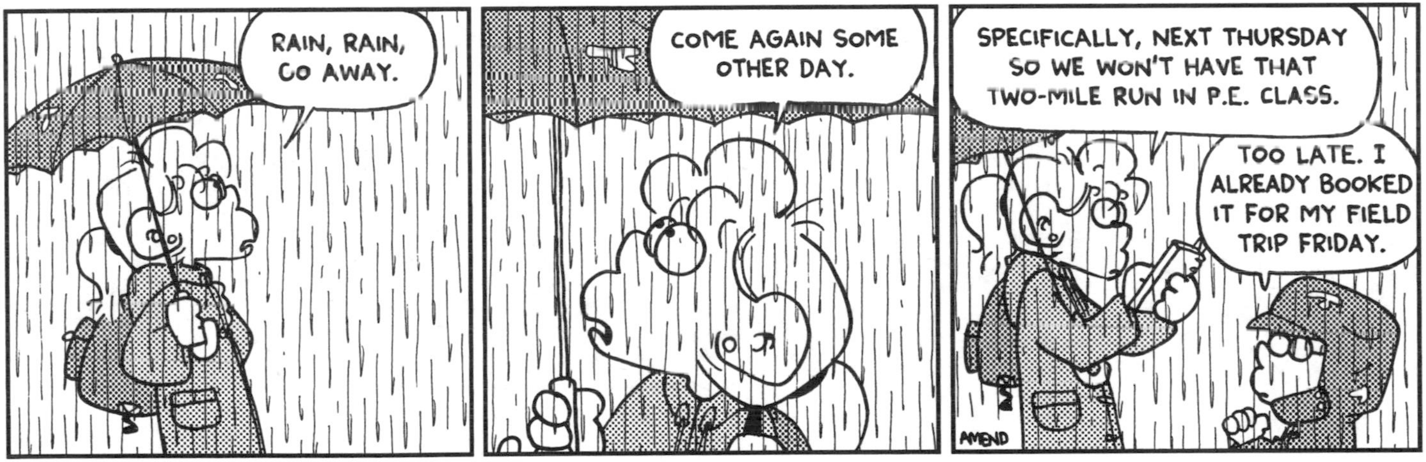
RAIN, RAIN, GO AWAY.
COME AGAIN SOME OTHER DAY.
SPECIFICALLY, NEXT THURSDAY SO WE WON'T HAVE THAT TWO-MILE RUN IN P.E. CLASS.
TOO LATE. I ALREADY BOOKED IT FOR MY FIELD TRIP FRIDAY.
AMEND

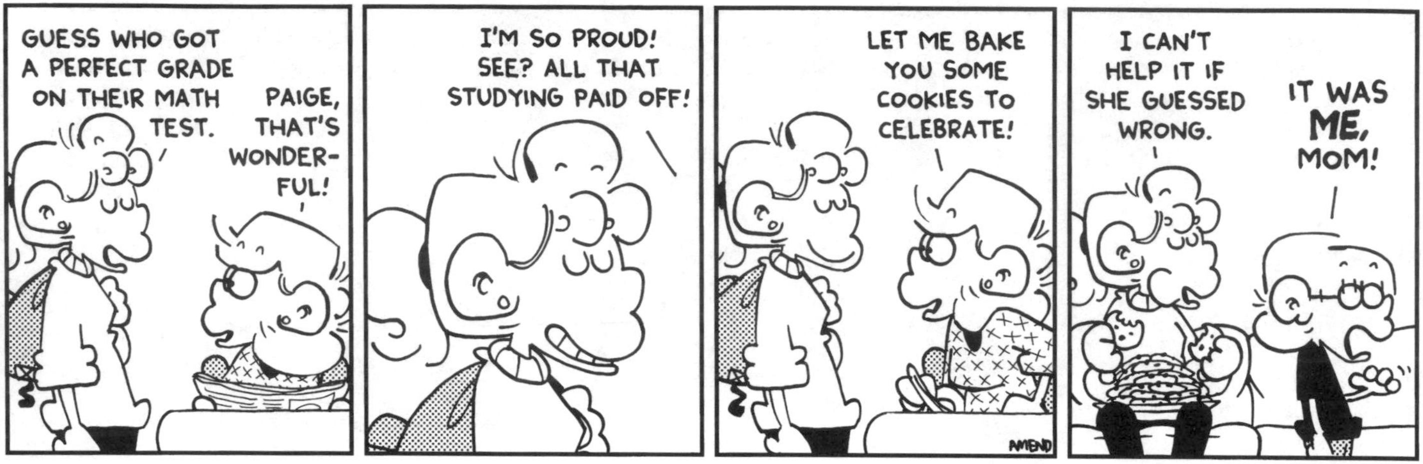
GUESS WHO GOT A PERFECT GRADE ON THEIR MATH TEST.
PAIGE, THAT'S WONDERFUL!
I'M SO PROUD! SEE? ALL THAT STUDYING PAID OFF!
LET ME BAKE YOU SOME COOKIES TO CELEBRATE!
AMEND
I CAN'T HELP IT IF SHE GUESSED WRONG.
IT WAS **ME,** MOM!

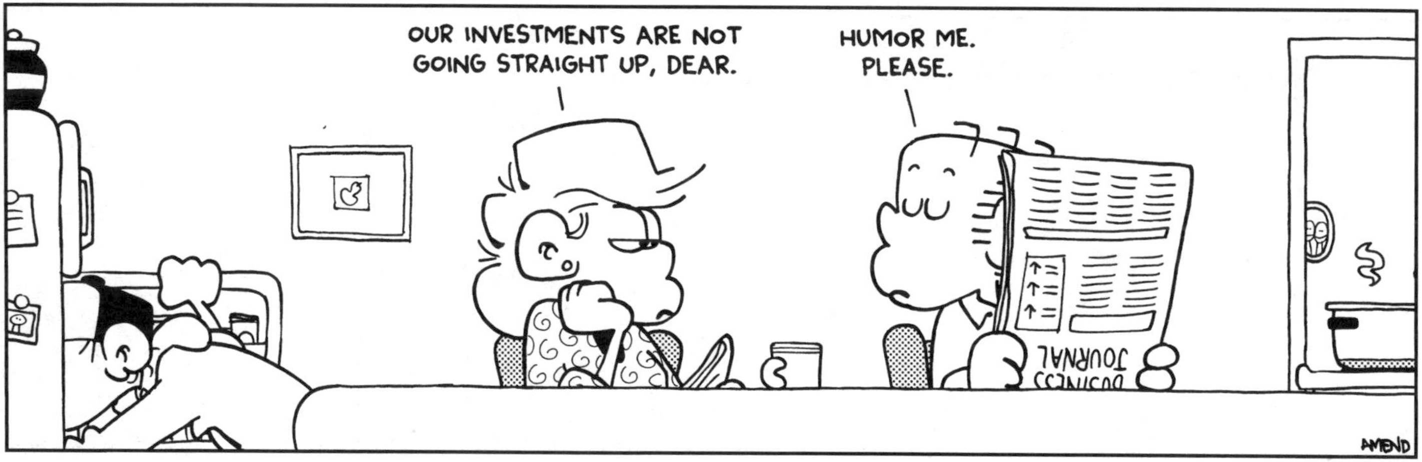
OUR INVESTMENTS ARE NOT GOING STRAIGHT UP, DEAR.
HUMOR ME. PLEASE.
AMEND

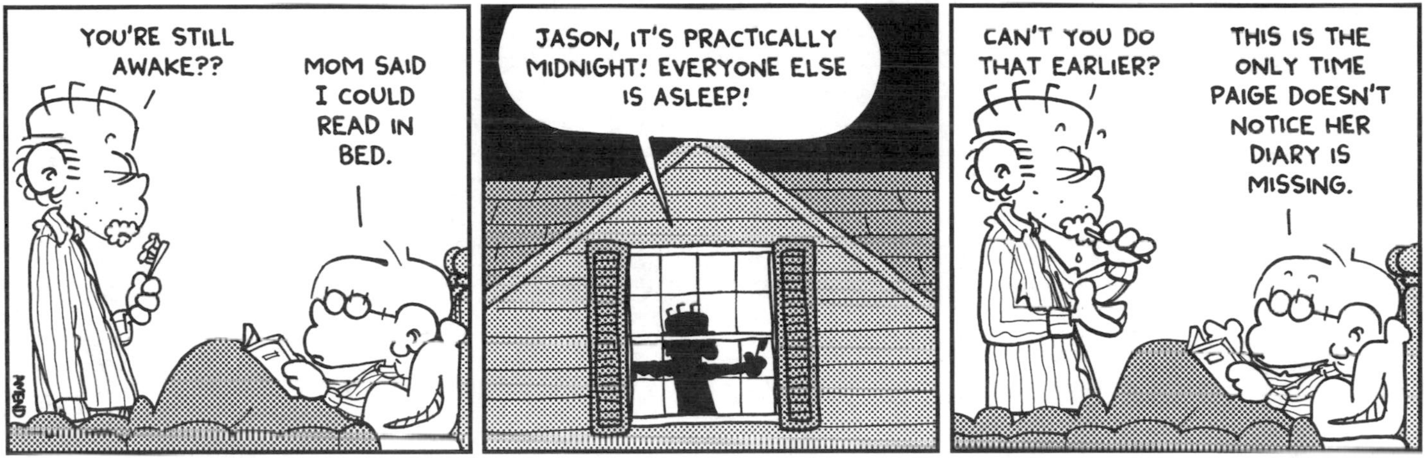
YOU'RE STILL AWAKE??
MOM SAID I COULD READ IN BED.
AMEND
JASON, IT'S PRACTICALLY MIDNIGHT! EVERYONE ELSE IS ASLEEP!
CAN'T YOU DO THAT EARLIER?
THIS IS THE ONLY TIME PAIGE DOESN'T NOTICE HER DIARY IS MISSING.

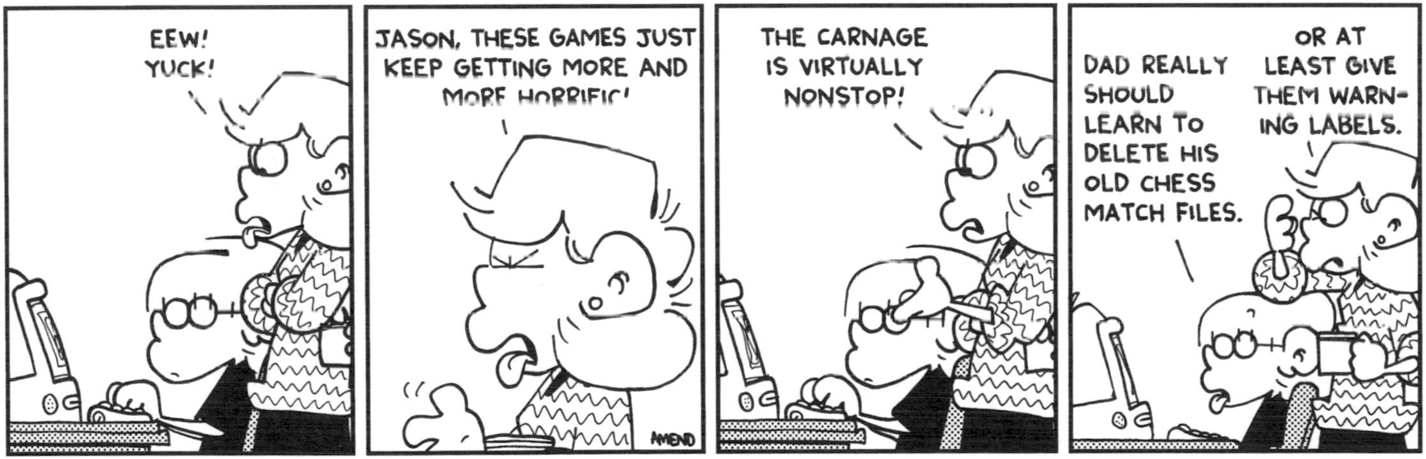
EEW! YUCK!
JASON, THESE GAMES JUST KEEP GETTING MORE AND MORE HORRIFIC!
AMEND
THE CARNAGE IS VIRTUALLY NONSTOP!
DAD REALLY SHOULD LEARN TO DELETE HIS OLD CHESS MATCH FILES.
OR AT LEAST GIVE THEM WARNING LABELS.

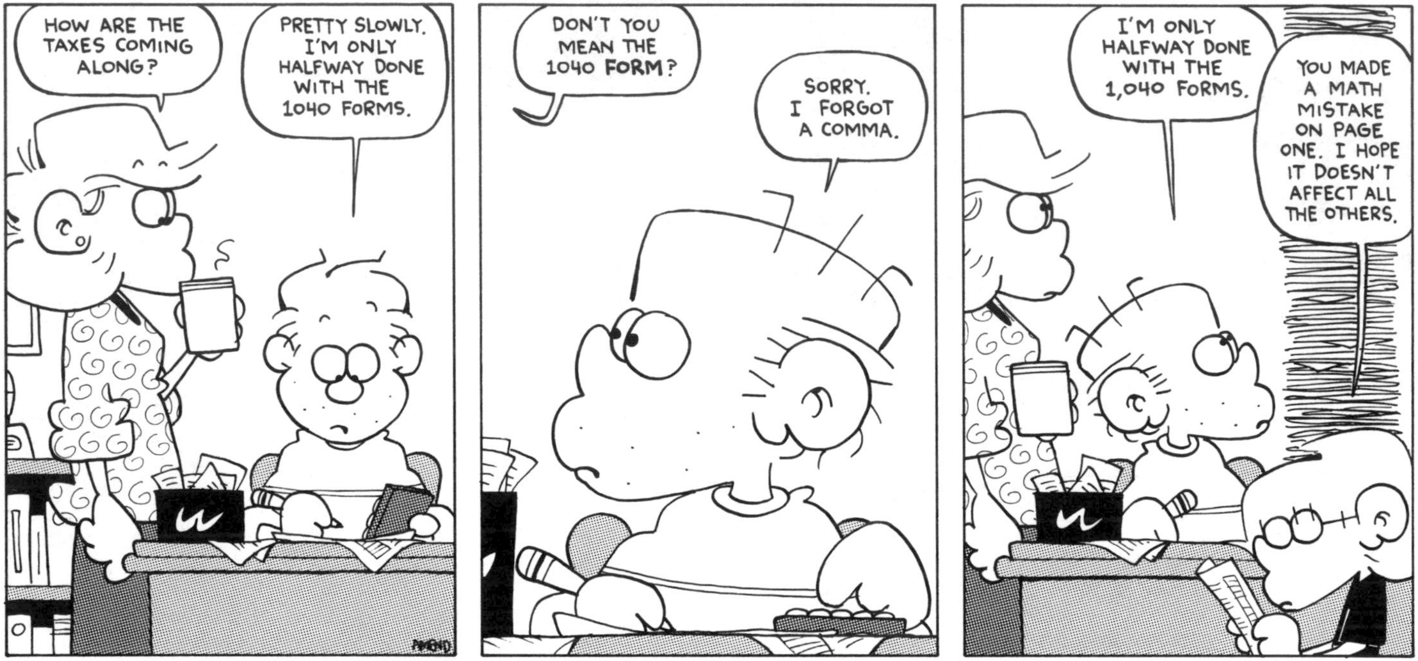
HOW ARE THE TAXES COMING ALONG?
PRETTY SLOWLY. I'M ONLY HALFWAY DONE WITH THE 1040 FORMS.
DON'T YOU MEAN THE 1040 **FORM**?
SORRY. I FORGOT A COMMA.
I'M ONLY HALFWAY DONE WITH THE 1,040 FORMS.
YOU MADE A MATH MISTAKE ON PAGE ONE. I HOPE IT DOESN'T AFFECT ALL THE OTHERS.

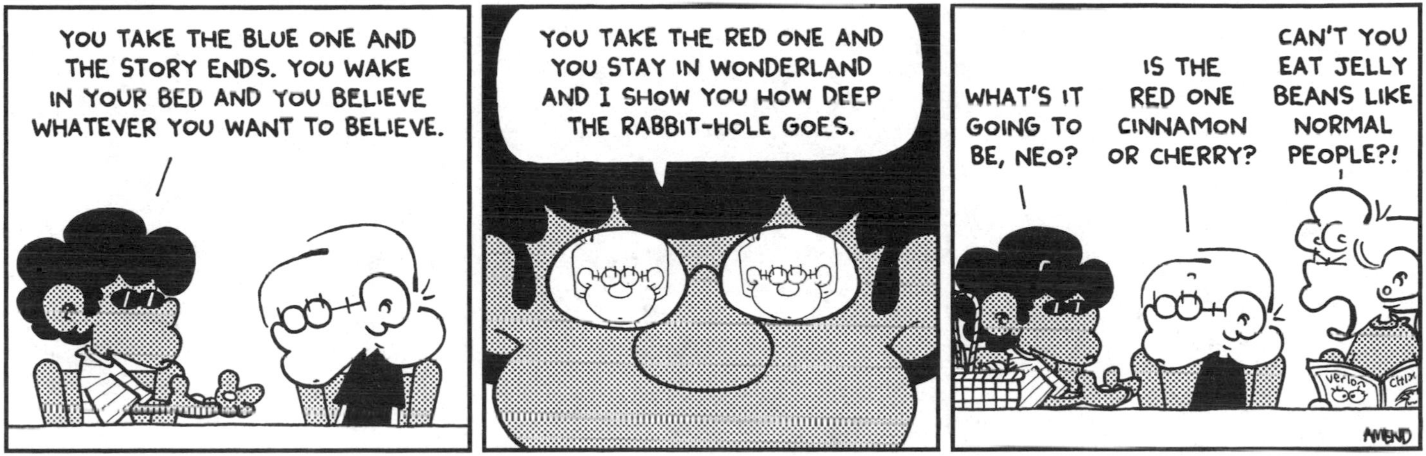
YOU TAKE THE BLUE ONE AND THE STORY ENDS. YOU WAKE IN YOUR BED AND YOU BELIEVE WHATEVER YOU WANT TO BELIEVE.
YOU TAKE THE RED ONE AND YOU STAY IN WONDERLAND AND I SHOW YOU HOW DEEP THE RABBIT-HOLE GOES.
WHAT'S IT GOING TO BE, NEO?
IS THE RED ONE CINNAMON OR CHERRY?
CAN'T YOU EAT JELLY BEANS LIKE NORMAL PEOPLE?!
AMEND

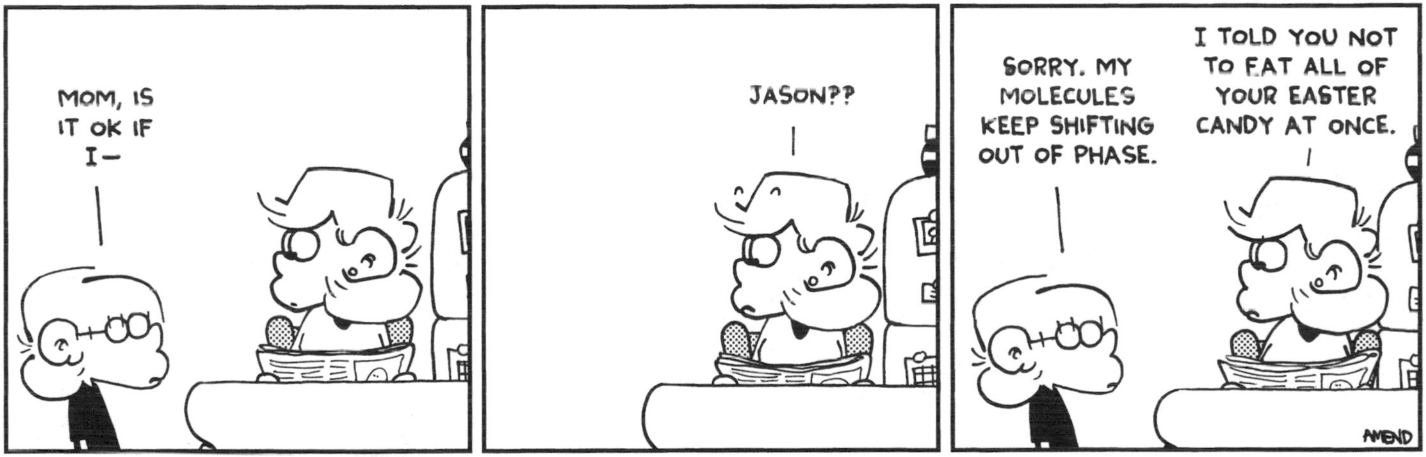
MOM, IS IT OK IF I—
JASON??
SORRY. MY MOLECULES KEEP SHIFTING OUT OF PHASE.
I TOLD YOU NOT TO EAT ALL OF YOUR EASTER CANDY AT ONCE.
AMEND

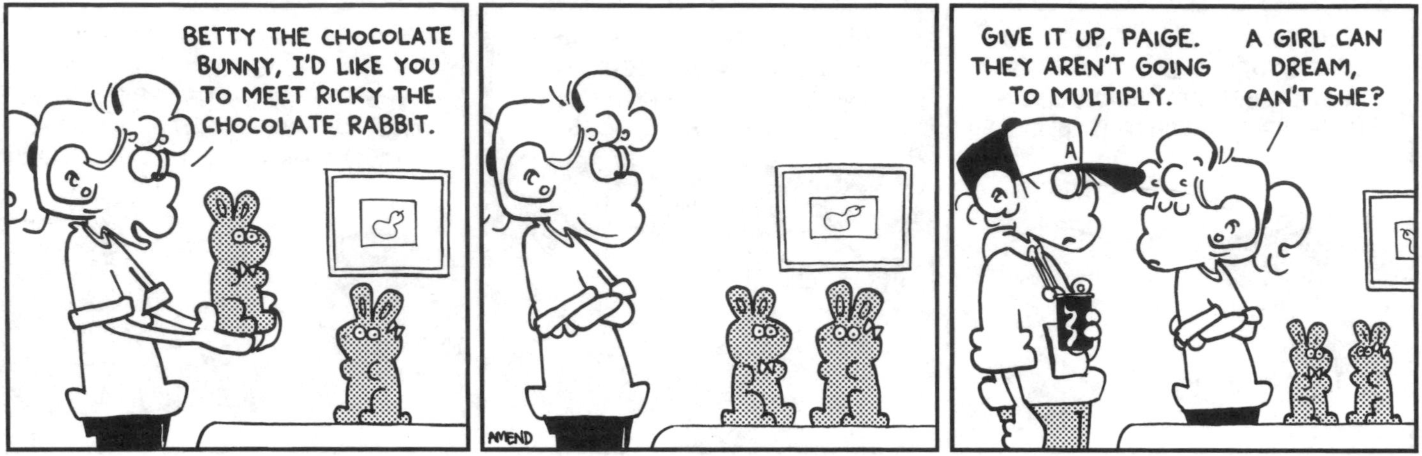
BETTY THE CHOCOLATE BUNNY, I'D LIKE YOU TO MEET RICKY THE CHOCOLATE RABBIT.
AMEND
GIVE IT UP, PAIGE. THEY AREN'T GOING TO MULTIPLY.
A GIRL CAN DREAM, CAN'T SHE?

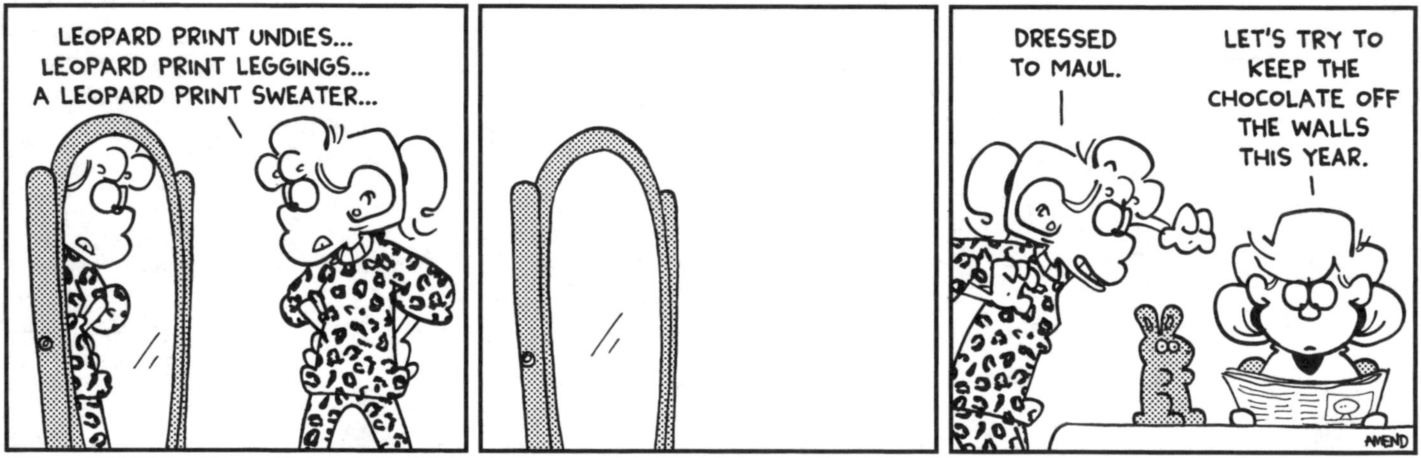
LEOPARD PRINT UNDIES... LEOPARD PRINT LEGGINGS... A LEOPARD PRINT SWEATER...
DRESSED TO MAUL.
LET'S TRY TO KEEP THE CHOCOLATE OFF THE WALLS THIS YEAR.
AMEND

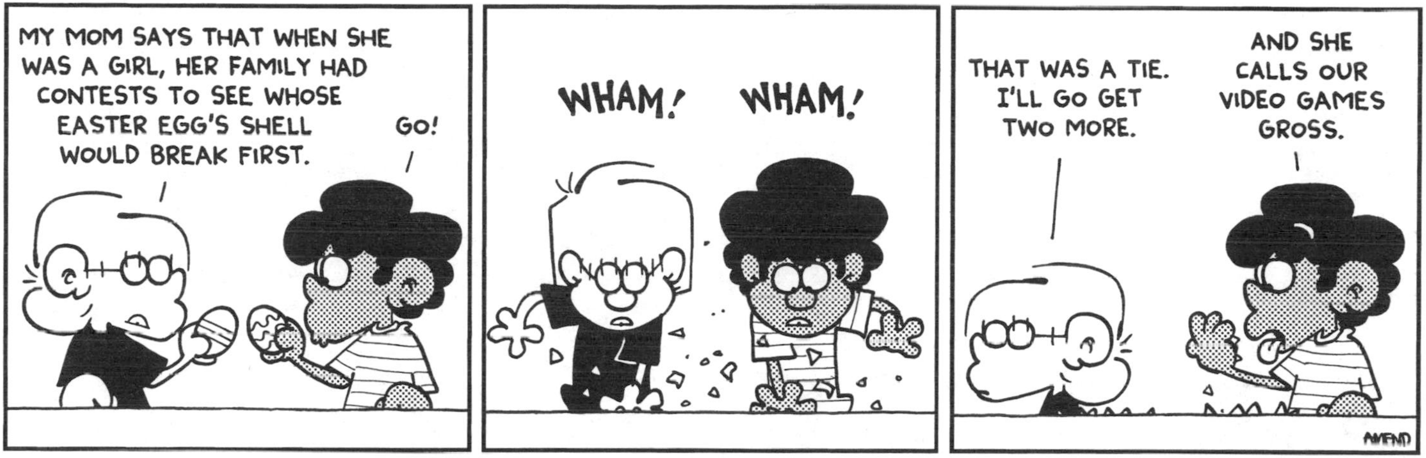
MY MOM SAYS THAT WHEN SHE WAS A GIRL, HER FAMILY HAD CONTESTS TO SEE WHOSE EASTER EGG'S SHELL WOULD BREAK FIRST.
GO!
WHAM!
WHAM!
THAT WAS A TIE. I'LL GO GET TWO MORE.
AND SHE CALLS OUR VIDEO GAMES GROSS.
AMEND

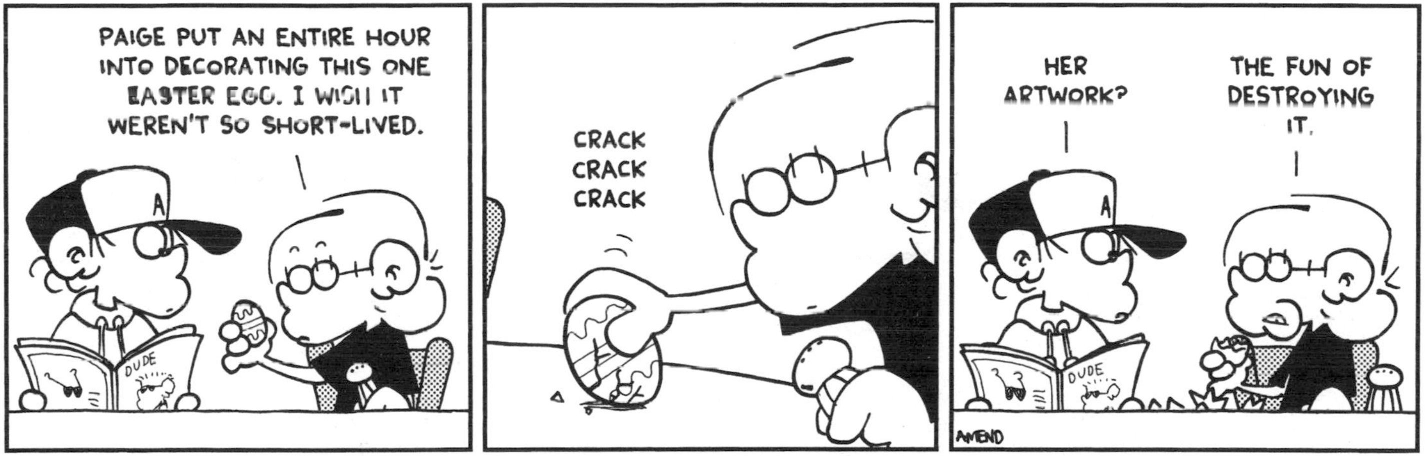
PAIGE PUT AN ENTIRE HOUR INTO DECORATING THIS ONE EASTER EGG. I WISH IT WEREN'T SO SHORT-LIVED.
DUDE
CRACK
CRACK
CRACK
HER ARTWORK?
THE FUN OF DESTROYING IT.
DUDE
AMEND

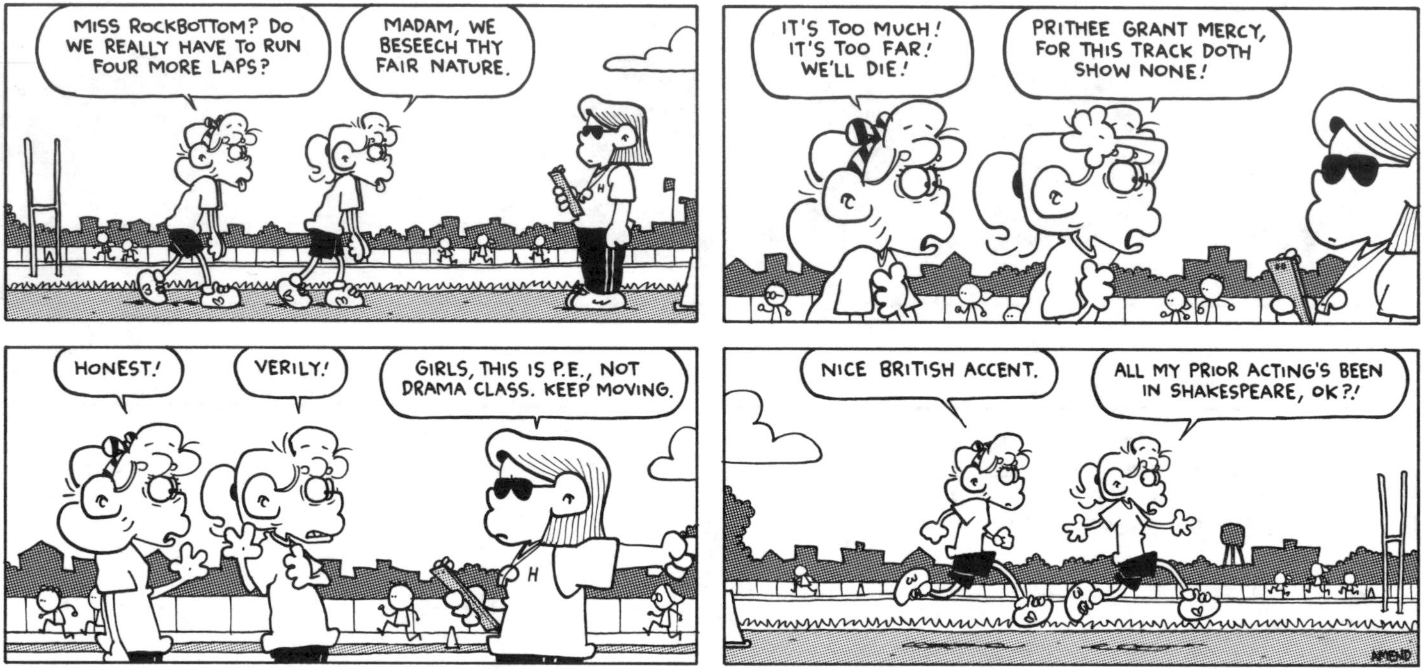
MISS ROCKBOTTOM? DO WE REALLY HAVE TO RUN FOUR MORE LAPS?
MADAM, WE BESEECH THY FAIR NATURE.
IT'S TOO MUCH! IT'S TOO FAR! WE'LL DIE!
PRITHEE GRANT MERCY, FOR THIS TRACK DOTH SHOW NONE!
HONEST!
VERILY!
GIRLS, THIS IS P.E., NOT DRAMA CLASS. KEEP MOVING.
NICE BRITISH ACCENT.
ALL MY PRIOR ACTING'S BEEN IN SHAKESPEARE, OK?!
AMEND

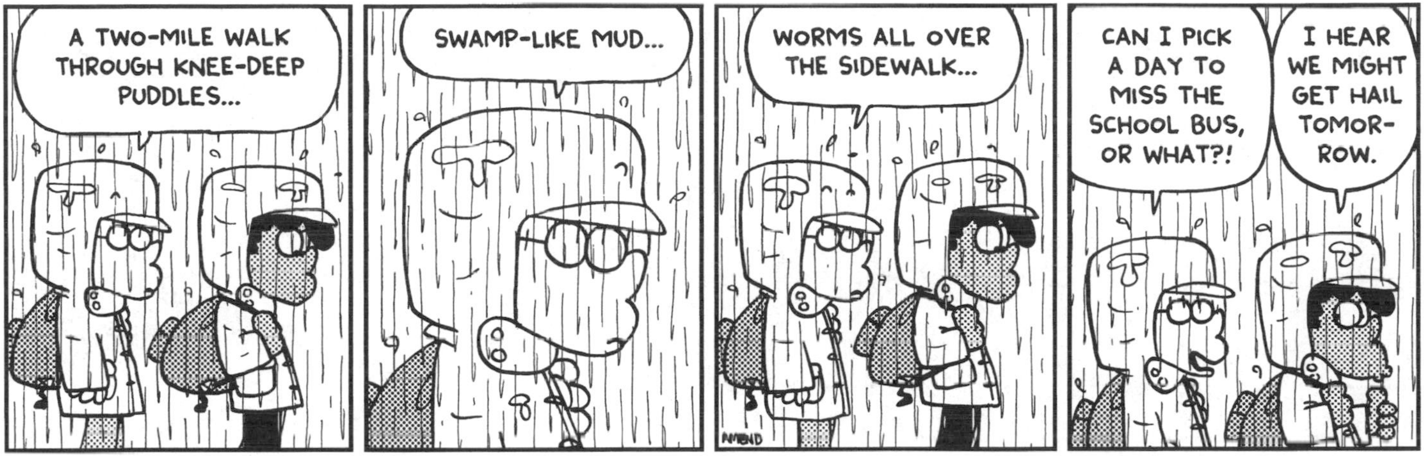
A TWO-MILE WALK THROUGH KNEE-DEEP PUDDLES...
SWAMP-LIKE MUD...
WORMS ALL OVER THE SIDEWALK...
CAN I PICK A DAY TO MISS THE SCHOOL BUS, OR WHAT?!
I HEAR WE MIGHT GET HAIL TOMOR-ROW.
AMEND

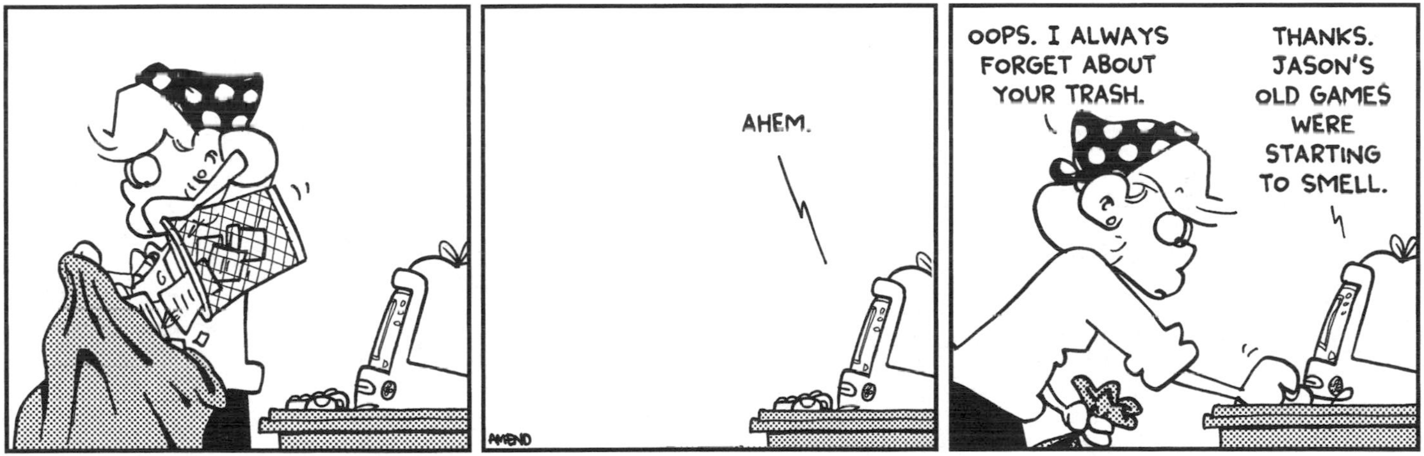
AHEM.
AMEND
OOPS. I ALWAYS FORGET ABOUT YOUR TRASH.
THANKS. JASON'S OLD GAMES WERE STARTING TO SMELL.

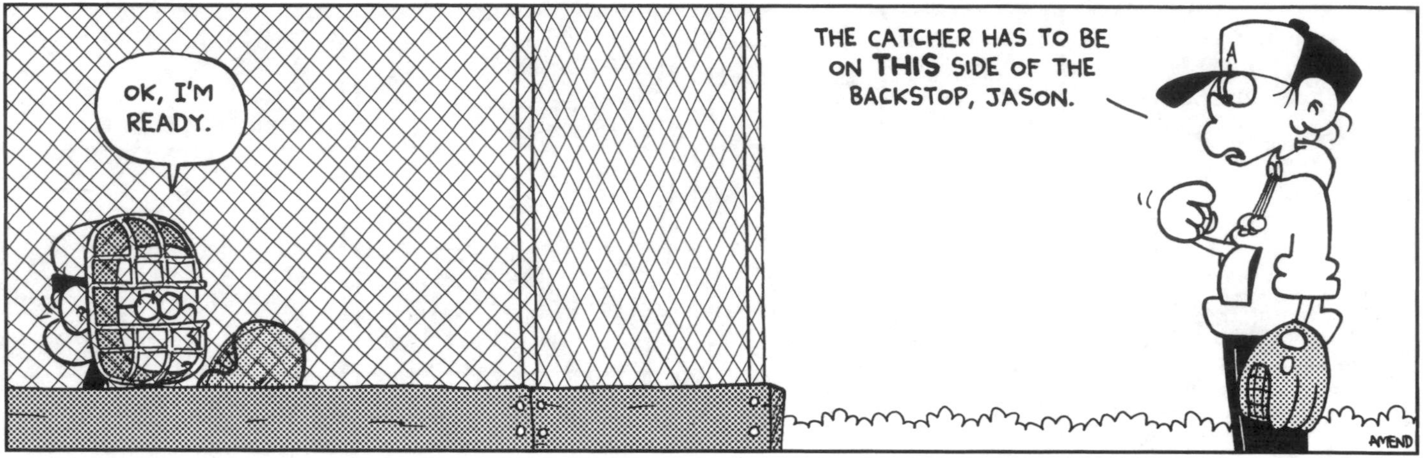
OK, I'M READY.
THE CATCHER HAS TO BE ON THIS SIDE OF THE BACKSTOP, JASON.
AMEND

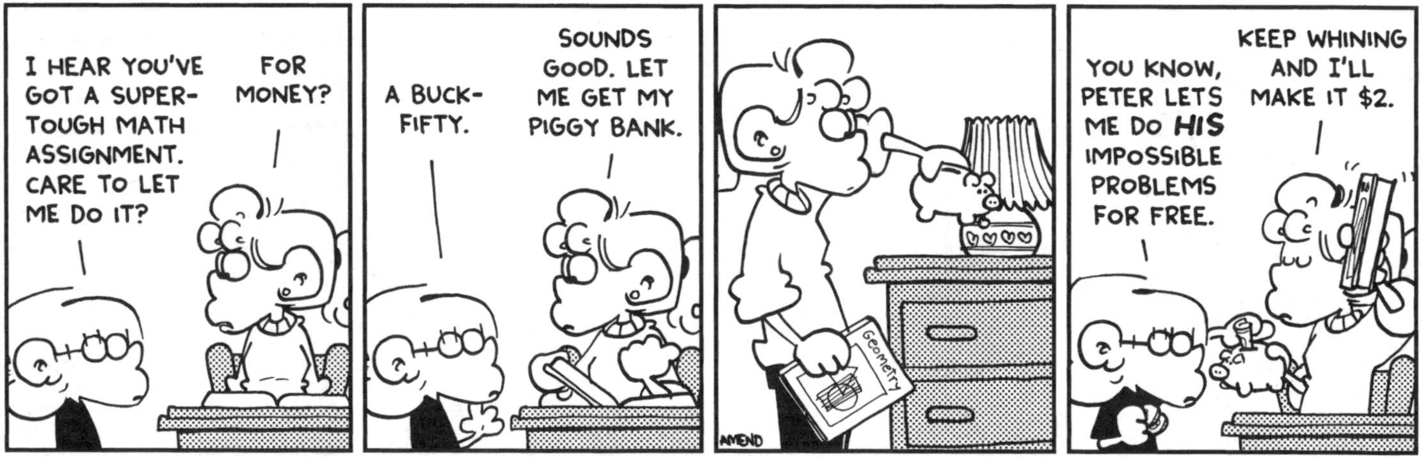
I HEAR YOU'VE GOT A SUPER-TOUGH MATH ASSIGNMENT. CARE TO LET ME DO IT?
FOR MONEY?
A BUCK-FIFTY.
SOUNDS GOOD. LET ME GET MY PIGGY BANK.
Geometry
AMEND
YOU KNOW, PETER LETS ME DO HIS IMPOSSIBLE PROBLEMS FOR FREE.
KEEP WHINING AND I'LL MAKE IT $2.

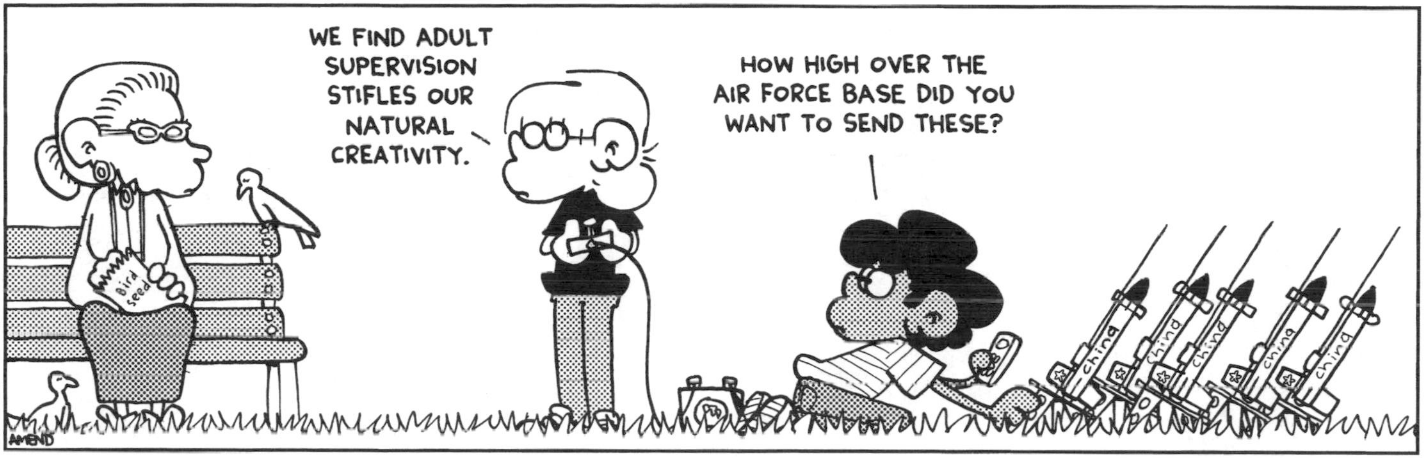

AMEND
Bird seed
WE FIND ADULT SUPERVISION STIFLES OUR NATURAL CREATIVITY.
HOW HIGH OVER THE AIR FORCE BASE DID YOU WANT TO SEND THESE?
china

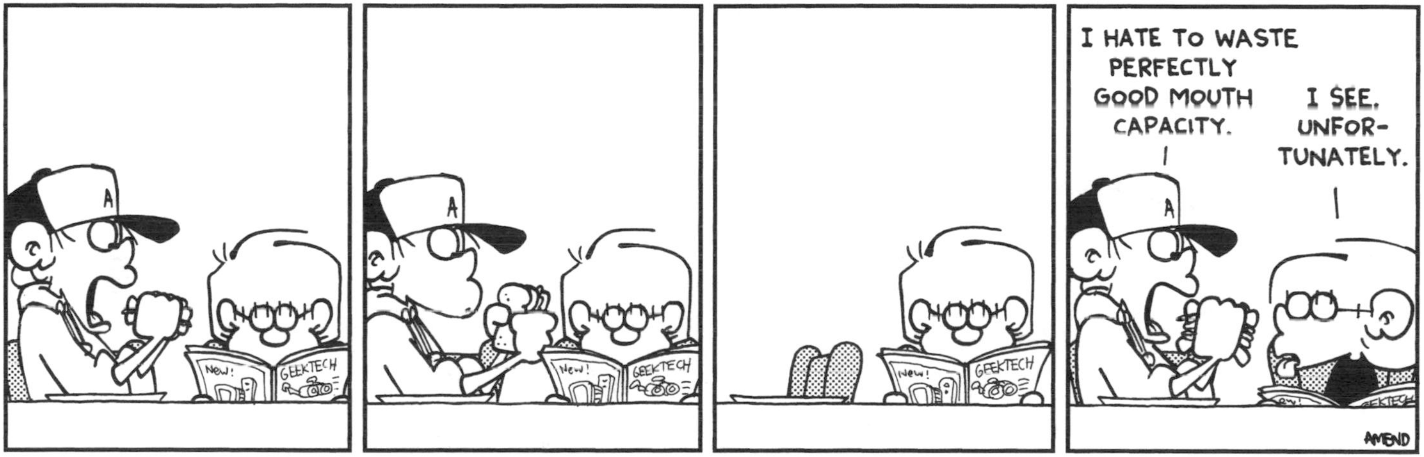

A
New!
GEEKTECH
I HATE TO WASTE PERFECTLY GOOD MOUTH CAPACITY.
I SEE. UNFORTUNATELY.
AMEND

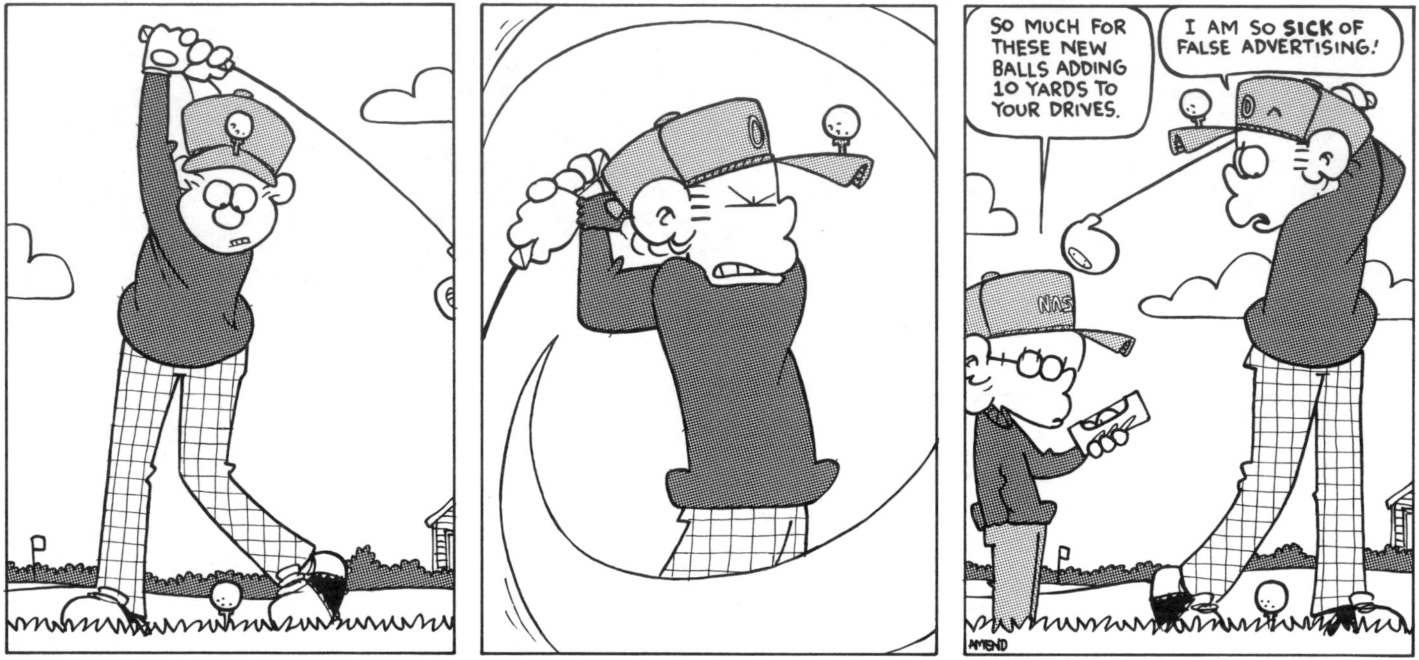
SO MUCH FOR THESE NEW BALLS ADDING 10 YARDS TO YOUR DRIVES.
I AM SO **SICK** OF FALSE ADVERTISING!
AMEND

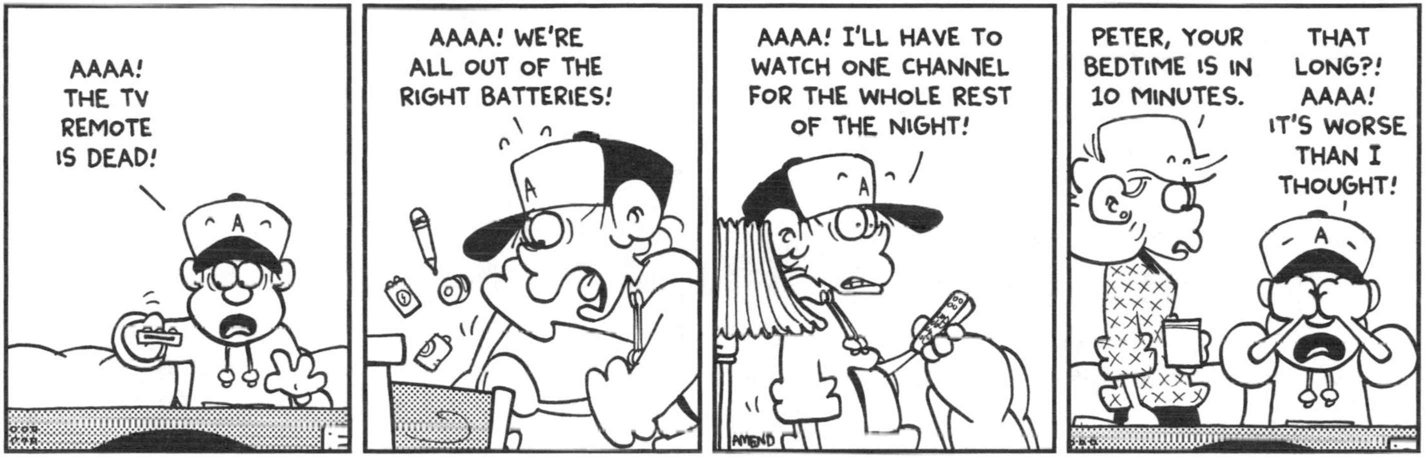
AAAA! THE TV REMOTE IS DEAD!
AAAA! WE'RE ALL OUT OF THE RIGHT BATTERIES!
AAAA! I'LL HAVE TO WATCH ONE CHANNEL FOR THE WHOLE REST OF THE NIGHT!
PETER, YOUR BEDTIME IS IN 10 MINUTES.
THAT LONG?! AAAA! IT'S WORSE THAN I THOUGHT!
AMEND

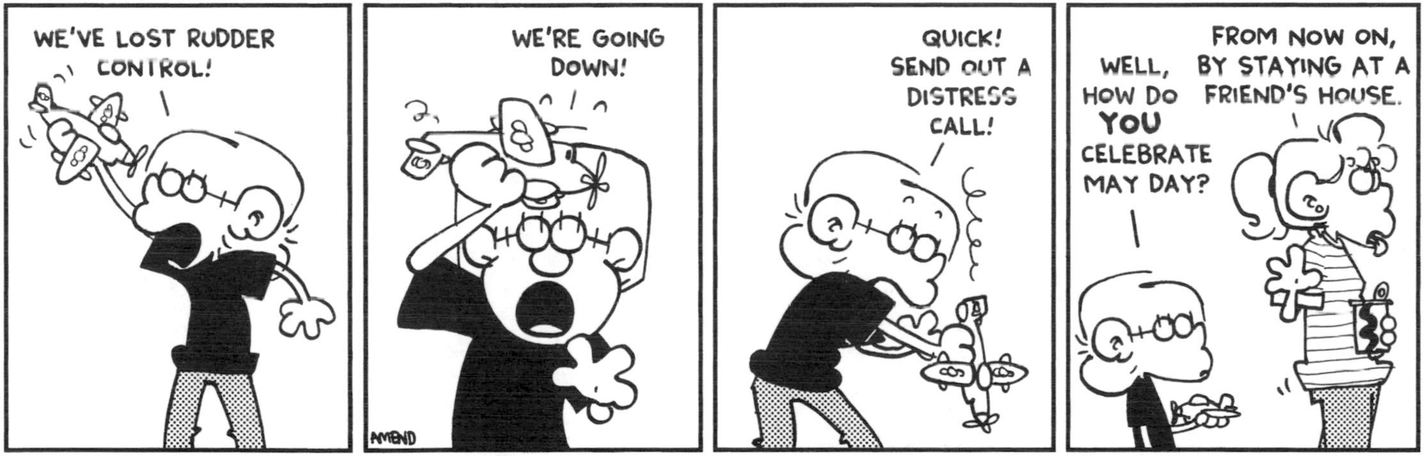
WE'VE LOST RUDDER CONTROL!
WE'RE GOING DOWN!
AMEND
QUICK! SEND OUT A DISTRESS CALL!
WELL, HOW DO **YOU** CELEBRATE MAY DAY?
FROM NOW ON, BY STAYING AT A FRIEND'S HOUSE.

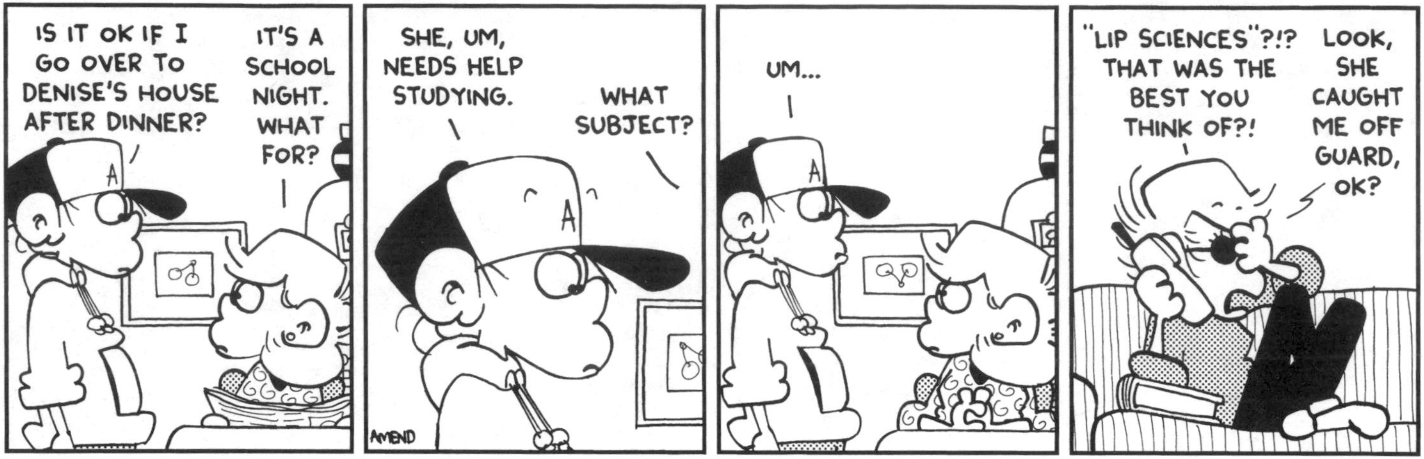
IS IT OK IF I GO OVER TO DENISE'S HOUSE AFTER DINNER?
IT'S A SCHOOL NIGHT. WHAT FOR?
SHE, UM, NEEDS HELP STUDYING.
WHAT SUBJECT?
AMEND
UM...
"LIP SCIENCES"?!? THAT WAS THE BEST YOU THINK OF?!
LOOK, SHE CAUGHT ME OFF GUARD, OK?

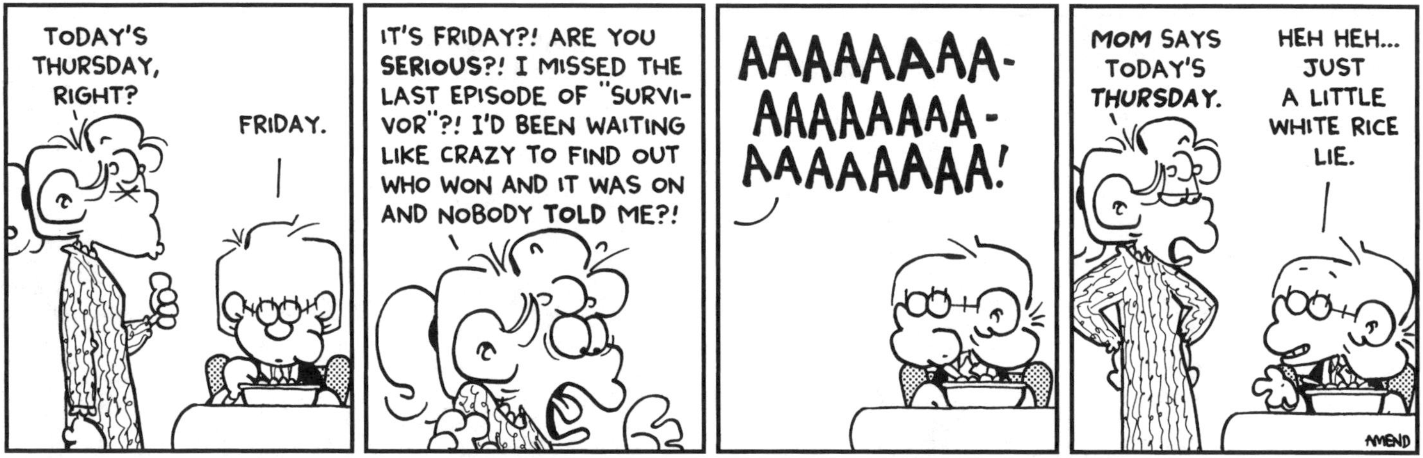
TODAY'S THURSDAY, RIGHT?
FRIDAY.
IT'S FRIDAY?! ARE YOU SERIOUS?! I MISSED THE LAST EPISODE OF "SURVIVOR"?! I'D BEEN WAITING LIKE CRAZY TO FIND OUT WHO WON AND IT WAS ON AND NOBODY TOLD ME?!
AAAAAAAA-AAAAAAAA-AAAAAAAA!
MOM SAYS TODAY'S THURSDAY.
HEH HEH... JUST A LITTLE WHITE RICE LIE.
AMEND

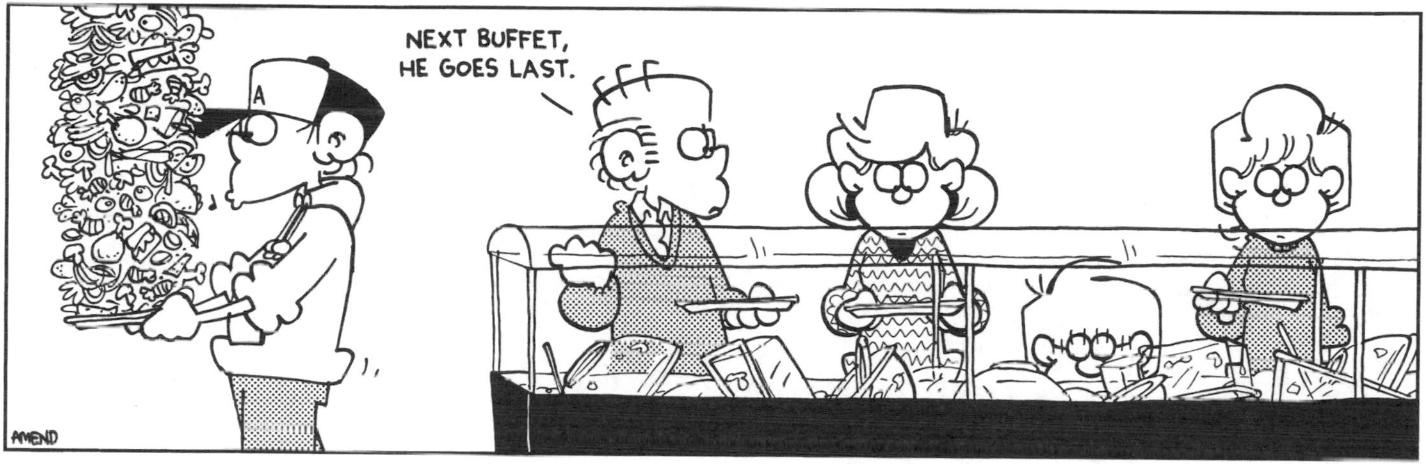
NEXT BUFFET, HE GOES LAST.
AMEND

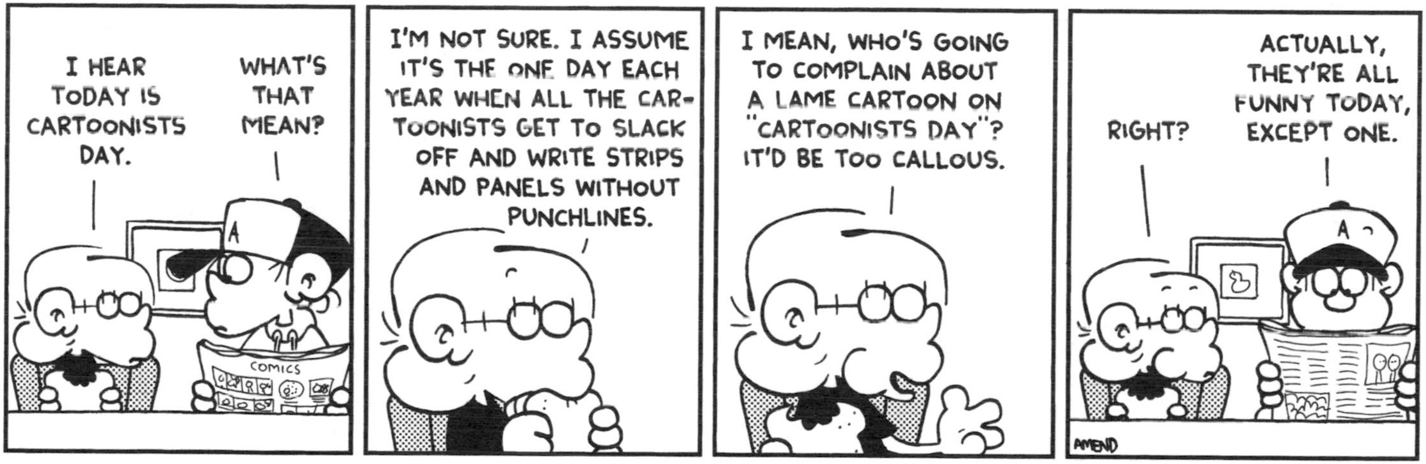
I HEAR TODAY IS CARTOONISTS DAY.
WHAT'S THAT MEAN?
COMICS
I'M NOT SURE. I ASSUME IT'S THE ONE DAY EACH YEAR WHEN ALL THE CARTOONISTS GET TO SLACK OFF AND WRITE STRIPS AND PANELS WITHOUT PUNCHLINES.
I MEAN, WHO'S GOING TO COMPLAIN ABOUT A LAME CARTOON ON "CARTOONISTS DAY"? IT'D BE TOO CALLOUS.
RIGHT?
ACTUALLY, THEY'RE ALL FUNNY TODAY, EXCEPT ONE.
AMEND

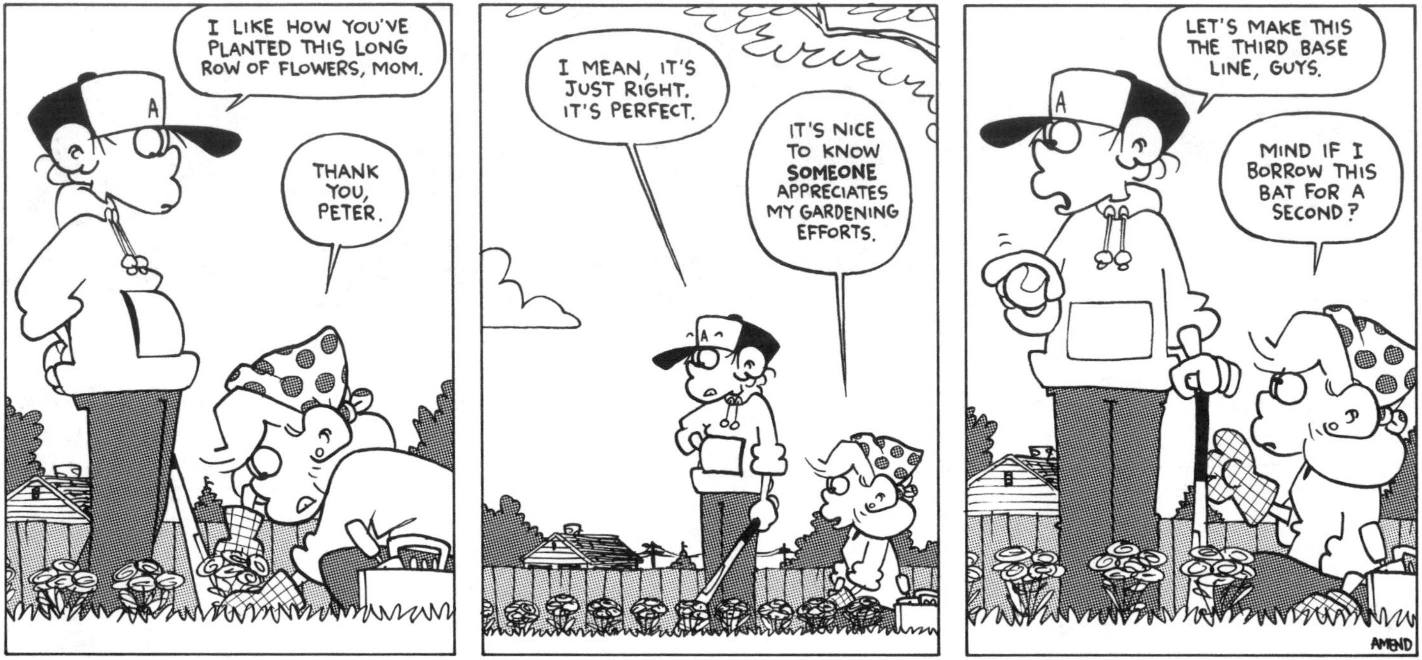
I LIKE HOW YOU'VE PLANTED THIS LONG ROW OF FLOWERS, MOM.
THANK YOU, PETER.
I MEAN, IT'S JUST RIGHT. IT'S PERFECT.
IT'S NICE TO KNOW **SOMEONE** APPRECIATES MY GARDENING EFFORTS.
LET'S MAKE THIS THE THIRD BASE LINE, GUYS.
MIND IF I BORROW THIS BAT FOR A SECOND?
AMEND

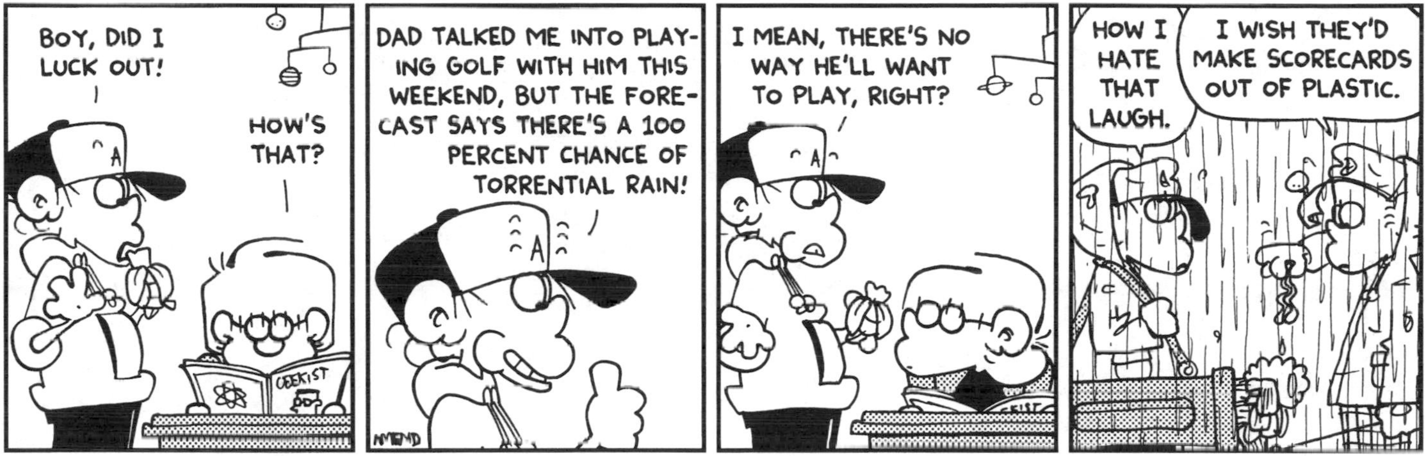
BOY, DID I LUCK OUT!
HOW'S THAT?
GEEKIST
DAD TALKED ME INTO PLAY-ING GOLF WITH HIM THIS WEEKEND, BUT THE FORE-CAST SAYS THERE'S A 100 PERCENT CHANCE OF TORRENTIAL RAIN!
AMEND
I MEAN, THERE'S NO WAY HE'LL WANT TO PLAY, RIGHT?
HOW I HATE THAT LAUGH.
I WISH THEY'D MAKE SCORECARDS OUT OF PLASTIC.

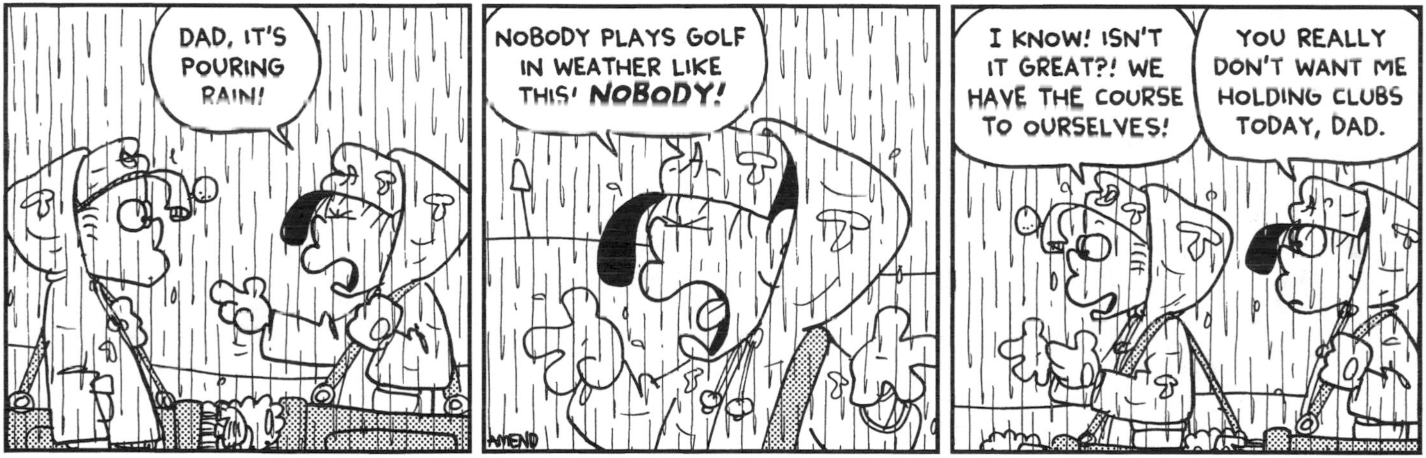
DAD, IT'S POURING RAIN!
NOBODY PLAYS GOLF IN WEATHER LIKE THIS! NOBODY!
AMEND
I KNOW! ISN'T IT GREAT?! WE HAVE THE COURSE TO OURSELVES!
YOU REALLY DON'T WANT ME HOLDING CLUBS TODAY, DAD.

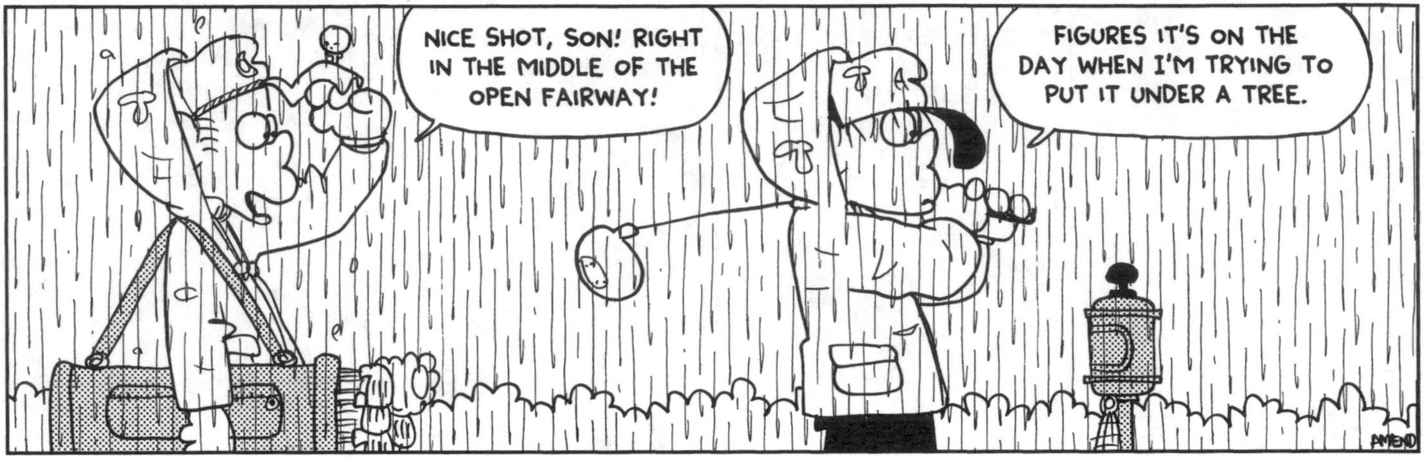
NICE SHOT, SON! RIGHT IN THE MIDDLE OF THE OPEN FAIRWAY!
FIGURES IT'S ON THE DAY WHEN I'M TRYING TO PUT IT UNDER A TREE.
AMEND

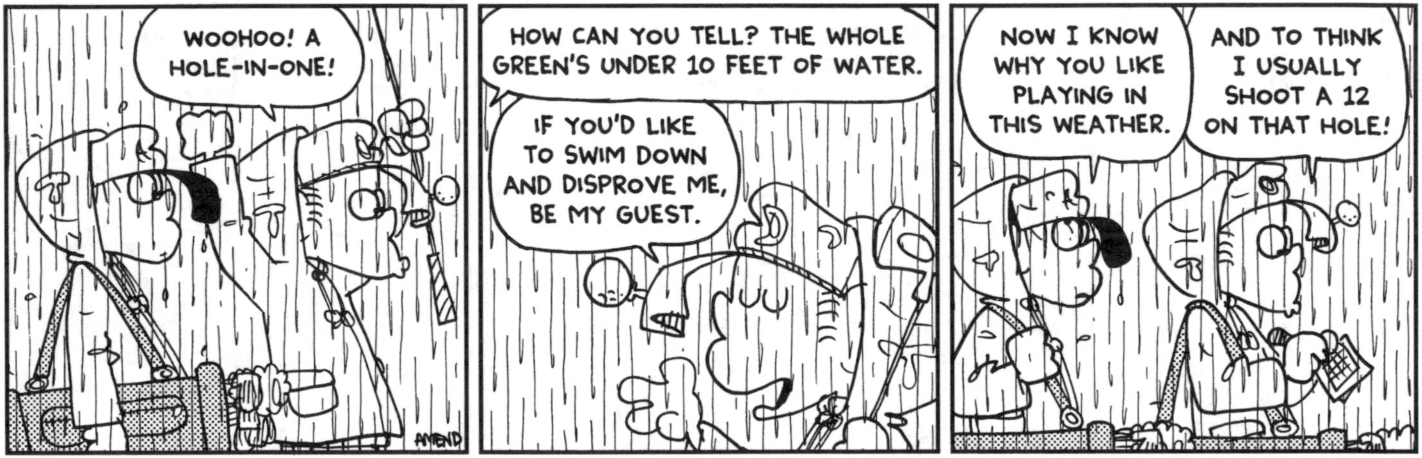
WOOHOO! A HOLE-IN-ONE!
AMEND
HOW CAN YOU TELL? THE WHOLE GREEN'S UNDER 10 FEET OF WATER.
IF YOU'D LIKE TO SWIM DOWN AND DISPROVE ME, BE MY GUEST.
NOW I KNOW WHY YOU LIKE PLAYING IN THIS WEATHER.
AND TO THINK I USUALLY SHOOT A 12 ON THAT HOLE!

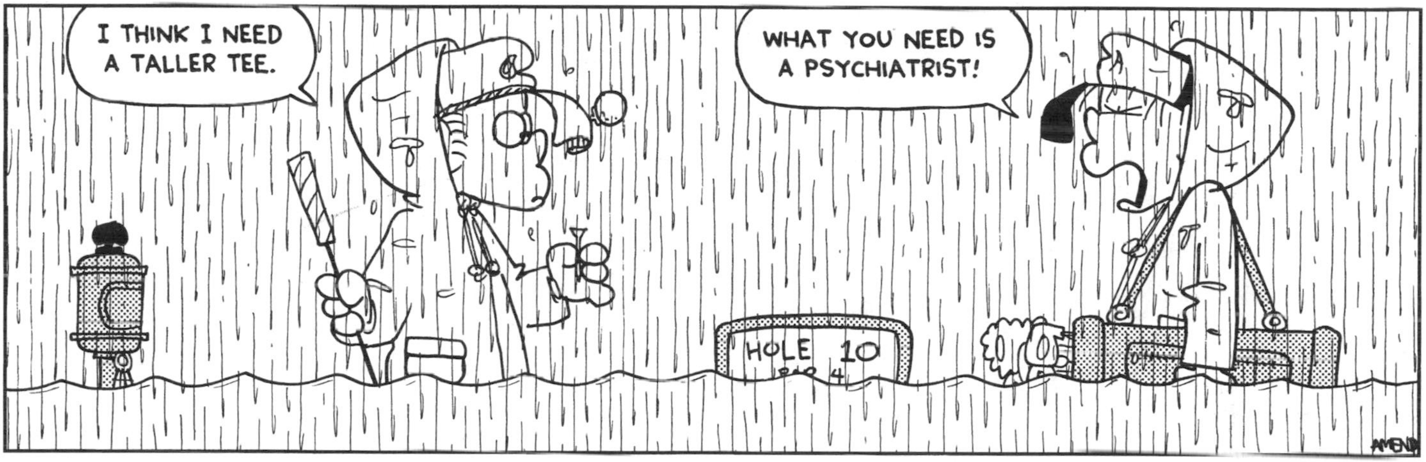
I THINK I NEED A TALLER TEE.
WHAT YOU NEED IS A PSYCHIATRIST!
HOLE 10
AMEND

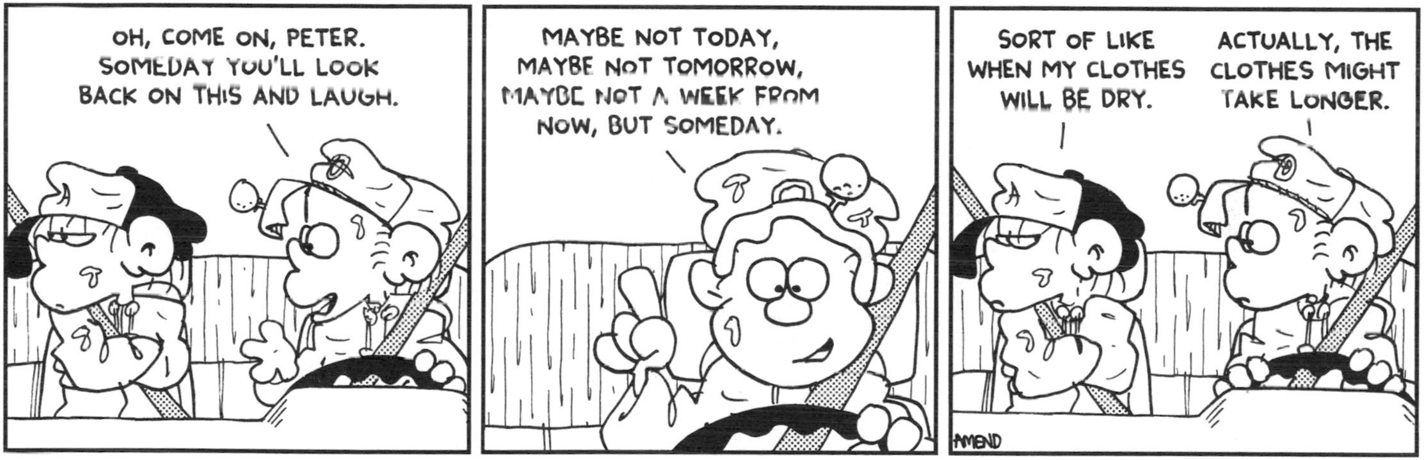
OH, COME ON, PETER. SOMEDAY YOU'LL LOOK BACK ON THIS AND LAUGH.
MAYBE NOT TODAY, MAYBE NOT TOMORROW, MAYBE NOT A WEEK FROM NOW, BUT SOMEDAY.
SORT OF LIKE WHEN MY CLOTHES WILL BE DRY.
ACTUALLY, THE CLOTHES MIGHT TAKE LONGER.
AMEND

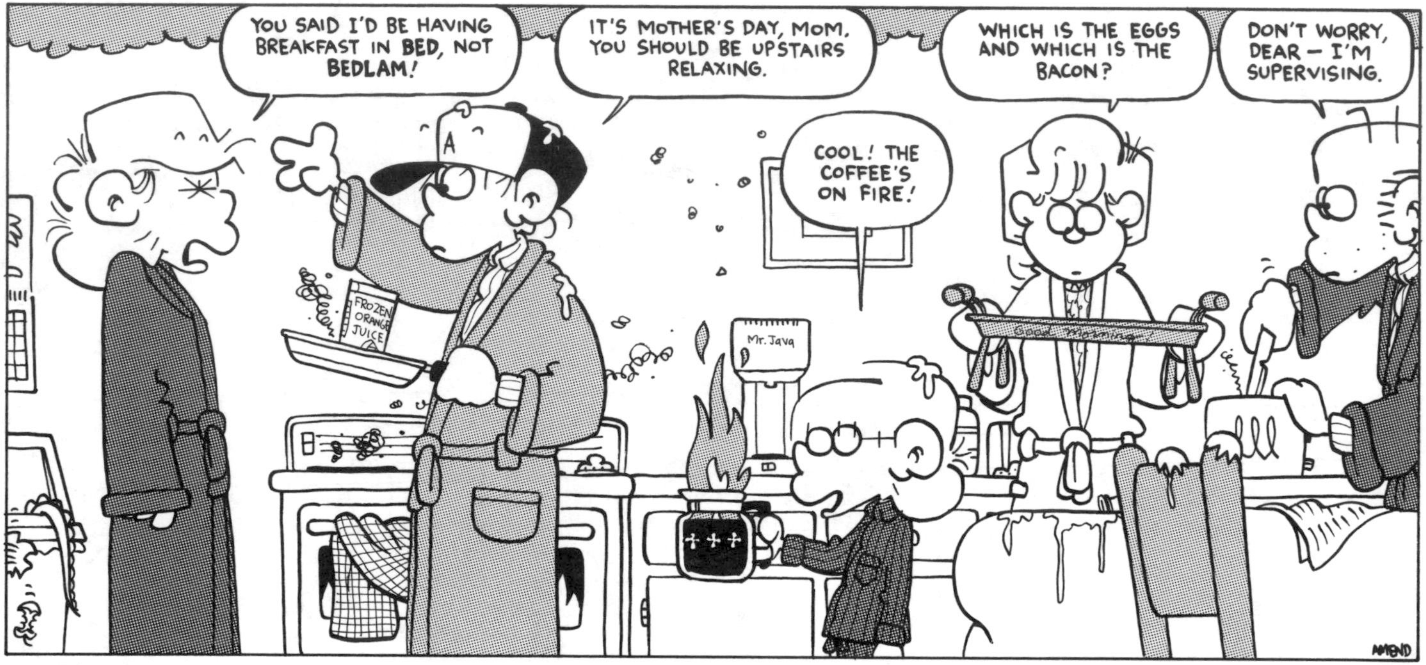
YOU SAID I'D BE HAVING BREAKFAST IN BED, NOT BEDLAM!
IT'S MOTHER'S DAY, MOM. YOU SHOULD BE UPSTAIRS RELAXING.
COOL! THE COFFEE'S ON FIRE!
WHICH IS THE EGGS AND WHICH IS THE BACON?
DON'T WORRY, DEAR – I'M SUPERVISING.
FROZEN ORANGE JUICE
Mr. Java
AMEND

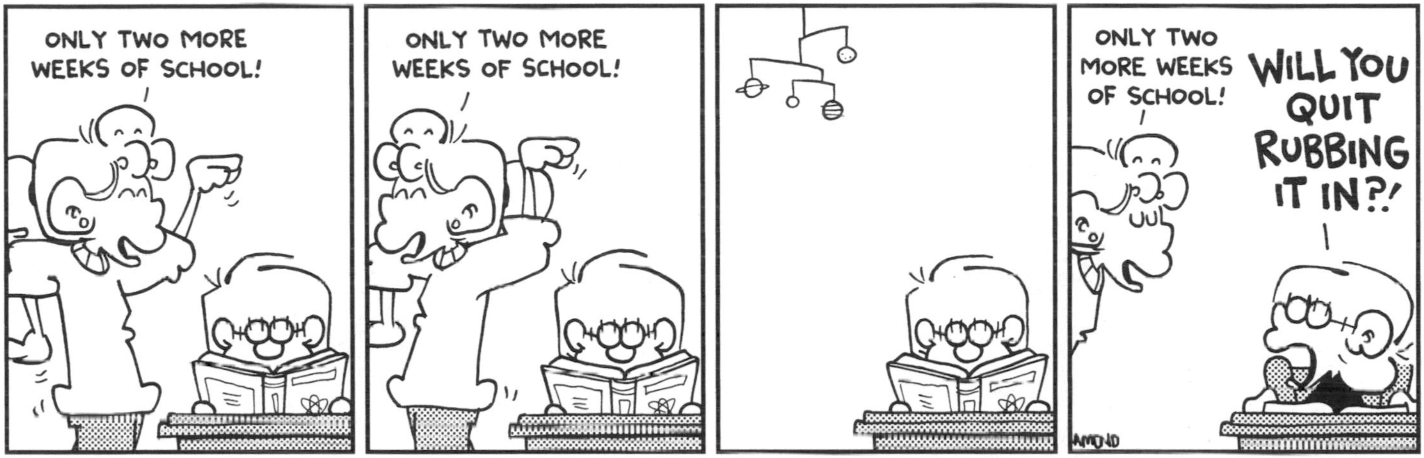
ONLY TWO MORE WEEKS OF SCHOOL!
ONLY TWO MORE WEEKS OF SCHOOL!
ONLY TWO MORE WEEKS OF SCHOOL!
WILL YOU QUIT RUBBING IT IN?!

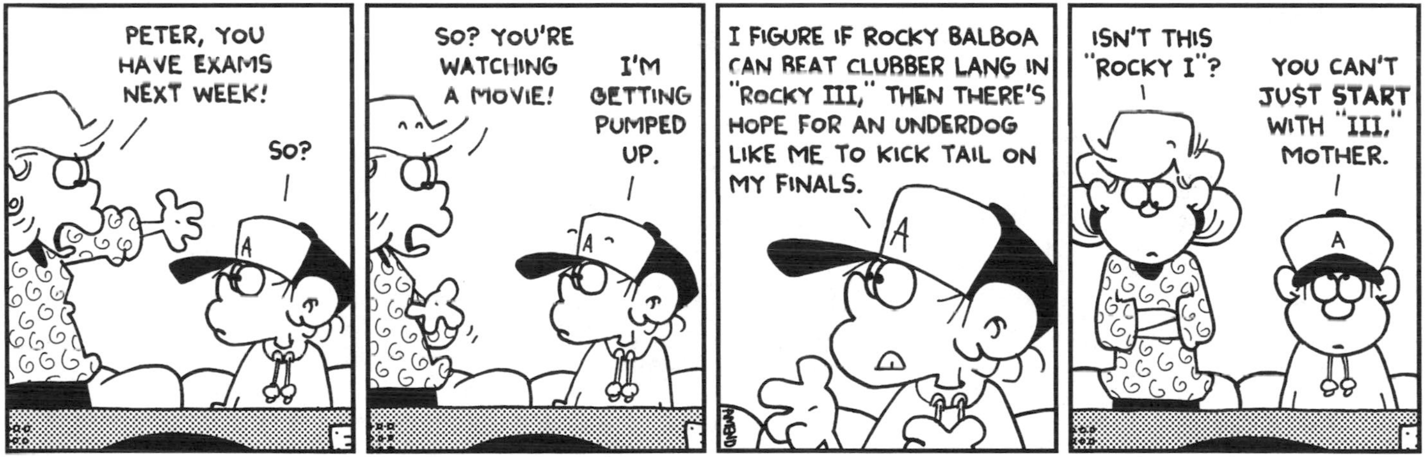
PETER, YOU HAVE EXAMS NEXT WEEK!
SO?
SO? YOU'RE WATCHING A MOVIE!
I'M GETTING PUMPED UP.
I FIGURE IF ROCKY BALBOA CAN BEAT CLUBBER LANG IN "ROCKY III," THEN THERE'S HOPE FOR AN UNDERDOG LIKE ME TO KICK TAIL ON MY FINALS.
ISN'T THIS "ROCKY I"?
YOU CAN'T JUST START WITH "III," MOTHER.

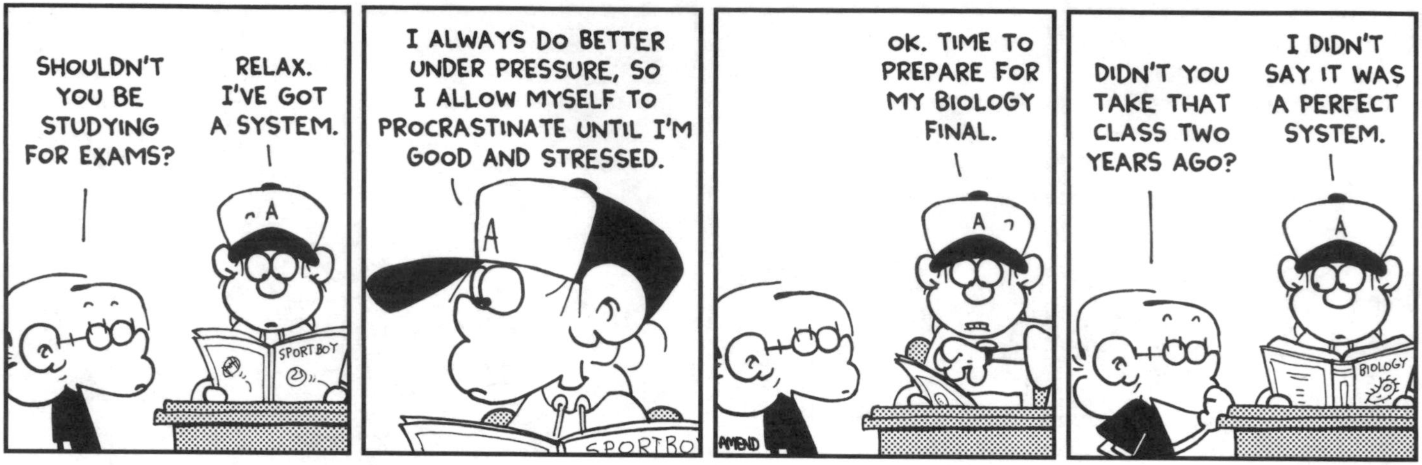
SHOULDN'T YOU BE STUDYING FOR EXAMS?
RELAX. I'VE GOT A SYSTEM.
SPORTBOY
I ALWAYS DO BETTER UNDER PRESSURE, SO I ALLOW MYSELF TO PROCRASTINATE UNTIL I'M GOOD AND STRESSED.
OK. TIME TO PREPARE FOR MY BIOLOGY FINAL.
AMEND
DIDN'T YOU TAKE THAT CLASS TWO YEARS AGO?
I DIDN'T SAY IT WAS A PERFECT SYSTEM.
BIOLOGY

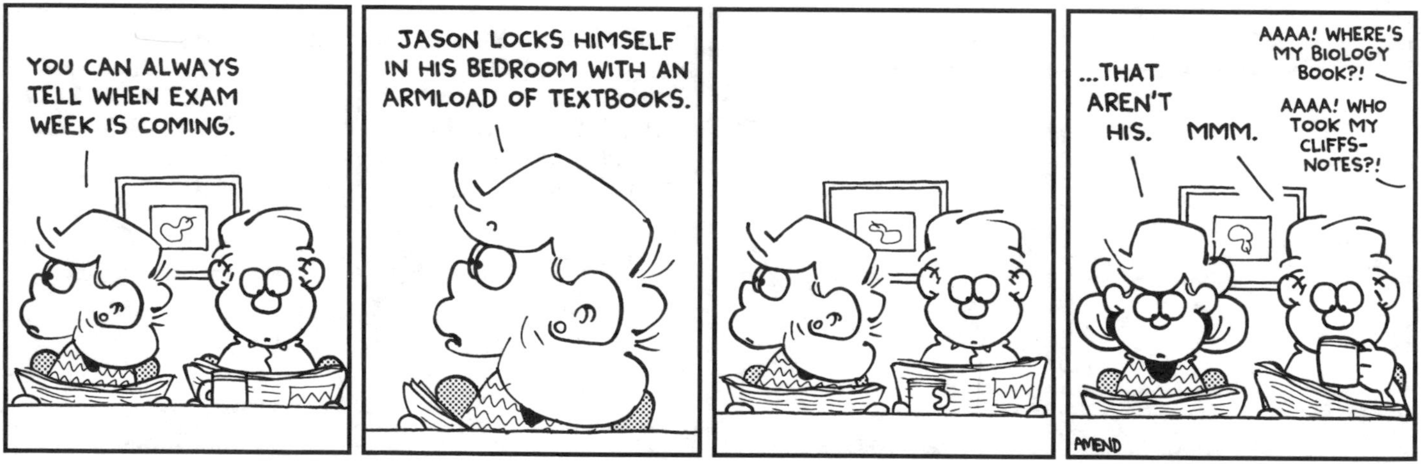
YOU CAN ALWAYS TELL WHEN EXAM WEEK IS COMING.
JASON LOCKS HIMSELF IN HIS BEDROOM WITH AN ARMLOAD OF TEXTBOOKS.
...THAT AREN'T HIS.
MMM.
AAAA! WHERE'S MY BIOLOGY BOOK?!
AAAA! WHO TOOK MY CLIFFS-NOTES?!
AMEND

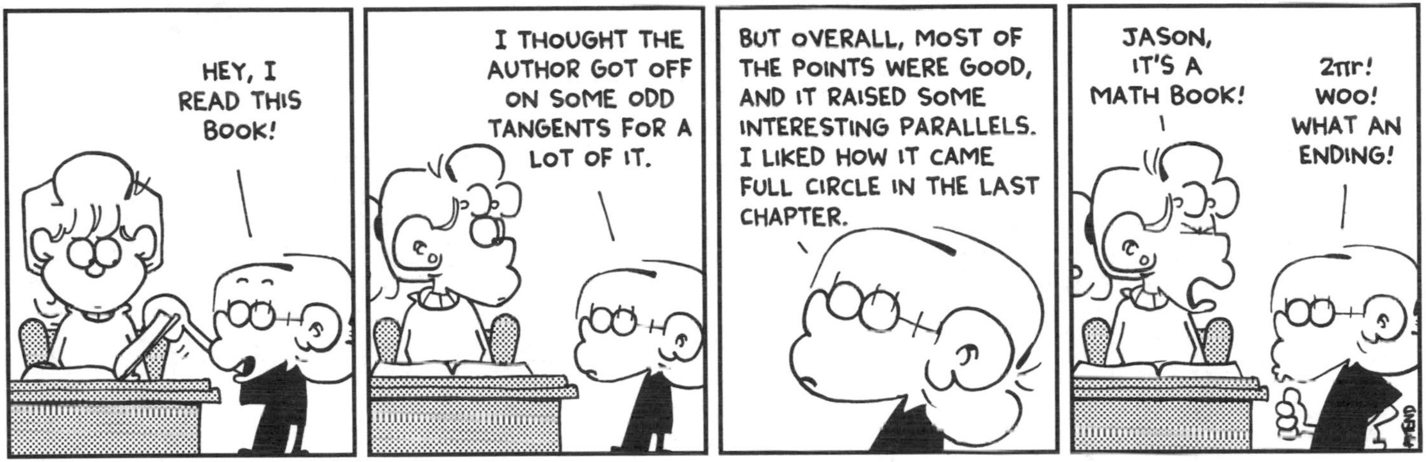
HEY, I READ THIS BOOK!
I THOUGHT THE AUTHOR GOT OFF ON SOME ODD TANGENTS FOR A LOT OF IT.
BUT OVERALL, MOST OF THE POINTS WERE GOOD, AND IT RAISED SOME INTERESTING PARALLELS. I LIKED HOW IT CAME FULL CIRCLE IN THE LAST CHAPTER.
JASON, IT'S A MATH BOOK!
2πr! WOO! WHAT AN ENDING!

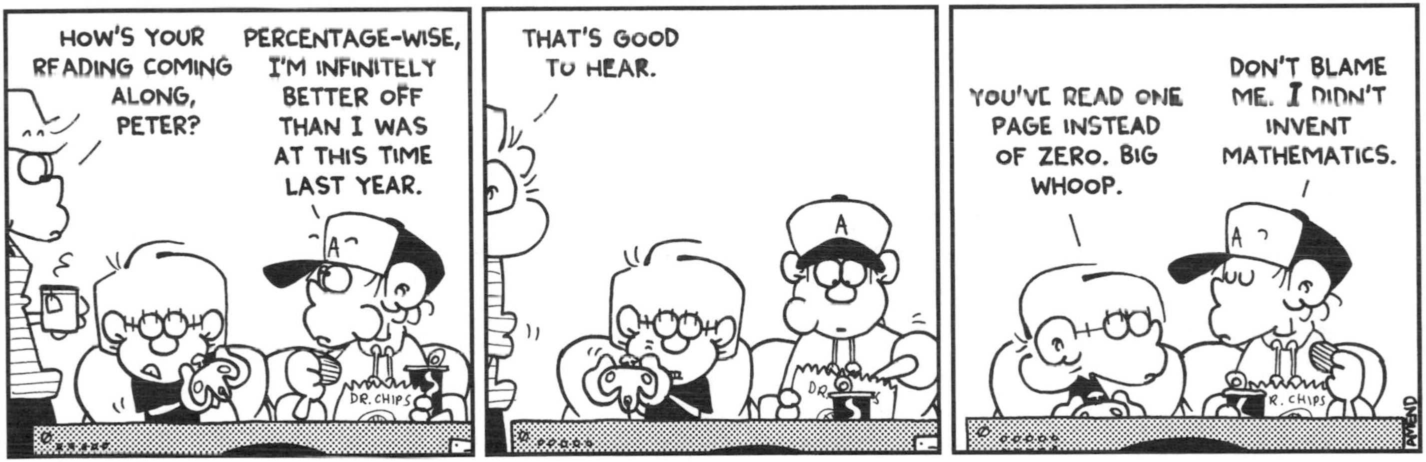
HOW'S YOUR READING COMING ALONG, PETER?
PERCENTAGE-WISE, I'M INFINITELY BETTER OFF THAN I WAS AT THIS TIME LAST YEAR.
THAT'S GOOD TO HEAR.
YOU'VE READ ONE PAGE INSTEAD OF ZERO. BIG WHOOP.
DON'T BLAME ME. I DIDN'T INVENT MATHEMATICS.

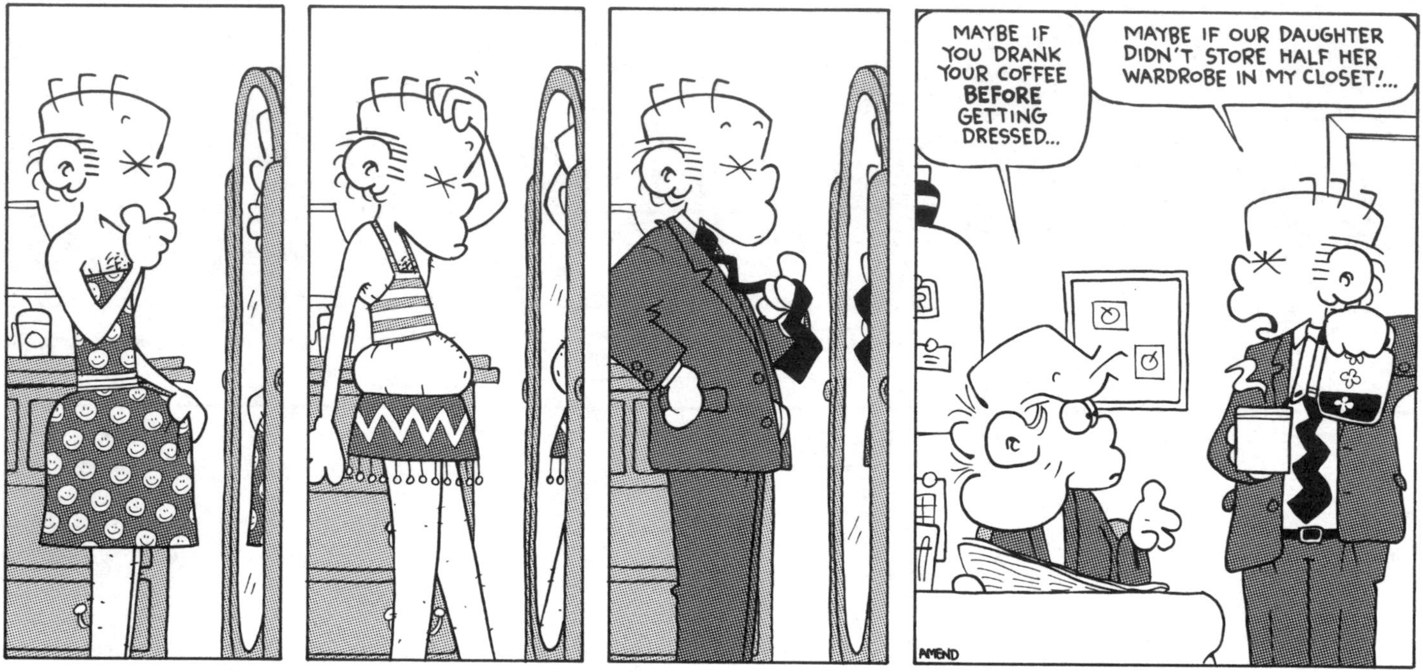
MAYBE IF YOU DRANK YOUR COFFEE **BEFORE** GETTING DRESSED...
MAYBE IF OUR DAUGHTER DIDN'T STORE HALF HER WARDROBE IN MY CLOSET!...
AMEND

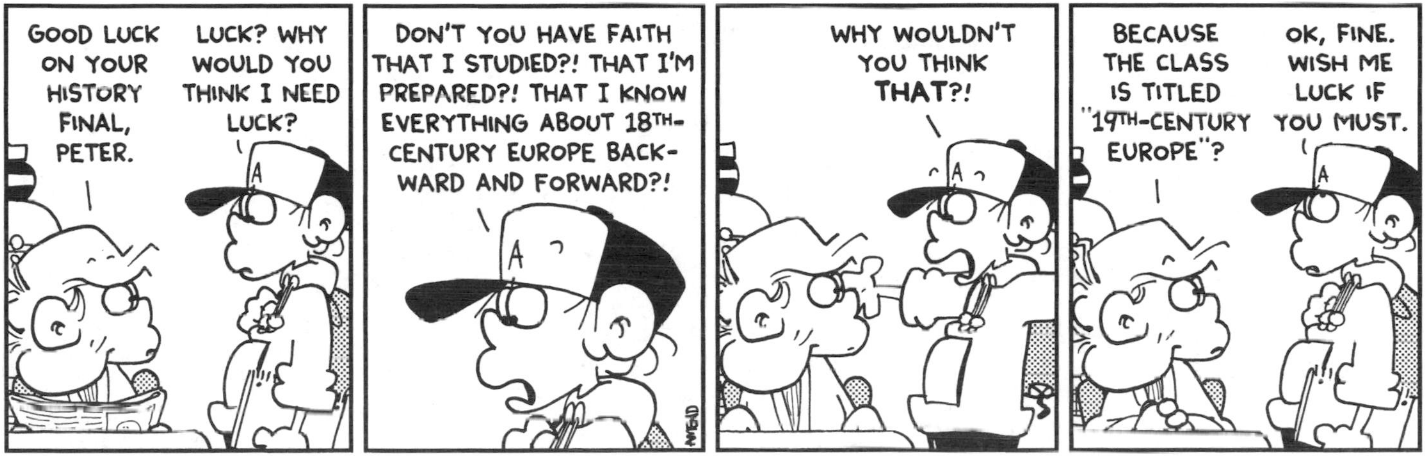
GOOD LUCK ON YOUR HISTORY FINAL, PETER.
LUCK? WHY WOULD YOU THINK I NEED LUCK?
DON'T YOU HAVE FAITH THAT I STUDIED?! THAT I'M PREPARED?! THAT I KNOW EVERYTHING ABOUT 18TH-CENTURY EUROPE BACKWARD AND FORWARD?!
WHY WOULDN'T YOU THINK THAT?!
BECAUSE THE CLASS IS TITLED "19TH-CENTURY EUROPE"?
OK, FINE. WISH ME LUCK IF YOU MUST.

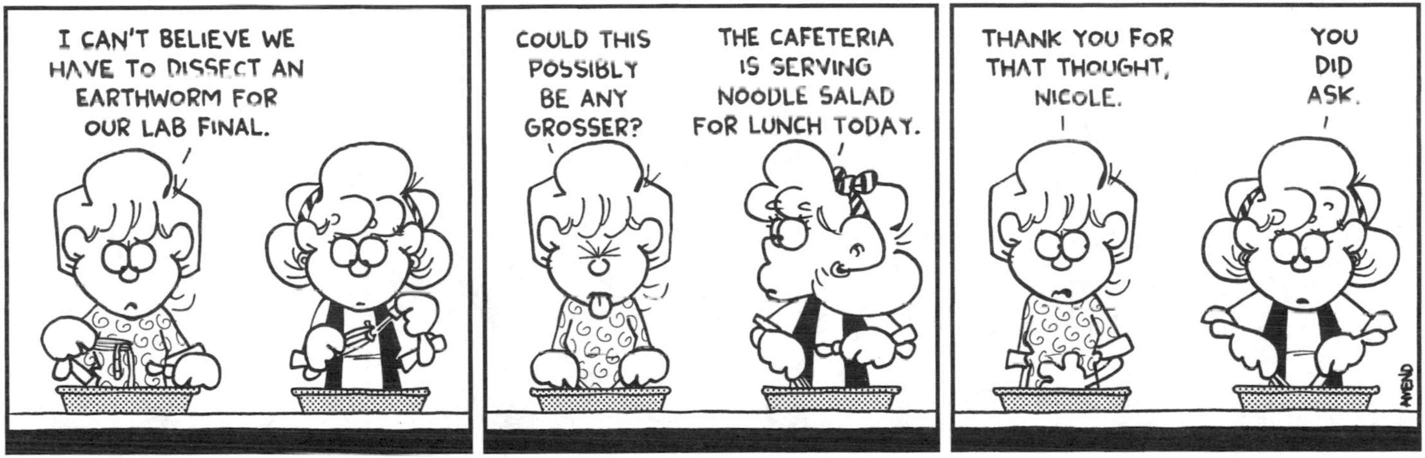
I CAN'T BELIEVE WE HAVE TO DISSECT AN EARTHWORM FOR OUR LAB FINAL.
COULD THIS POSSIBLY BE ANY GROSSER?
THE CAFETERIA IS SERVING NOODLE SALAD FOR LUNCH TODAY.
THANK YOU FOR THAT THOUGHT, NICOLE.
YOU DID ASK.

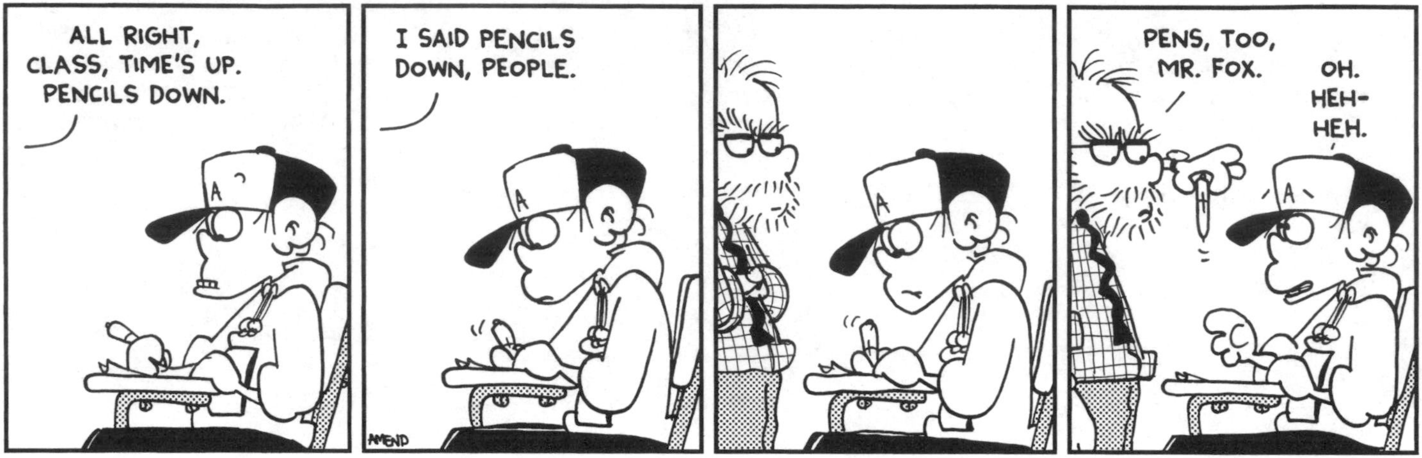
ALL RIGHT, CLASS, TIME'S UP. PENCILS DOWN.
I SAID PENCILS DOWN, PEOPLE.
AMEND
PENS, TOO, MR. FOX.
OH. HEH-HEH.

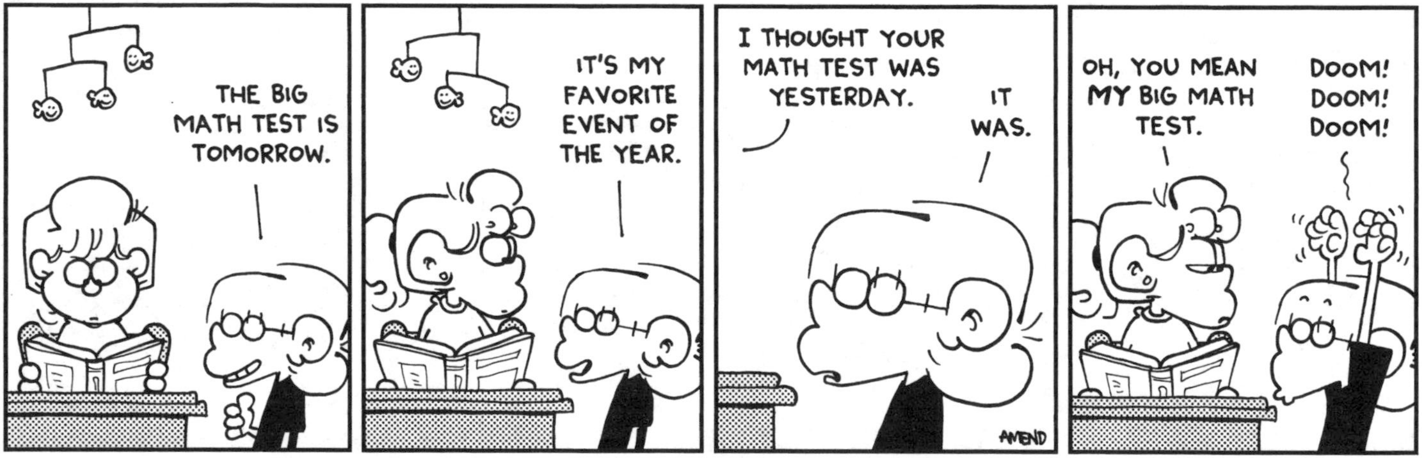
THE BIG MATH TEST IS TOMORROW.
IT'S MY FAVORITE EVENT OF THE YEAR.
I THOUGHT YOUR MATH TEST WAS YESTERDAY.
IT WAS.
AMEND
OH, YOU MEAN MY BIG MATH TEST.
DOOM! DOOM! DOOM!

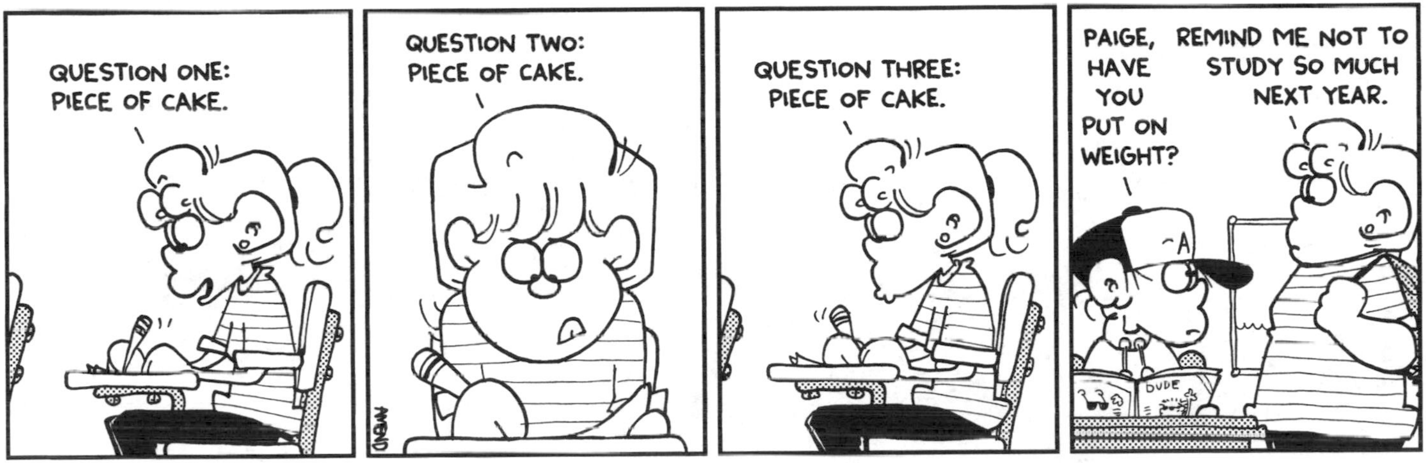
QUESTION ONE: PIECE OF CAKE.
QUESTION TWO: PIECE OF CAKE.
QUESTION THREE: PIECE OF CAKE.
PAIGE, HAVE YOU PUT ON WEIGHT?
REMIND ME NOT TO STUDY SO MUCH NEXT YEAR.
DUDE
AMEND

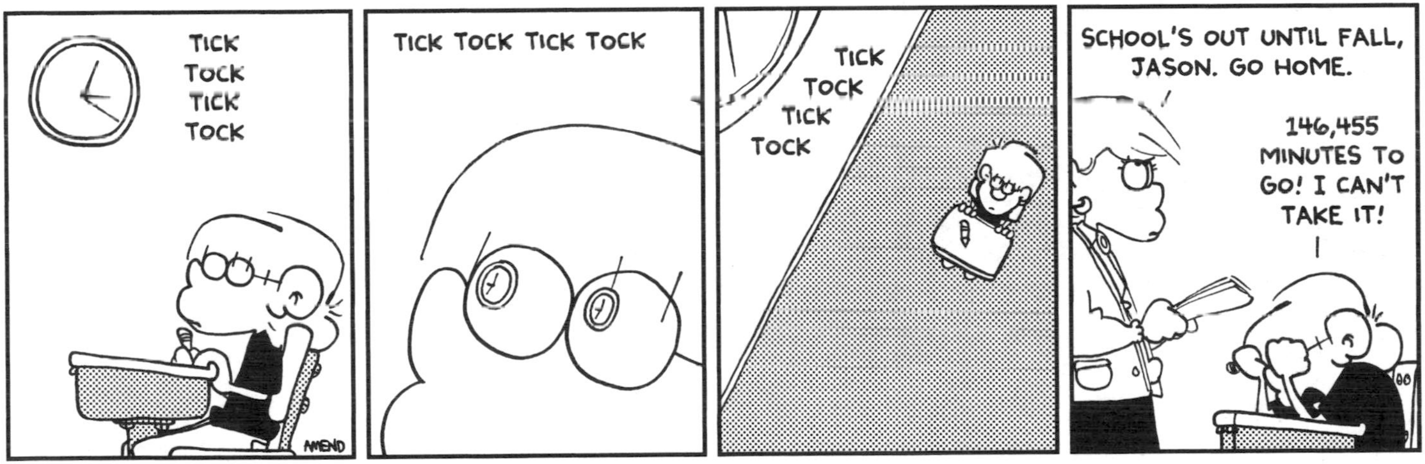
TICK TOCK TICK TOCK
AMEND
TICK TOCK TICK TOCK
TICK TOCK TICK TOCK
SCHOOL'S OUT UNTIL FALL, JASON. GO HOME.
146,455 MINUTES TO GO! I CAN'T TAKE IT!

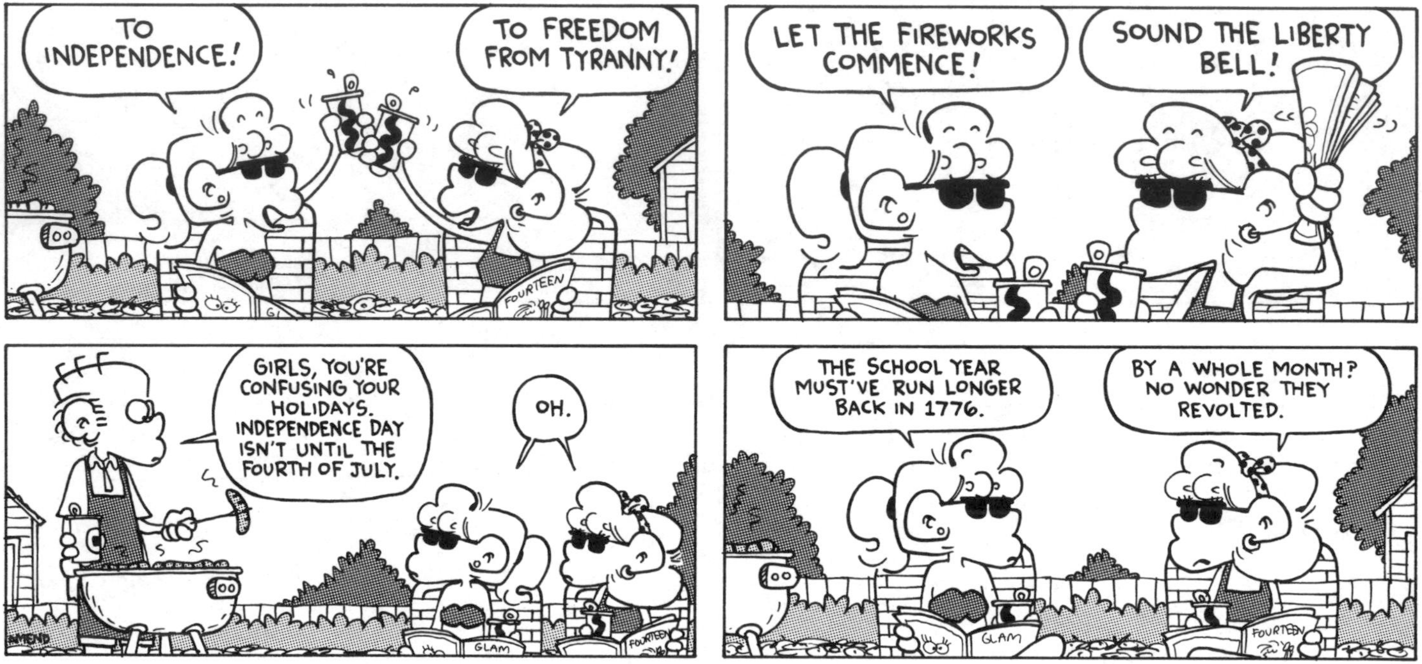
TO INDEPENDENCE!
TO FREEDOM FROM TYRANNY!
LET THE FIREWORKS COMMENCE!
SOUND THE LIBERTY BELL!
GIRLS, YOU'RE CONFUSING YOUR HOLIDAYS. INDEPENDENCE DAY ISN'T UNTIL THE FOURTH OF JULY.
OH.
THE SCHOOL YEAR MUST'VE RUN LONGER BACK IN 1776.
BY A WHOLE MONTH? NO WONDER THEY REVOLTED.

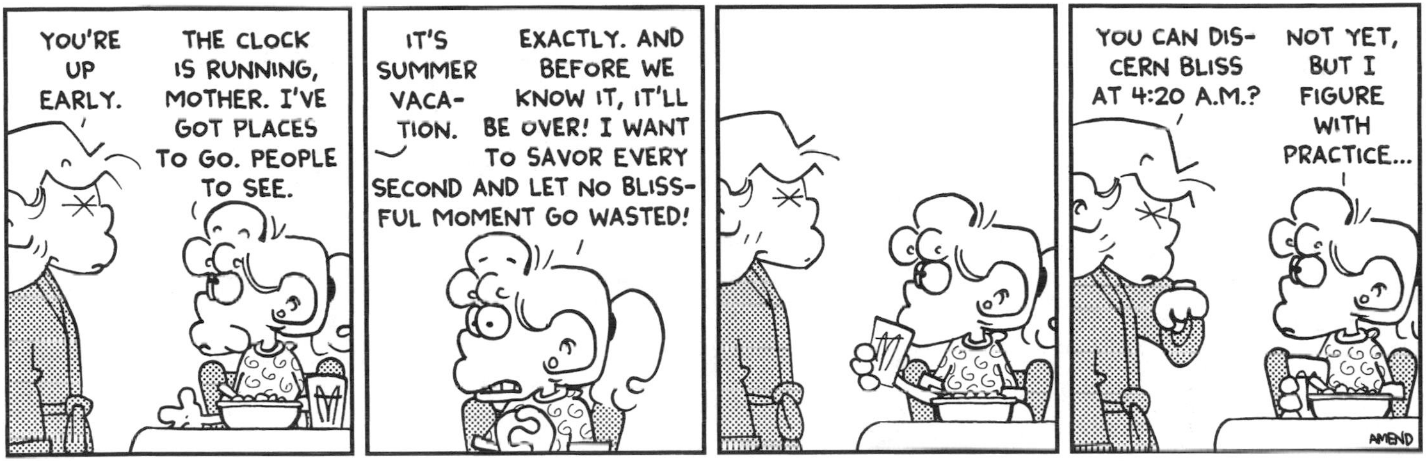
YOU'RE UP EARLY.
THE CLOCK IS RUNNING, MOTHER. I'VE GOT PLACES TO GO. PEOPLE TO SEE.
IT'S SUMMER VACATION.
EXACTLY. AND BEFORE WE KNOW IT, IT'LL BE OVER! I WANT TO SAVOR EVERY SECOND AND LET NO BLISSFUL MOMENT GO WASTED!
YOU CAN DISCERN BLISS AT 4:20 A.M.?
NOT YET, BUT I FIGURE WITH PRACTICE...
AMEND

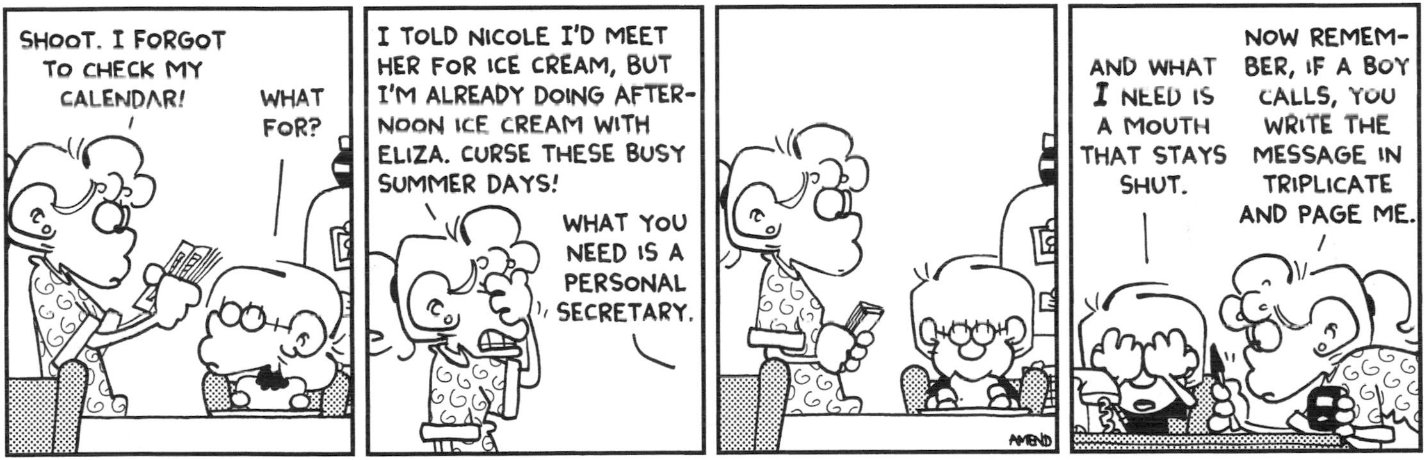
SHOOT. I FORGOT TO CHECK MY CALENDAR!
WHAT FOR?
I TOLD NICOLE I'D MEET HER FOR ICE CREAM, BUT I'M ALREADY DOING AFTERNOON ICE CREAM WITH ELIZA. CURSE THESE BUSY SUMMER DAYS!
WHAT YOU NEED IS A PERSONAL SECRETARY.
AMEND
NOW REMEMBER, IF A BOY CALLS, YOU WRITE THE MESSAGE IN TRIPLICATE AND PAGE ME.
AND WHAT I NEED IS A MOUTH THAT STAYS SHUT.

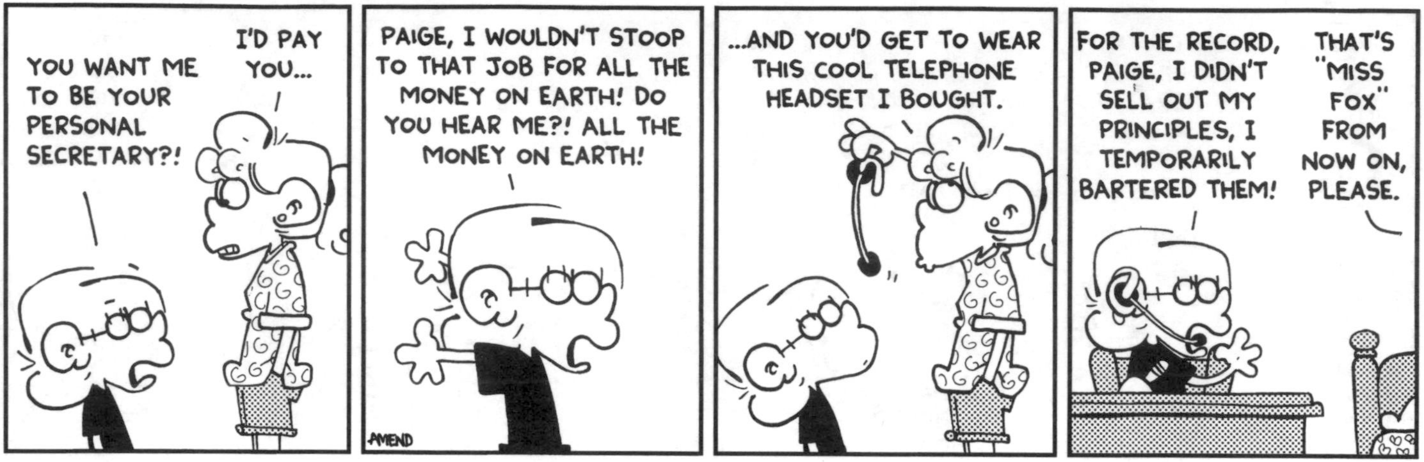
YOU WANT ME TO BE YOUR PERSONAL SECRETARY?!
I'D PAY YOU...
PAIGE, I WOULDN'T STOOP TO THAT JOB FOR ALL THE MONEY ON EARTH! DO YOU HEAR ME?! ALL THE MONEY ON EARTH!
AMEND
...AND YOU'D GET TO WEAR THIS COOL TELEPHONE HEADSET I BOUGHT.
FOR THE RECORD, PAIGE, I DIDN'T SELL OUT MY PRINCIPLES, I TEMPORARILY BARTERED THEM!
THAT'S "MISS FOX" FROM NOW ON, PLEASE.

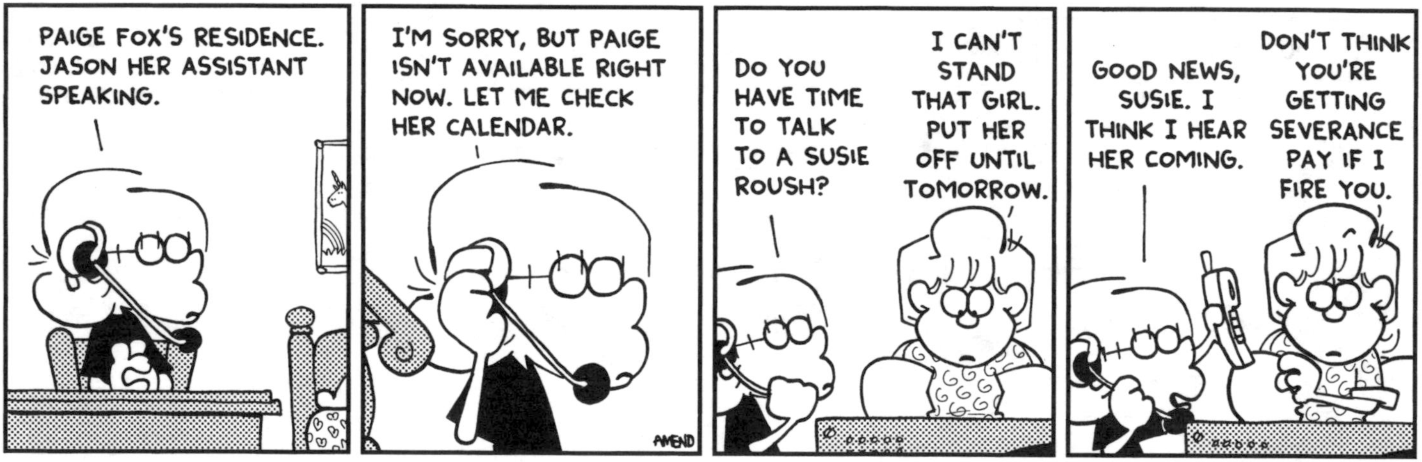
PAIGE FOX'S RESIDENCE. JASON HER ASSISTANT SPEAKING.
I'M SORRY, BUT PAIGE ISN'T AVAILABLE RIGHT NOW. LET ME CHECK HER CALENDAR.
AMEND
DO YOU HAVE TIME TO TALK TO A SUSIE ROUSH?
I CAN'T STAND THAT GIRL. PUT HER OFF UNTIL TOMORROW.
GOOD NEWS, SUSIE. I THINK I HEAR HER COMING.
DON'T THINK YOU'RE GETTING SEVERANCE PAY IF I FIRE YOU.

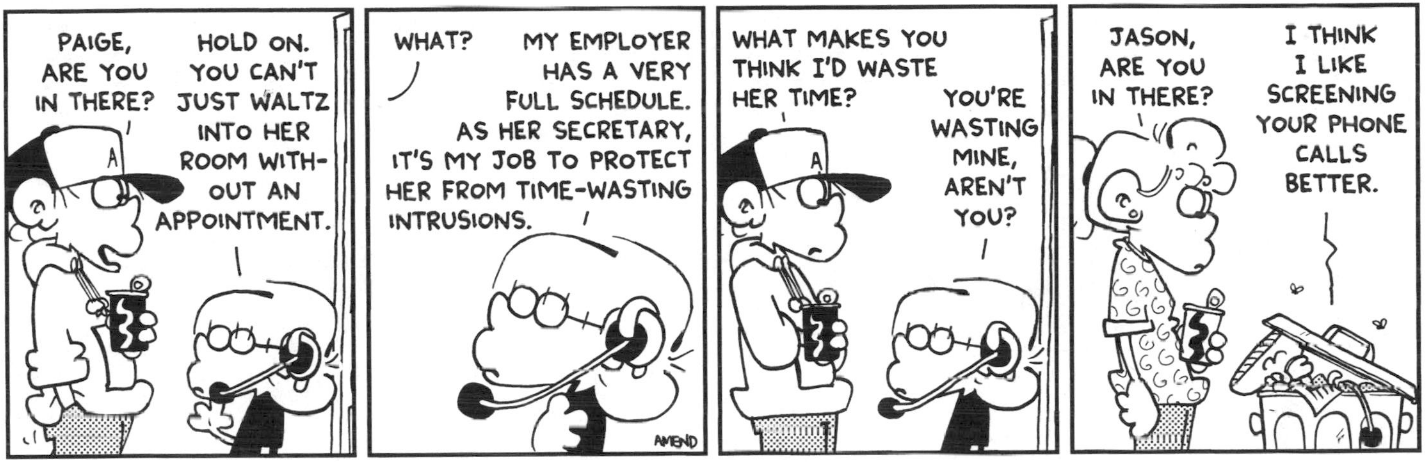
PAIGE, ARE YOU IN THERE?
HOLD ON. YOU CAN'T JUST WALTZ INTO HER ROOM WITHOUT AN APPOINTMENT.
WHAT?
MY EMPLOYER HAS A VERY FULL SCHEDULE. AS HER SECRETARY, IT'S MY JOB TO PROTECT HER FROM TIME-WASTING INTRUSIONS.
AMEND
WHAT MAKES YOU THINK I'D WASTE HER TIME?
YOU'RE WASTING MINE, AREN'T YOU?
JASON, ARE YOU IN THERE?
I THINK I LIKE SCREENING YOUR PHONE CALLS BETTER.

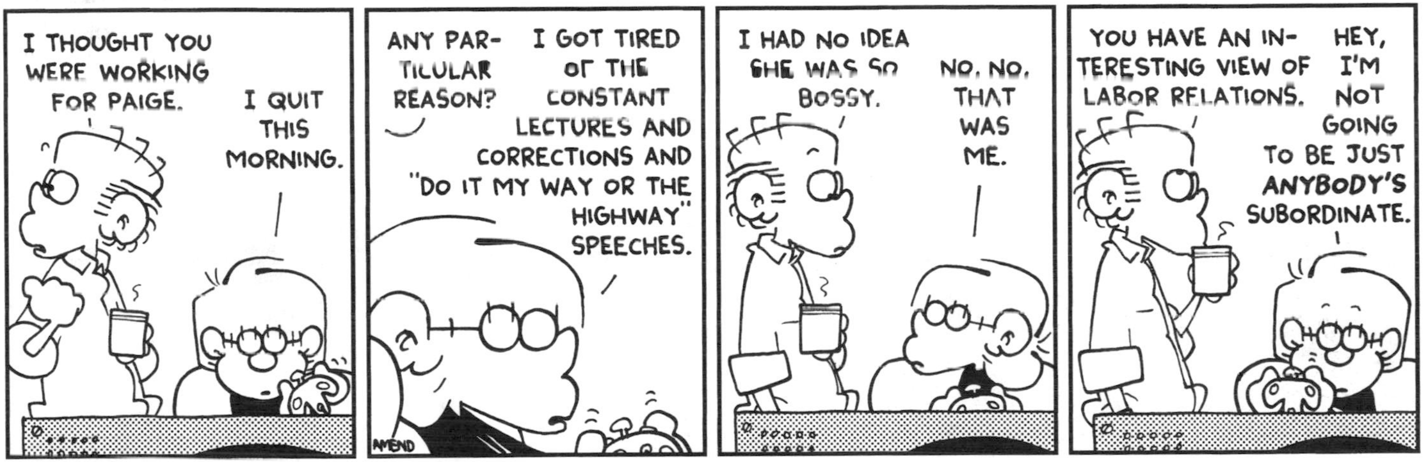
I THOUGHT YOU WERE WORKING FOR PAIGE.
I QUIT THIS MORNING.
ANY PARTICULAR REASON?
I GOT TIRED OF THE CONSTANT LECTURES AND CORRECTIONS AND "DO IT MY WAY OR THE HIGHWAY" SPEECHES.
AMEND
I HAD NO IDEA SHE WAS SO BOSSY.
NO, NO. THAT WAS ME.
YOU HAVE AN INTERESTING VIEW OF LABOR RELATIONS.
HEY, I'M NOT GOING TO BE JUST ANYBODY'S SUBORDINATE.

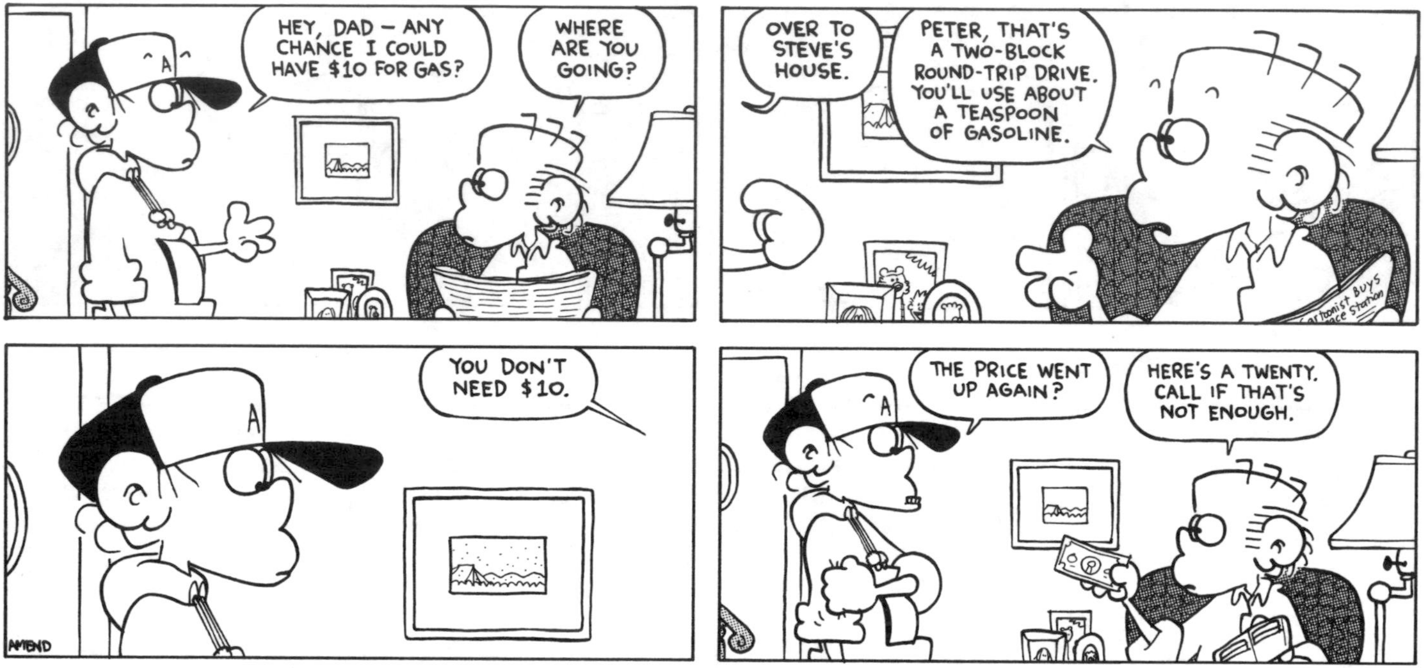
HEY, DAD – ANY CHANCE I COULD HAVE $10 FOR GAS?
WHERE ARE YOU GOING?
OVER TO STEVE'S HOUSE.
PETER, THAT'S A TWO-BLOCK ROUND-TRIP DRIVE. YOU'LL USE ABOUT A TEASPOON OF GASOLINE.
Cartoonist Buys
YOU DON'T NEED $10.
AMEND
THE PRICE WENT UP AGAIN?
HERE'S A TWENTY. CALL IF THAT'S NOT ENOUGH.

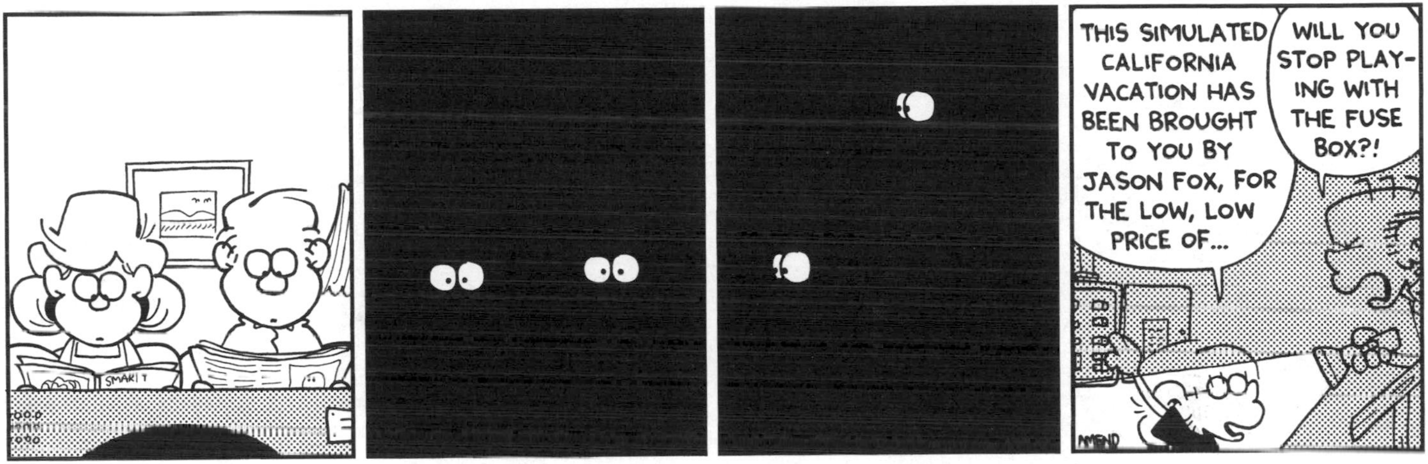
SMAKIT
THIS SIMULATED CALIFORNIA VACATION HAS BEEN BROUGHT TO YOU BY JASON FOX, FOR THE LOW, LOW PRICE OF...
WILL YOU STOP PLAYING WITH THE FUSE BOX?!
AMEND

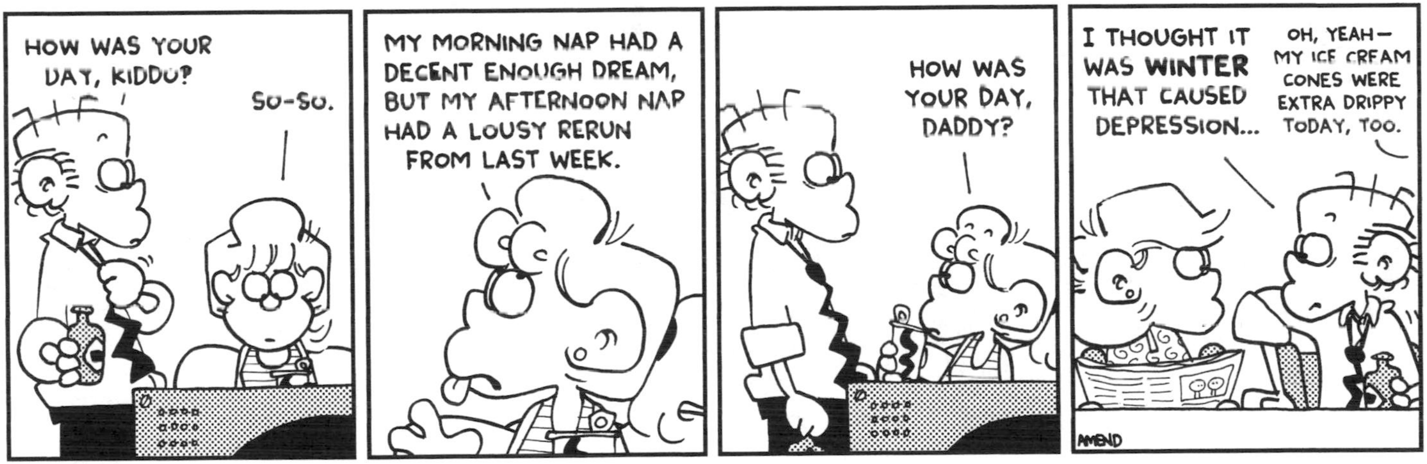
HOW WAS YOUR DAY, KIDDO?
SO-SO.
MY MORNING NAP HAD A DECENT ENOUGH DREAM, BUT MY AFTERNOON NAP HAD A LOUSY RERUN FROM LAST WEEK.
HOW WAS YOUR DAY, DADDY?
I THOUGHT IT WAS **WINTER** THAT CAUSED DEPRESSION...
OH, YEAH— MY ICE CREAM CONES WERE EXTRA DRIPPY TODAY, TOO.
AMEND

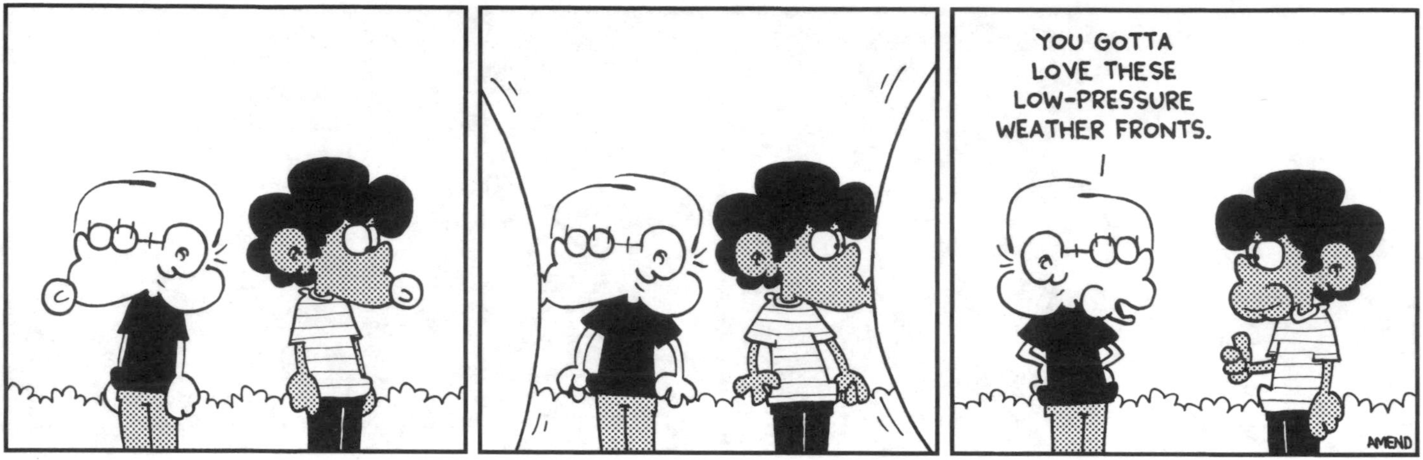
YOU GOTTA LOVE THESE LOW-PRESSURE WEATHER FRONTS.
AMEND

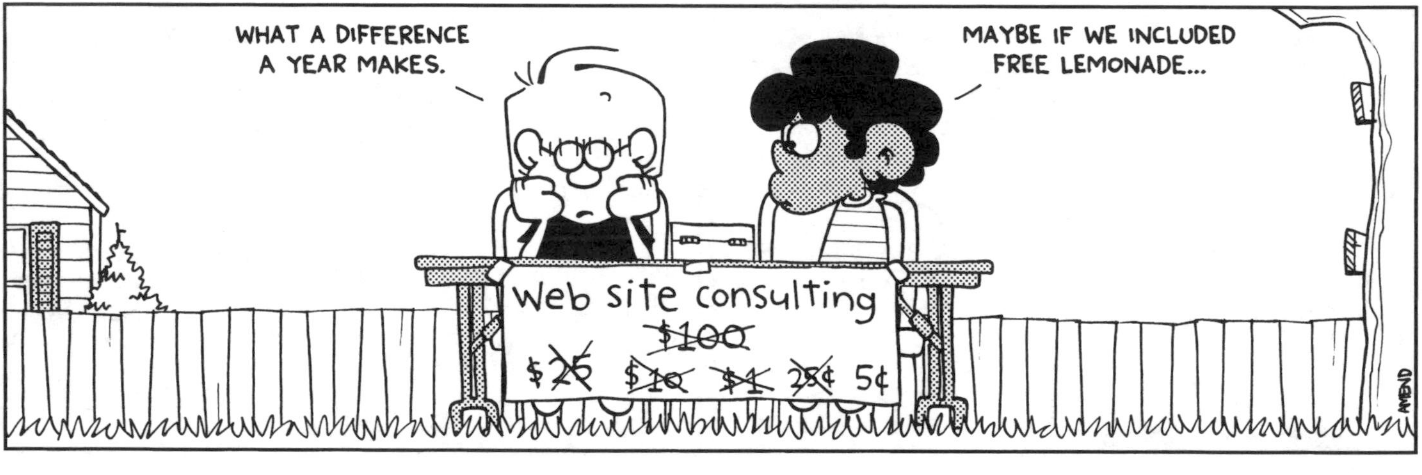
WHAT A DIFFERENCE A YEAR MAKES.
MAYBE IF WE INCLUDED FREE LEMONADE...
Web site consulting
$100
$25 $10 $1 25¢ 5¢
AMEND

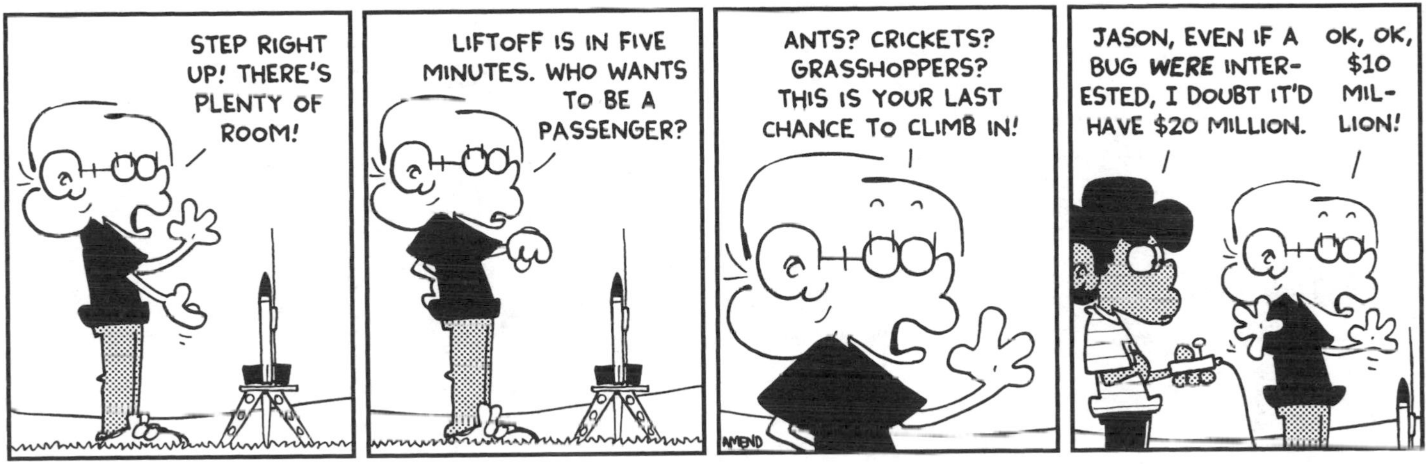
STEP RIGHT UP! THERE'S PLENTY OF ROOM!
LIFTOFF IS IN FIVE MINUTES. WHO WANTS TO BE A PASSENGER?
ANTS? CRICKETS? GRASSHOPPERS? THIS IS YOUR LAST CHANCE TO CLIMB IN!
AMEND
JASON, EVEN IF A BUG WERE INTERESTED, I DOUBT IT'D HAVE $20 MILLION.
OK, OK, $10 MILLION!

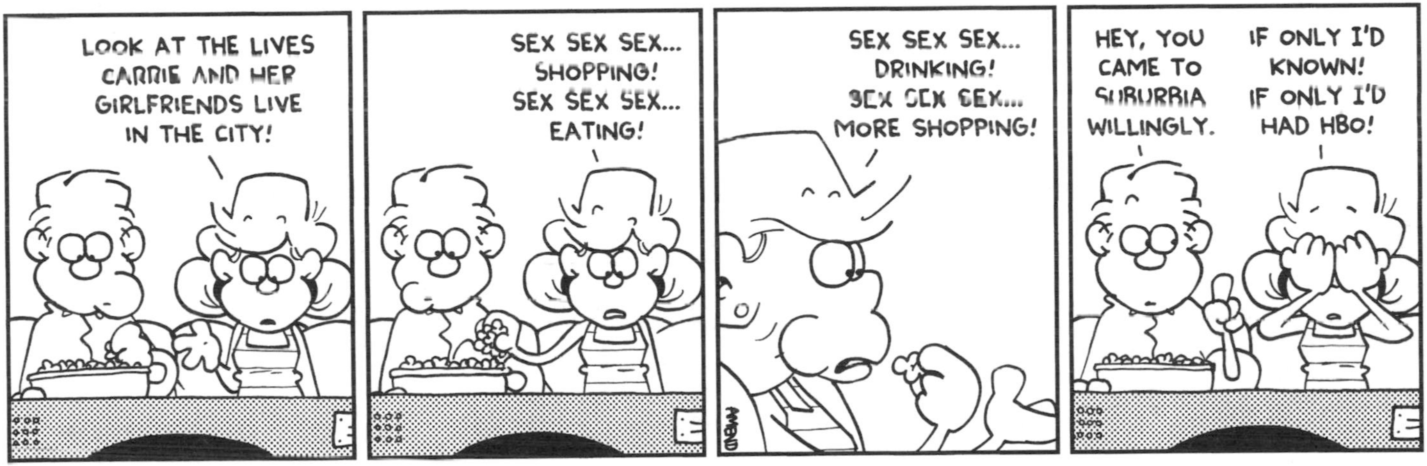
LOOK AT THE LIVES CARRIE AND HER GIRLFRIENDS LIVE IN THE CITY!
SEX SEX SEX... SHOPPING! SEX SEX SEX... EATING!
SEX SEX SEX... DRINKING! SEX SEX SEX... MORE SHOPPING!
AMEND
HEY, YOU CAME TO SUBURBIA WILLINGLY.
IF ONLY I'D KNOWN! IF ONLY I'D HAD HBO!

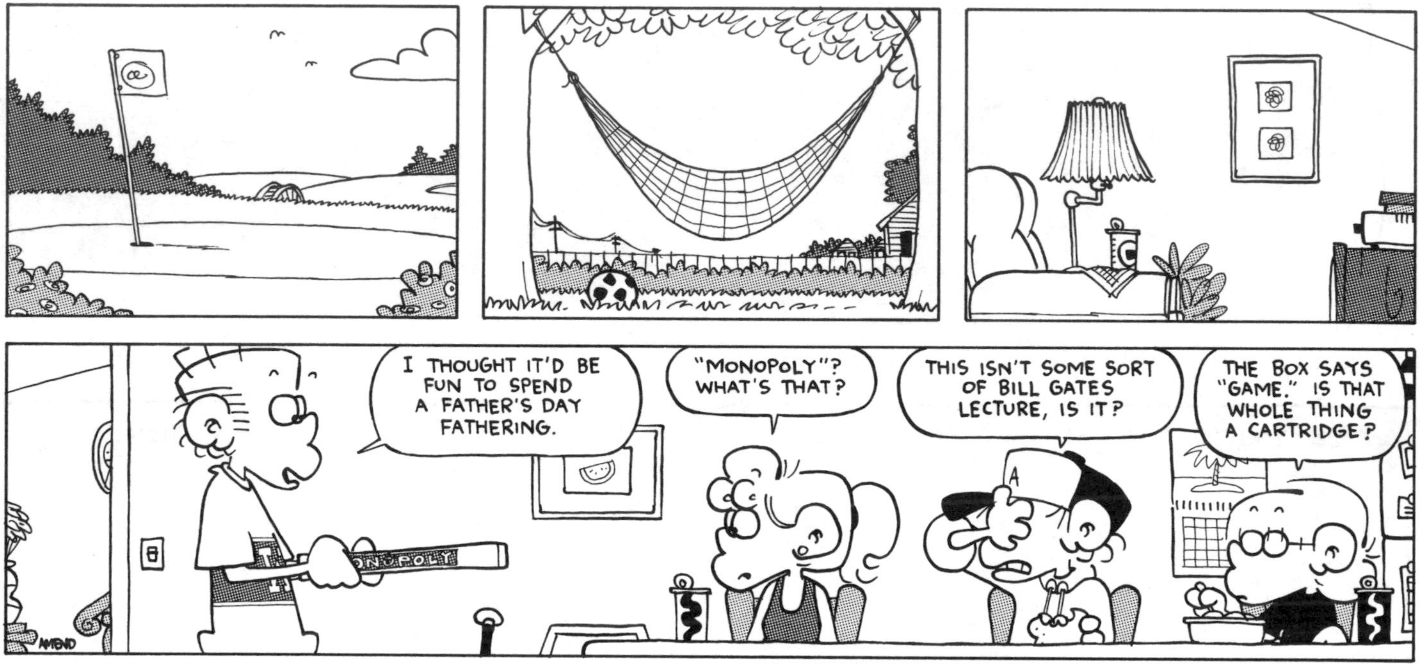
MONOPOLY
I THOUGHT IT'D BE FUN TO SPEND A FATHER'S DAY FATHERING.
"MONOPOLY"? WHAT'S THAT?
THIS ISN'T SOME SORT OF BILL GATES LECTURE, IS IT?
THE BOX SAYS "GAME." IS THAT WHOLE THING A CARTRIDGE?
AMEND

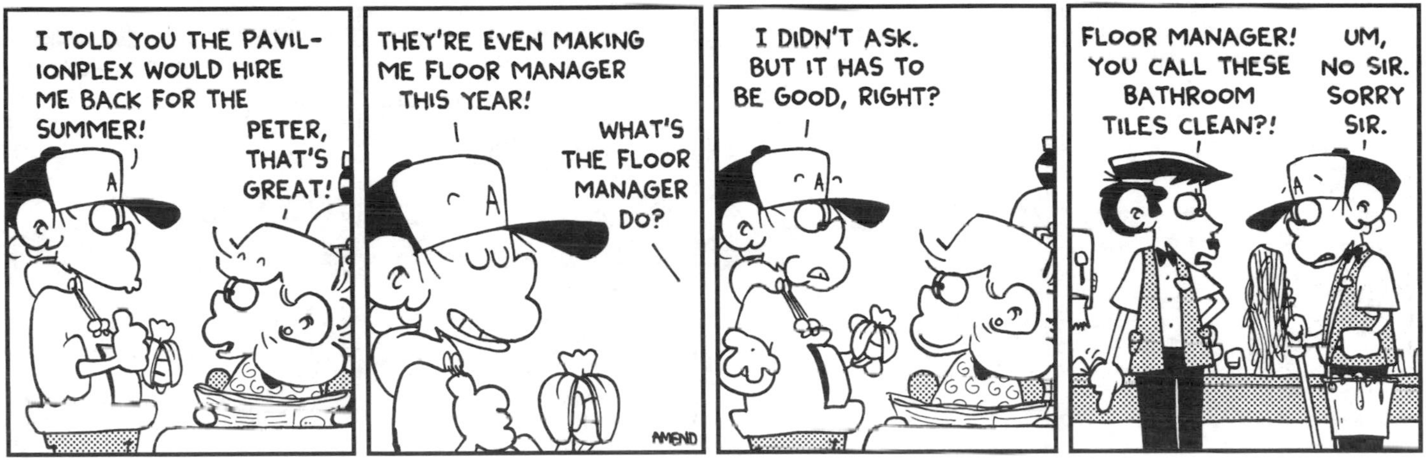
I TOLD YOU THE PAVIL-IONPLEX WOULD HIRE ME BACK FOR THE SUMMER!
PETER, THAT'S GREAT!
THEY'RE EVEN MAKING ME FLOOR MANAGER THIS YEAR!
WHAT'S THE FLOOR MANAGER DO?
AMEND
I DIDN'T ASK. BUT IT HAS TO BE GOOD, RIGHT?
FLOOR MANAGER! YOU CALL THESE BATHROOM TILES CLEAN?!
UM, NO SIR. SORRY SIR.

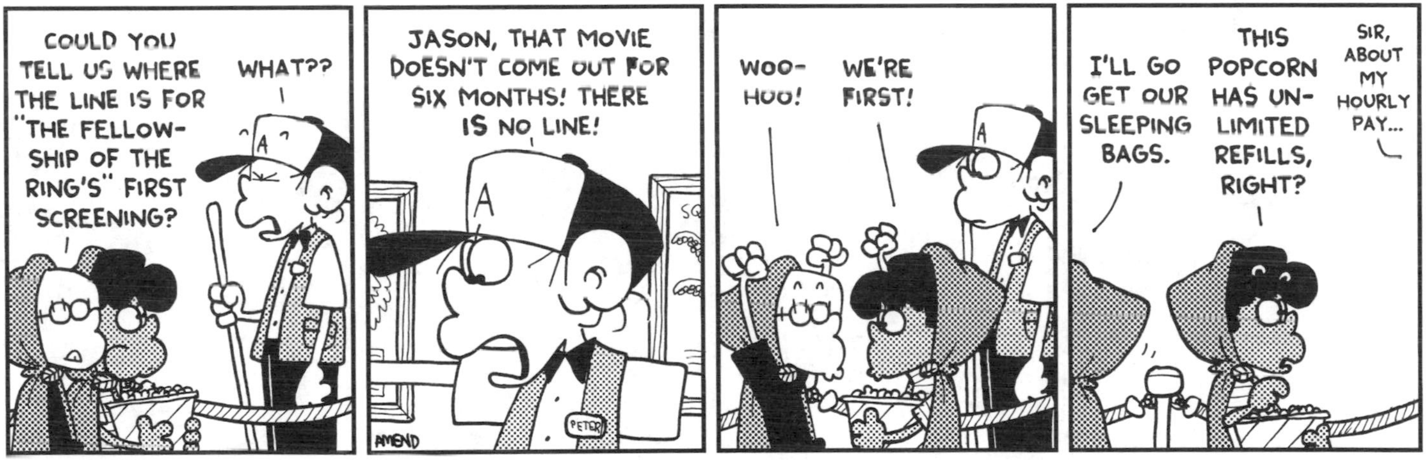
COULD YOU TELL US WHERE THE LINE IS FOR "THE FELLOW-SHIP OF THE RING'S" FIRST SCREENING?
WHAT??
JASON, THAT MOVIE DOESN'T COME OUT FOR SIX MONTHS! THERE IS NO LINE!
PETER
AMEND
WOO-HOO!
WE'RE FIRST!
I'LL GO GET OUR SLEEPING BAGS.
THIS POPCORN HAS UN-LIMITED REFILLS, RIGHT?
SIR, ABOUT MY HOURLY PAY...

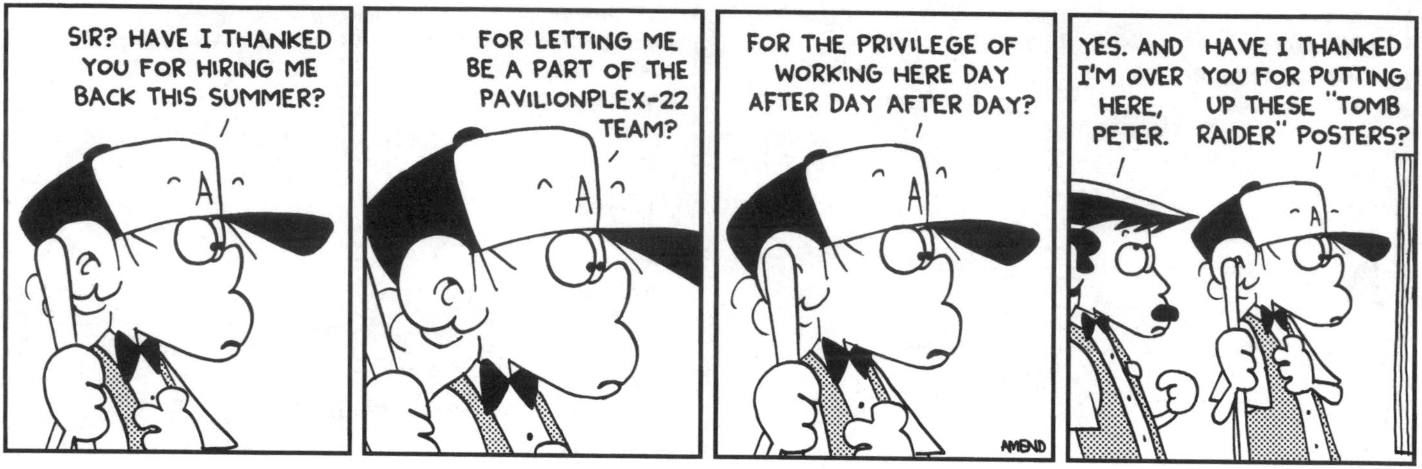
SIR? HAVE I THANKED YOU FOR HIRING ME BACK THIS SUMMER?
FOR LETTING ME BE A PART OF THE PAVILIONPLEX-22 TEAM?
FOR THE PRIVILEGE OF WORKING HERE DAY AFTER DAY AFTER DAY?
AMEND
YES. AND I'M OVER HERE, PETER.
HAVE I THANKED YOU FOR PUTTING UP THESE "TOMB RAIDER" POSTERS?

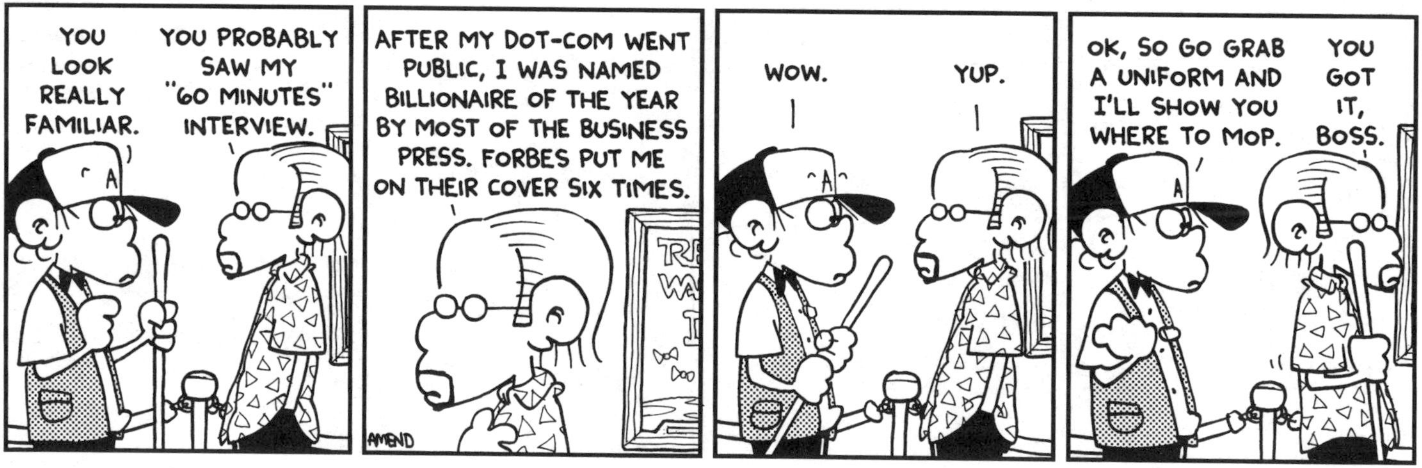
YOU LOOK REALLY FAMILIAR.
YOU PROBABLY SAW MY "60 MINUTES" INTERVIEW.
AFTER MY DOT-COM WENT PUBLIC, I WAS NAMED BILLIONAIRE OF THE YEAR BY MOST OF THE BUSINESS PRESS. FORBES PUT ME ON THEIR COVER SIX TIMES.
AMEND
WOW.
YUP.
OK, SO GO GRAB A UNIFORM AND I'LL SHOW YOU WHERE TO MOP.
YOU GOT IT, BOSS.

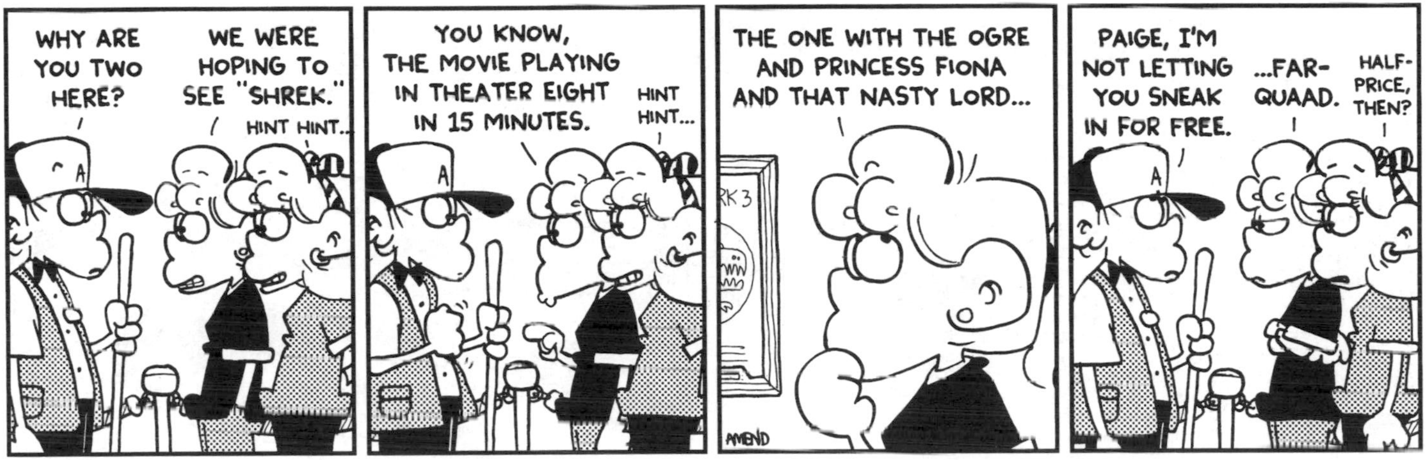
WHY ARE YOU TWO HERE?
WE WERE HOPING TO SEE "SHREK."
HINT HINT...
YOU KNOW, THE MOVIE PLAYING IN THEATER EIGHT IN 15 MINUTES.
HINT HINT...
THE ONE WITH THE OGRE AND PRINCESS FIONA AND THAT NASTY LORD...
AMEND
PAIGE, I'M NOT LETTING YOU SNEAK IN FOR FREE.
...FAR-QUAAD.
HALF-PRICE, THEN?

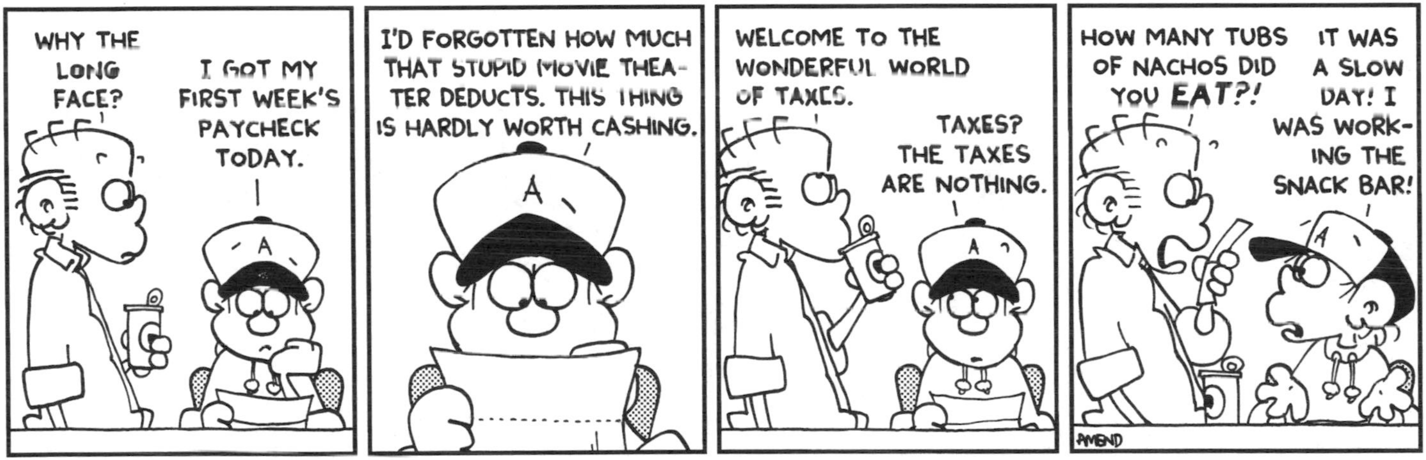
WHY THE LONG FACE?
I GOT MY FIRST WEEK'S PAYCHECK TODAY.
I'D FORGOTTEN HOW MUCH THAT STUPID MOVIE THEATER DEDUCTS. THIS THING IS HARDLY WORTH CASHING.
WELCOME TO THE WONDERFUL WORLD OF TAXES.
TAXES? THE TAXES ARE NOTHING.
HOW MANY TUBS OF NACHOS DID YOU EAT?!
IT WAS A SLOW DAY! I WAS WORKING THE SNACK BAR!
AMEND

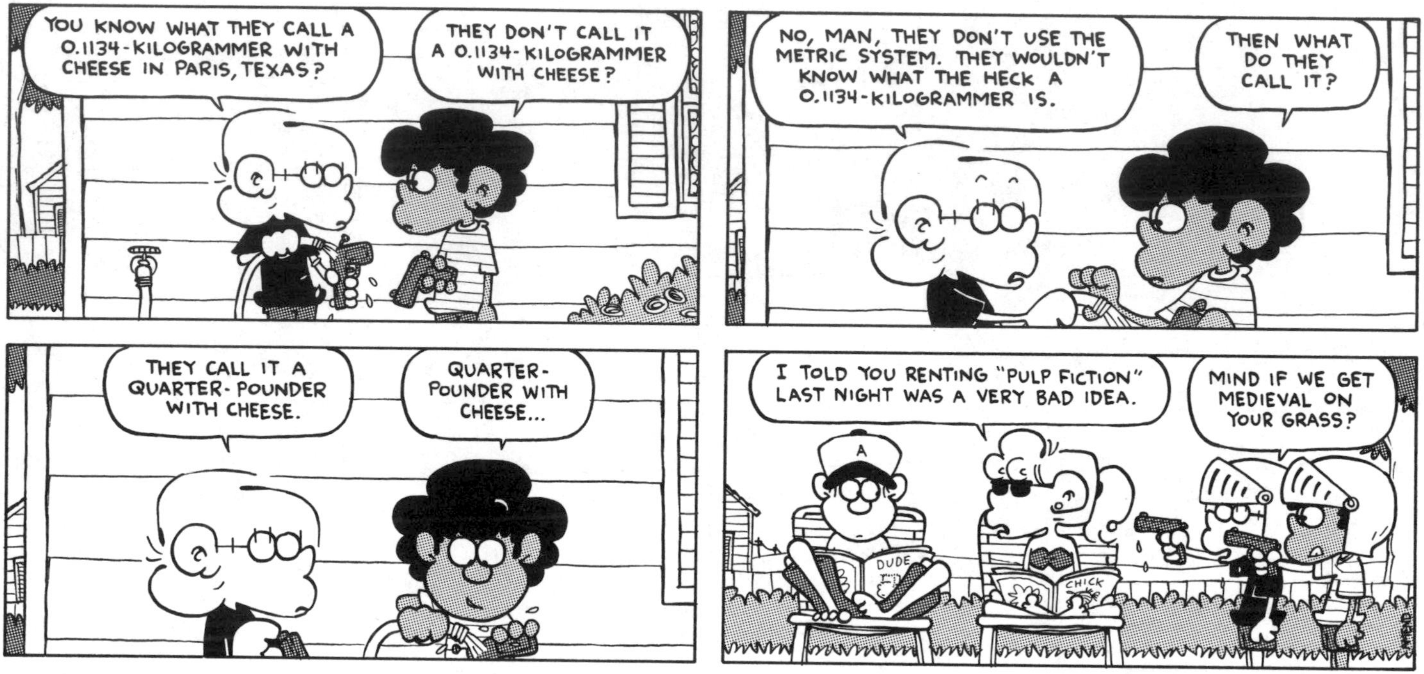
YOU KNOW WHAT THEY CALL A 0.1134-KILOGRAMMER WITH CHEESE IN PARIS, TEXAS?
THEY DON'T CALL IT A 0.1134-KILOGRAMMER WITH CHEESE?
NO, MAN, THEY DON'T USE THE METRIC SYSTEM. THEY WOULDN'T KNOW WHAT THE HECK A 0.1134-KILOGRAMMER IS.
THEN WHAT DO THEY CALL IT?
THEY CALL IT A QUARTER-POUNDER WITH CHEESE.
QUARTER-POUNDER WITH CHEESE...
I TOLD YOU RENTING "PULP FICTION" LAST NIGHT WAS A VERY BAD IDEA.
MIND IF WE GET MEDIEVAL ON YOUR GRASS?
DUDE
CHICK

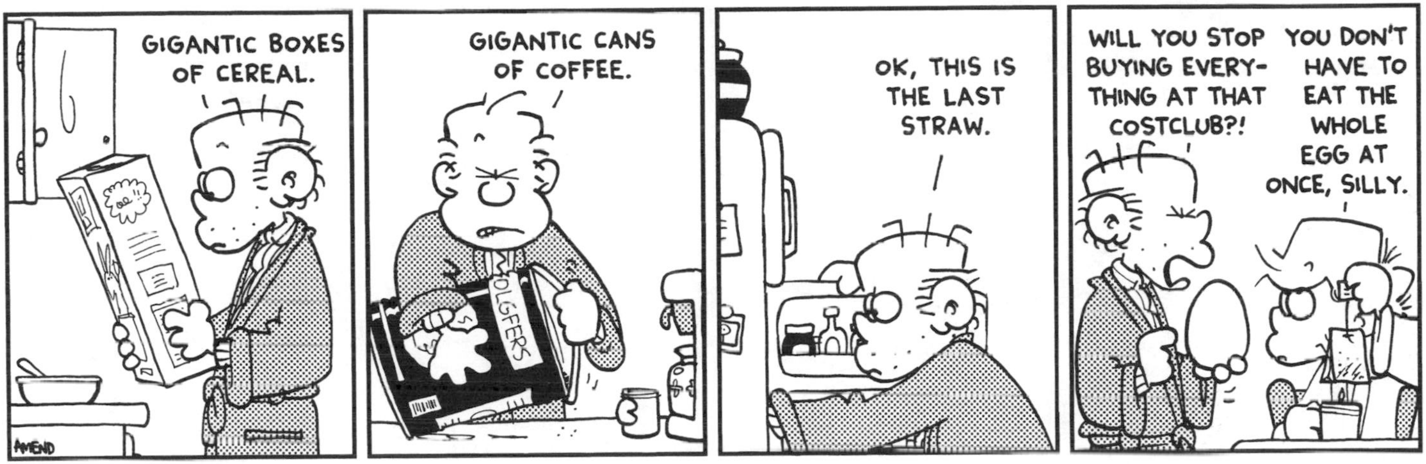
GIGANTIC BOXES OF CEREAL.
GIGANTIC CANS OF COFFEE.
OK, THIS IS THE LAST STRAW.
WILL YOU STOP BUYING EVERY-THING AT THAT COSTCLUB?!
YOU DON'T HAVE TO EAT THE WHOLE EGG AT ONCE, SILLY.

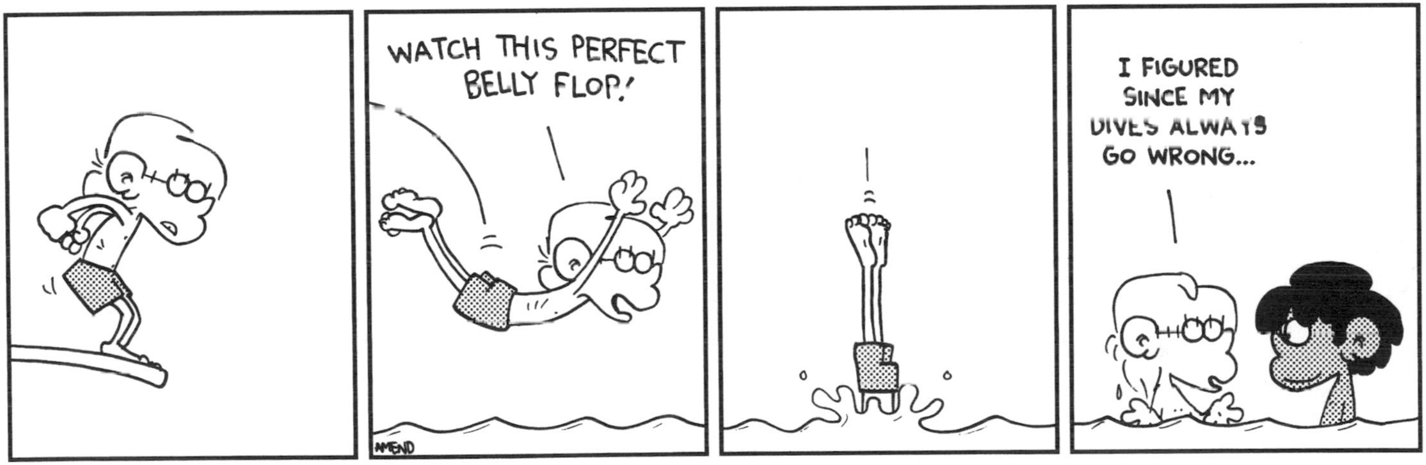
WATCH THIS PERFECT BELLY FLOP!
I FIGURED SINCE MY DIVES ALWAYS GO WRONG...

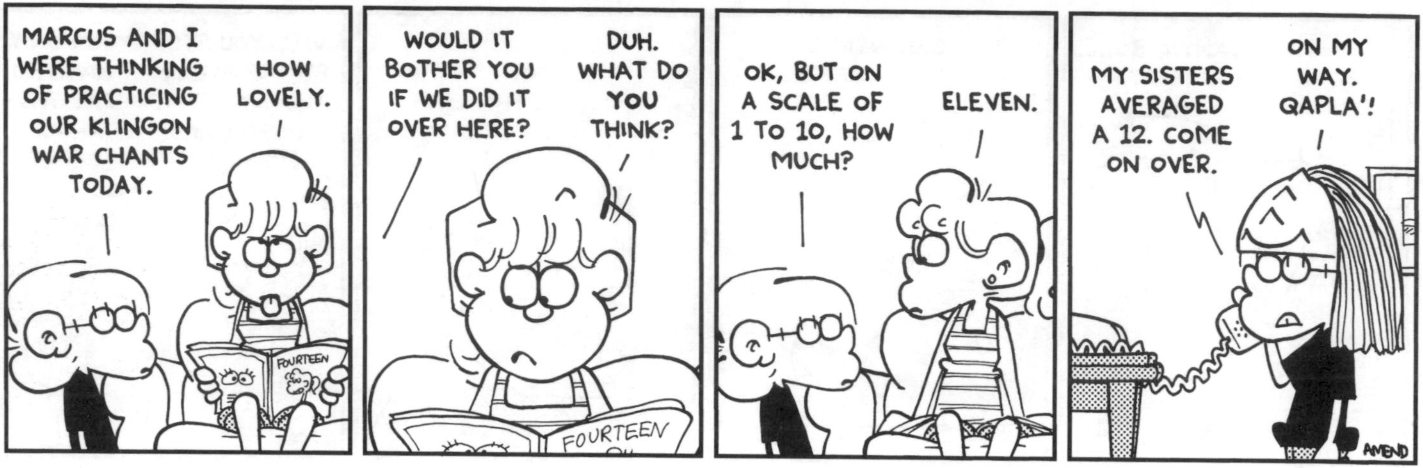
MARCUS AND I WERE THINKING OF PRACTICING OUR KLINGON WAR CHANTS TODAY.
HOW LOVELY.
FOURTEEN
WOULD IT BOTHER YOU IF WE DID IT OVER HERE?
DUH. WHAT DO YOU THINK?
FOURTEEN
OK, BUT ON A SCALE OF 1 TO 10, HOW MUCH?
ELEVEN.
MY SISTERS AVERAGED A 12. COME ON OVER.
ON MY WAY. QAPLA'!
AMEND

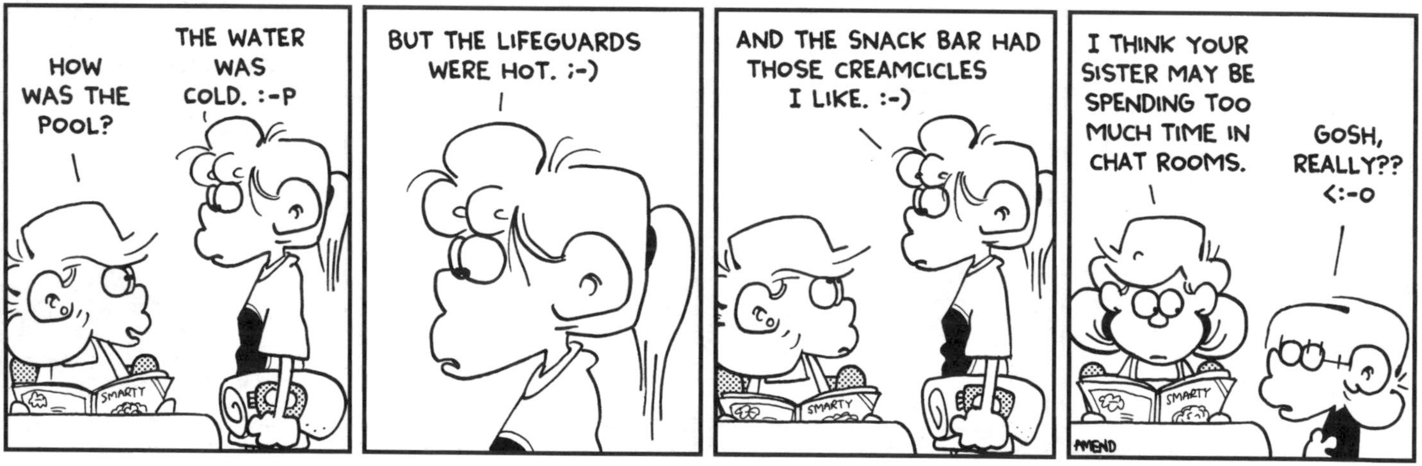
HOW WAS THE POOL?
THE WATER WAS COLD. :-P
SMARTY
BUT THE LIFEGUARDS WERE HOT. ;-)
AND THE SNACK BAR HAD THOSE CREAMCICLES I LIKE. :-)
SMARTY
I THINK YOUR SISTER MAY BE SPENDING TOO MUCH TIME IN CHAT ROOMS.
GOSH, REALLY?? <:-O
SMARTY
AMEND

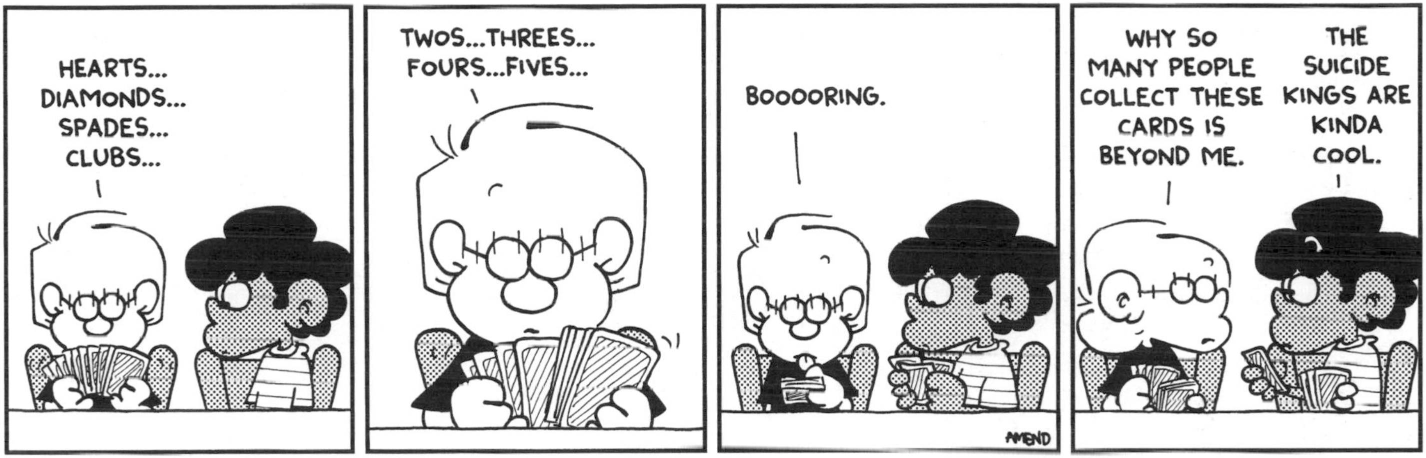
HEARTS... DIAMONDS... SPADES... CLUBS...
TWOS...THREES... FOURS...FIVES...
BOOOORING.
WHY SO MANY PEOPLE COLLECT THESE CARDS IS BEYOND ME.
THE SUICIDE KINGS ARE KINDA COOL.
AMEND

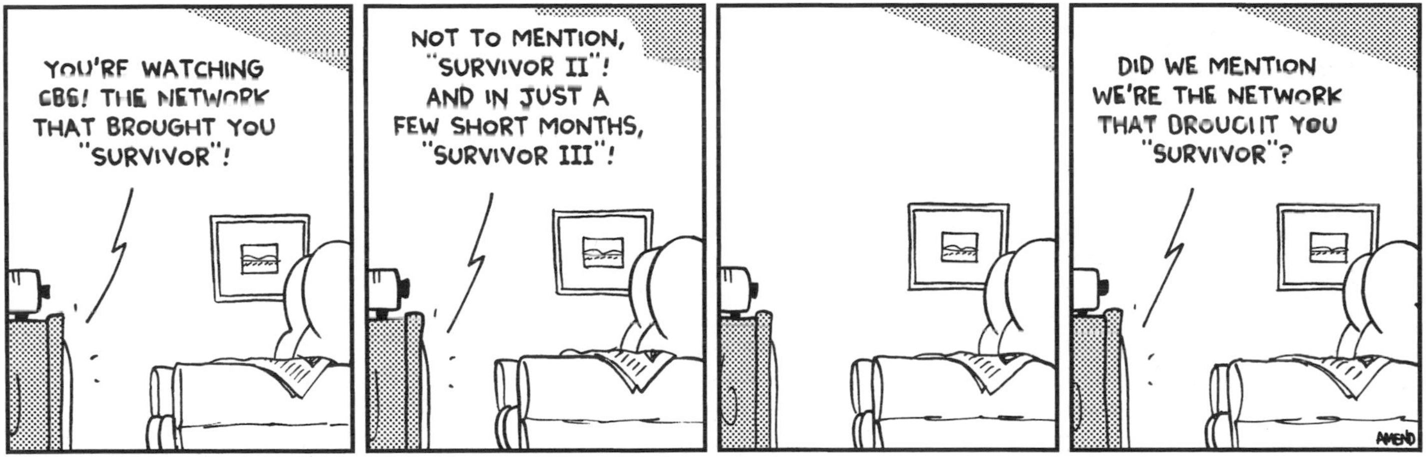
YOU'RE WATCHING CBS! THE NETWORK THAT BROUGHT YOU "SURVIVOR"!
NOT TO MENTION, "SURVIVOR II"! AND IN JUST A FEW SHORT MONTHS, "SURVIVOR III"!
DID WE MENTION WE'RE THE NETWORK THAT BROUGHT YOU "SURVIVOR"?
AMEND

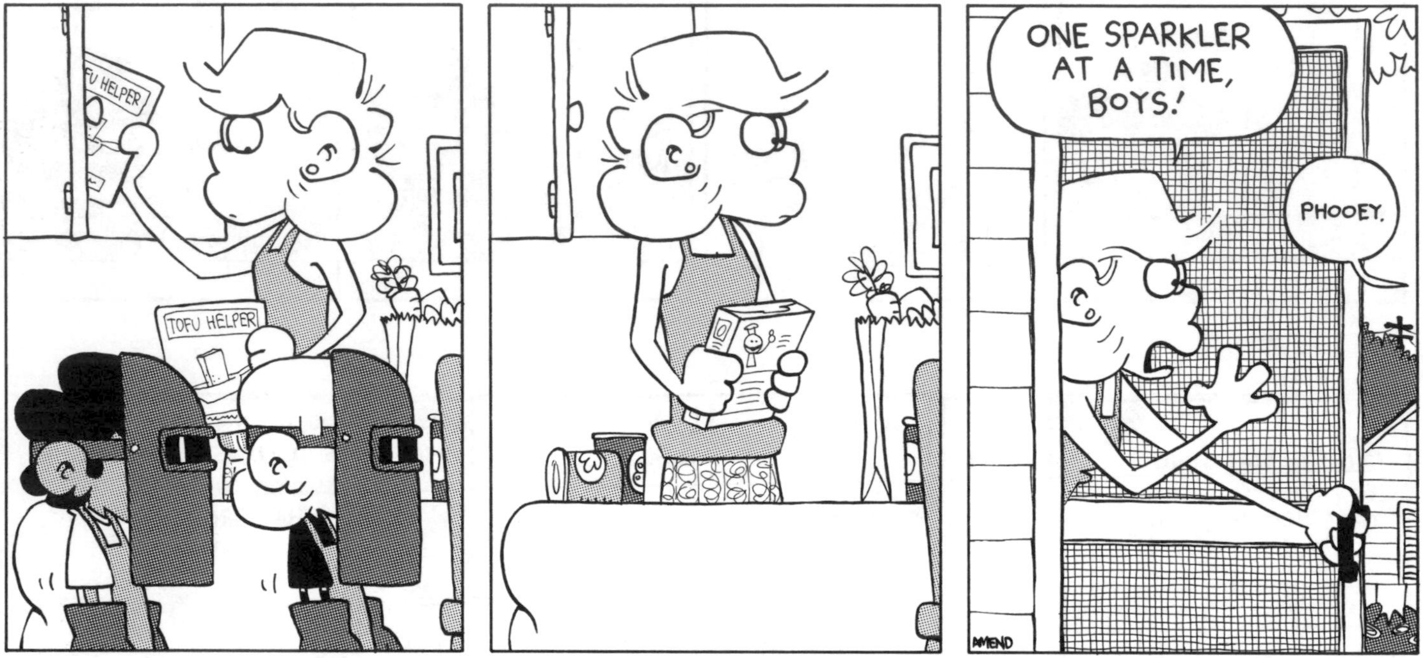
TOFU HELPER
TOFU HELPER
ONE SPARKLER AT A TIME, BOYS!
PHOOEY.
AMEND

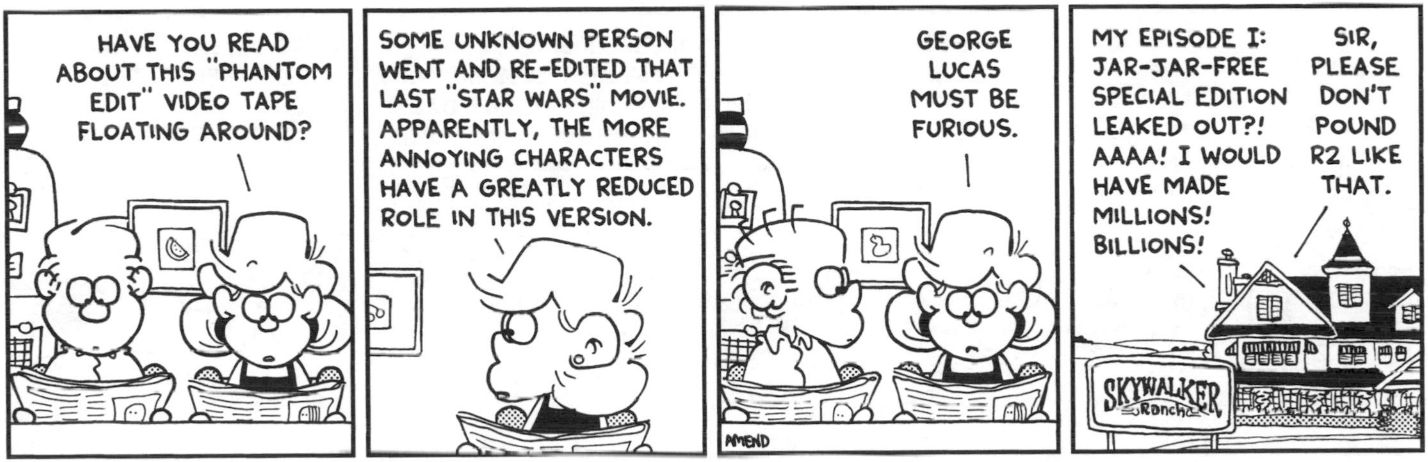
HAVE YOU READ ABOUT THIS "PHANTOM EDIT" VIDEO TAPE FLOATING AROUND?
SOME UNKNOWN PERSON WENT AND RE-EDITED THAT LAST "STAR WARS" MOVIE. APPARENTLY, THE MORE ANNOYING CHARACTERS HAVE A GREATLY REDUCED ROLE IN THIS VERSION.
GEORGE LUCAS MUST BE FURIOUS.
AMEND
MY EPISODE I: JAR-JAR-FREE SPECIAL EDITION LEAKED OUT?! AAAA! I WOULD HAVE MADE MILLIONS! BILLIONS!
SIR, PLEASE DON'T POUND R2 LIKE THAT.
SKYWALKER Ranch

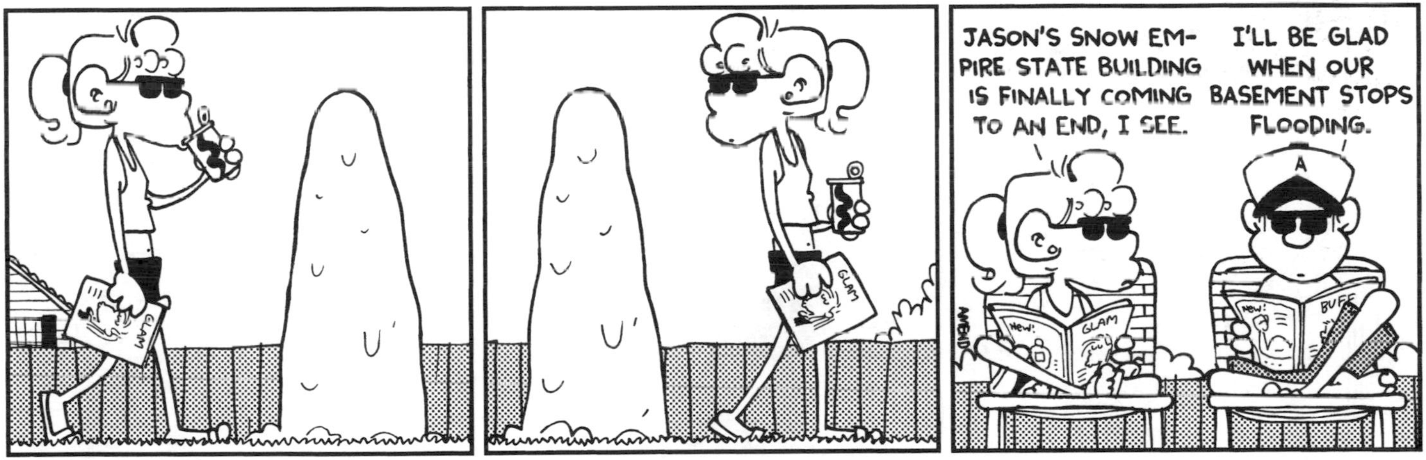
GLAM
AMEND
JASON'S SNOW EMPIRE STATE BUILDING IS FINALLY COMING TO AN END, I SEE.
I'LL BE GLAD WHEN OUR BASEMENT STOPS FLOODING.
New!
GLAM
BUFF

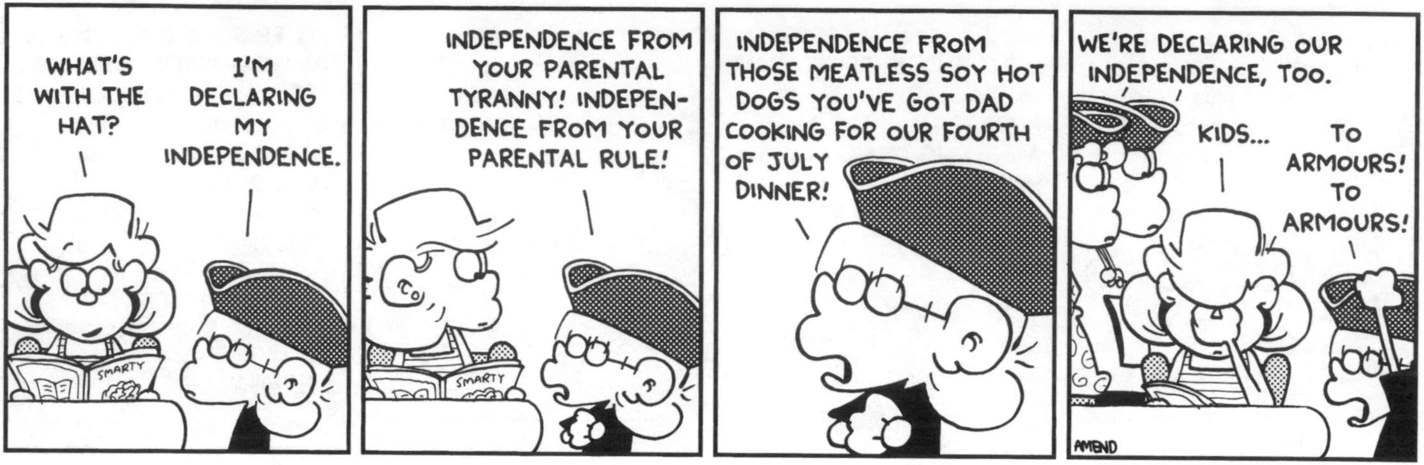
WHAT'S WITH THE HAT?
I'M DECLARING MY INDEPENDENCE.
INDEPENDENCE FROM YOUR PARENTAL TYRANNY! INDEPENDENCE FROM YOUR PARENTAL RULE!
INDEPENDENCE FROM THOSE MEATLESS SOY HOT DOGS YOU'VE GOT DAD COOKING FOR OUR FOURTH OF JULY DINNER!
WE'RE DECLARING OUR INDEPENDENCE, TOO.
KIDS...
TO ARMOURS! TO ARMOURS!
AMEND

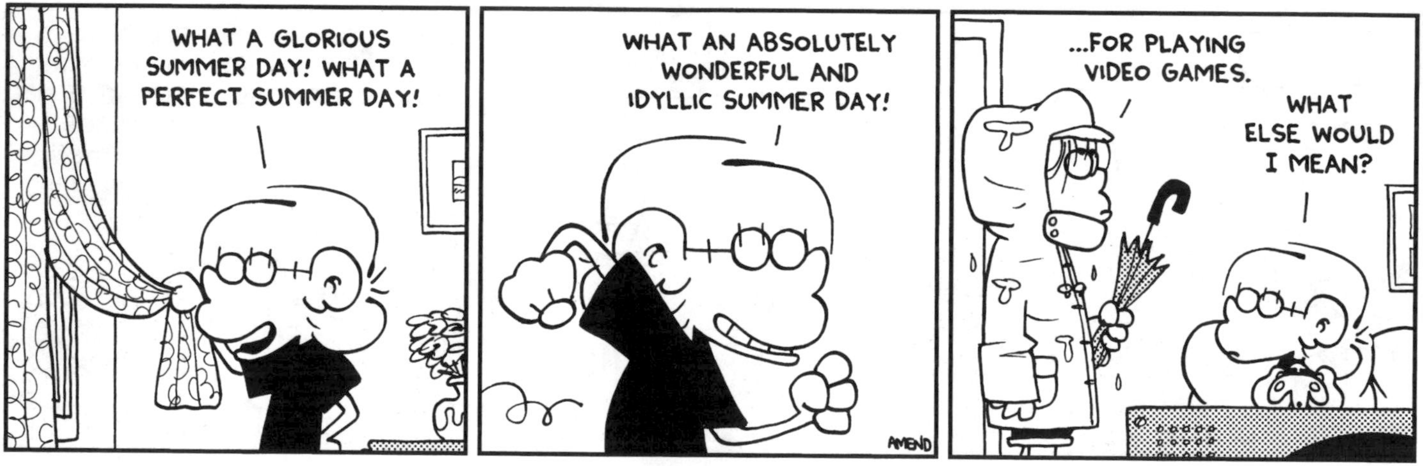
WHAT A GLORIOUS SUMMER DAY! WHAT A PERFECT SUMMER DAY!
WHAT AN ABSOLUTELY WONDERFUL AND IDYLLIC SUMMER DAY!
AMEND
...FOR PLAYING VIDEO GAMES.
WHAT ELSE WOULD I MEAN?

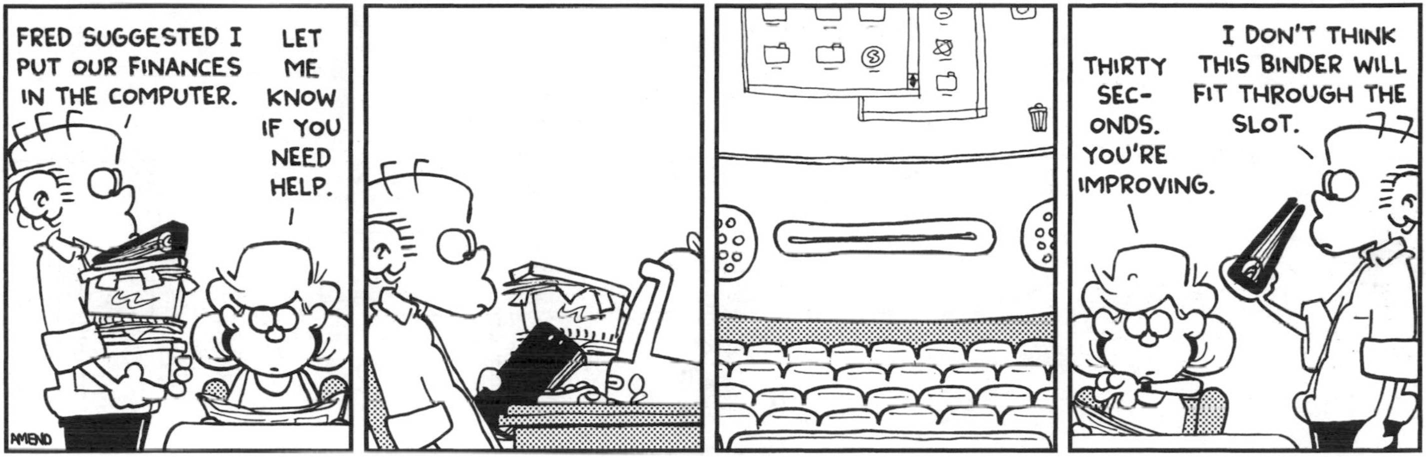
FRED SUGGESTED I PUT OUR FINANCES IN THE COMPUTER.
LET ME KNOW IF YOU NEED HELP.
THIRTY SEC- ONDS. YOU'RE IMPROVING.
I DON'T THINK THIS BINDER WILL FIT THROUGH THE SLOT.
AMEND

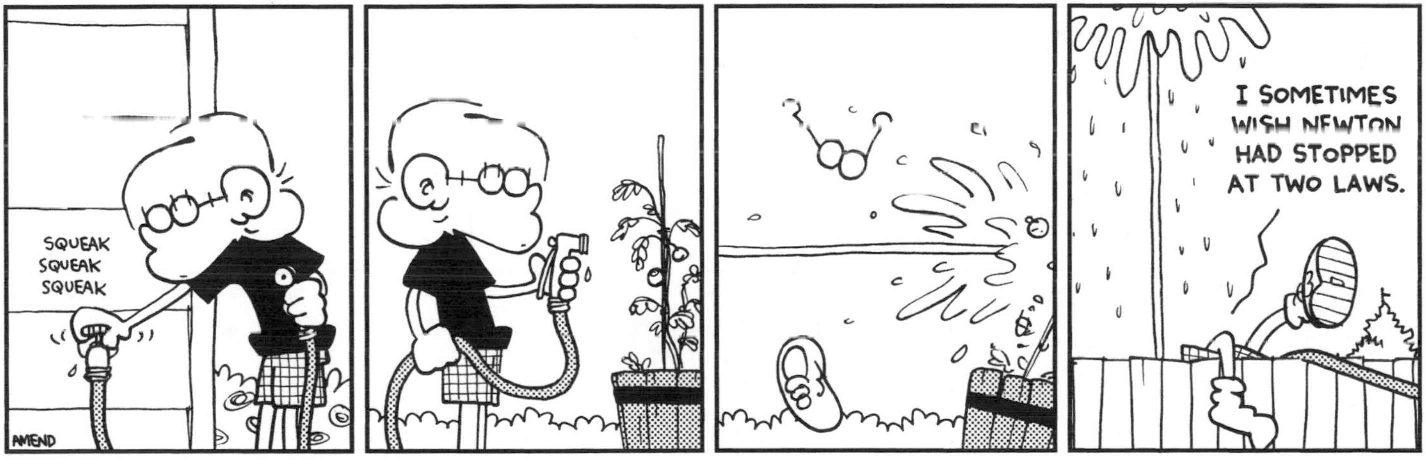
SQUEAK SQUEAK SQUEAK
I SOMETIMES WISH NEWTON HAD STOPPED AT TWO LAWS.
AMEND

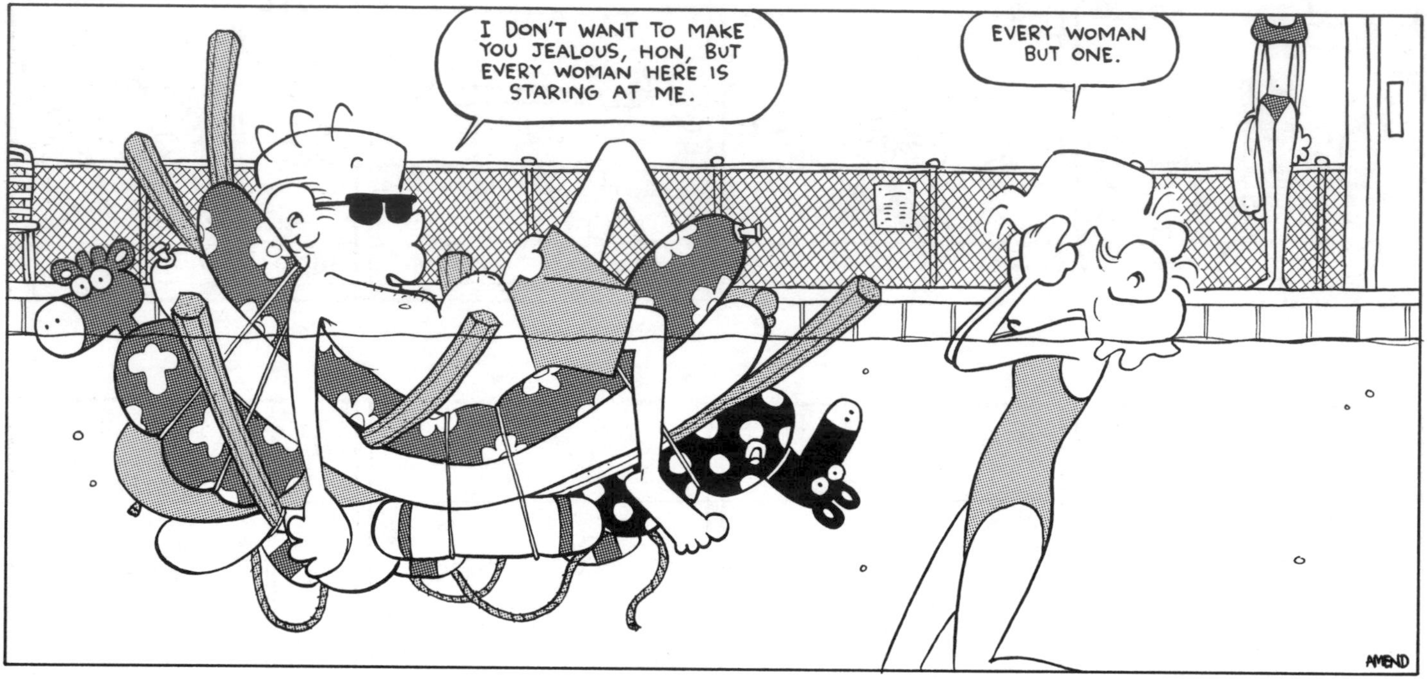
I DON'T WANT TO MAKE YOU JEALOUS, HON, BUT EVERY WOMAN HERE IS STARING AT ME.
EVERY WOMAN BUT ONE.
AMEND

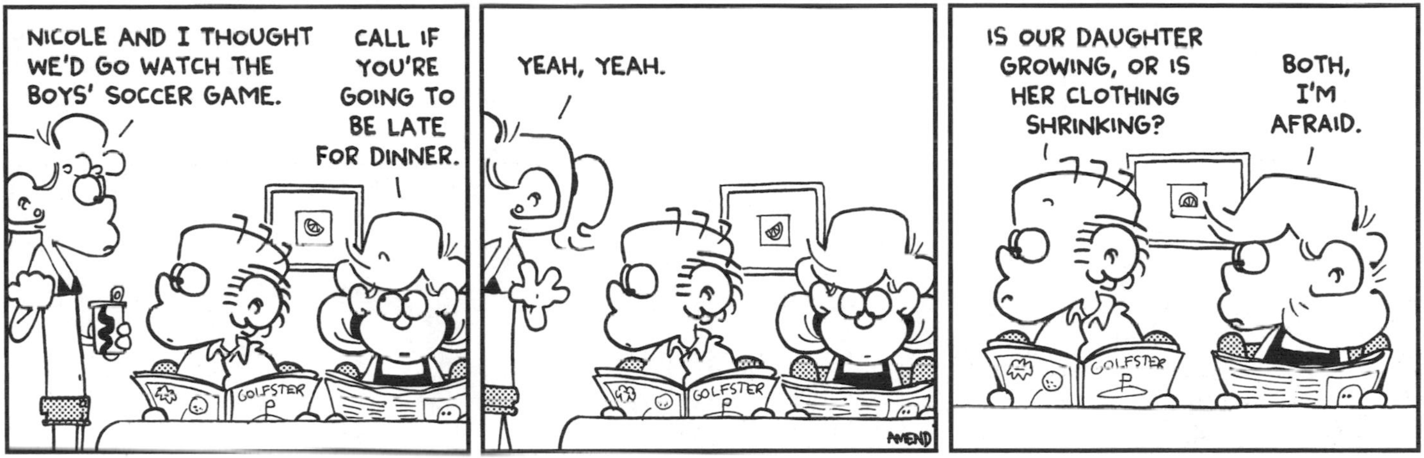
NICOLE AND I THOUGHT WE'D GO WATCH THE BOYS' SOCCER GAME.
CALL IF YOU'RE GOING TO BE LATE FOR DINNER.
GOLFSTER
YEAH, YEAH.
GOLFSTER
AMEND
IS OUR DAUGHTER GROWING, OR IS HER CLOTHING SHRINKING?
BOTH, I'M AFRAID.
GOLFSTER

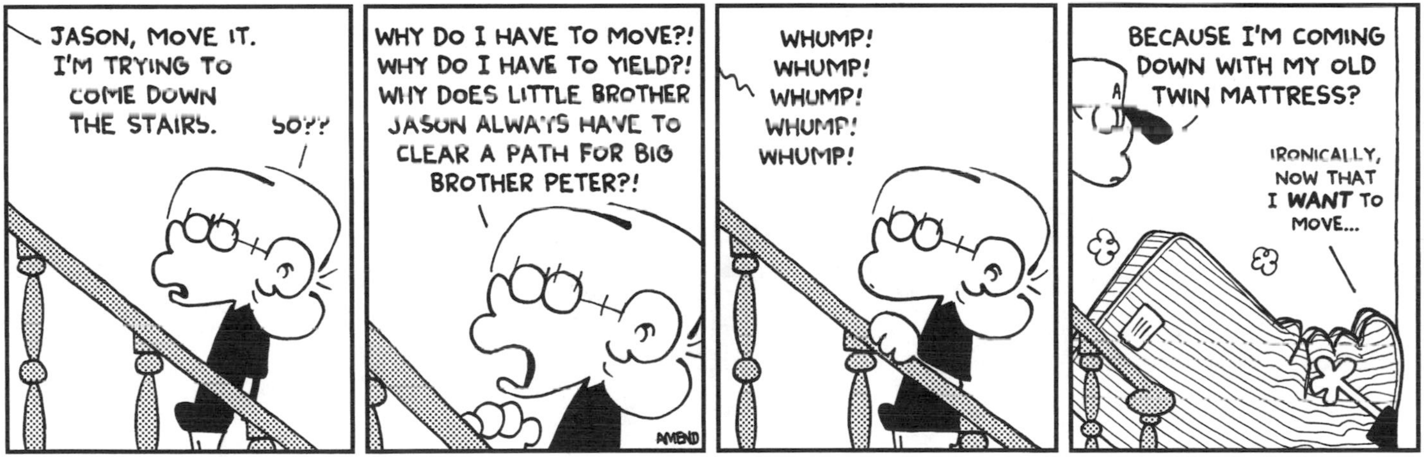
JASON, MOVE IT. I'M TRYING TO COME DOWN THE STAIRS.
SO??
WHY DO I HAVE TO MOVE?! WHY DO I HAVE TO YIELD?! WHY DOES LITTLE BROTHER JASON ALWAYS HAVE TO CLEAR A PATH FOR BIG BROTHER PETER?!
AMEND
WHUMP! WHUMP! WHUMP! WHUMP! WHUMP!
BECAUSE I'M COMING DOWN WITH MY OLD TWIN MATTRESS?
IRONICALLY, NOW THAT I **WANT** TO MOVE...

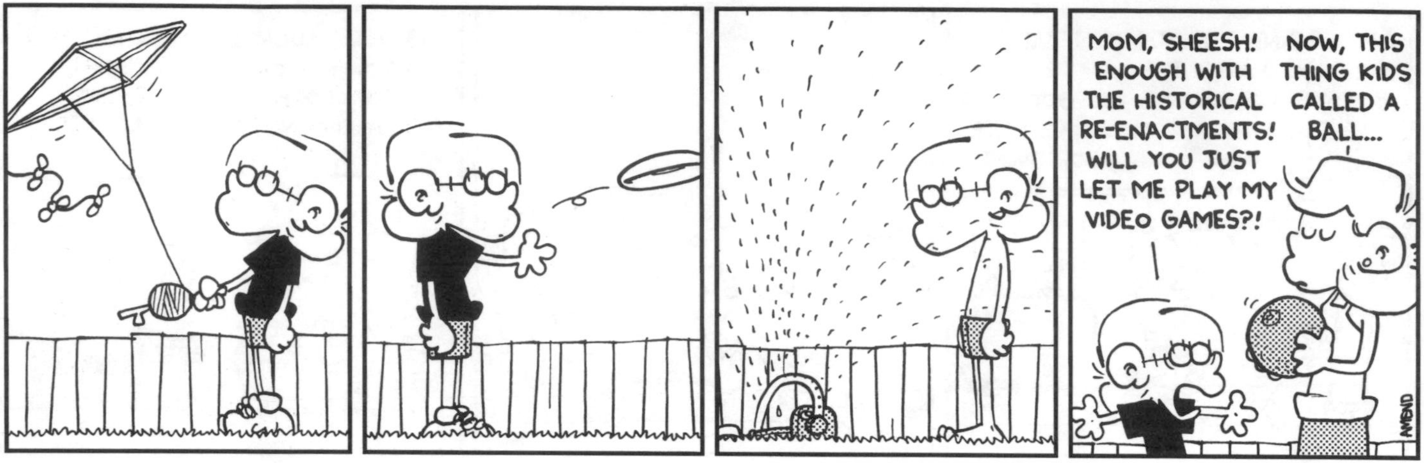
MOM, SHEESH! ENOUGH WITH THE HISTORICAL RE-ENACTMENTS! WILL YOU JUST LET ME PLAY MY VIDEO GAMES?!
NOW, THIS THING KIDS CALLED A BALL...
AMEND

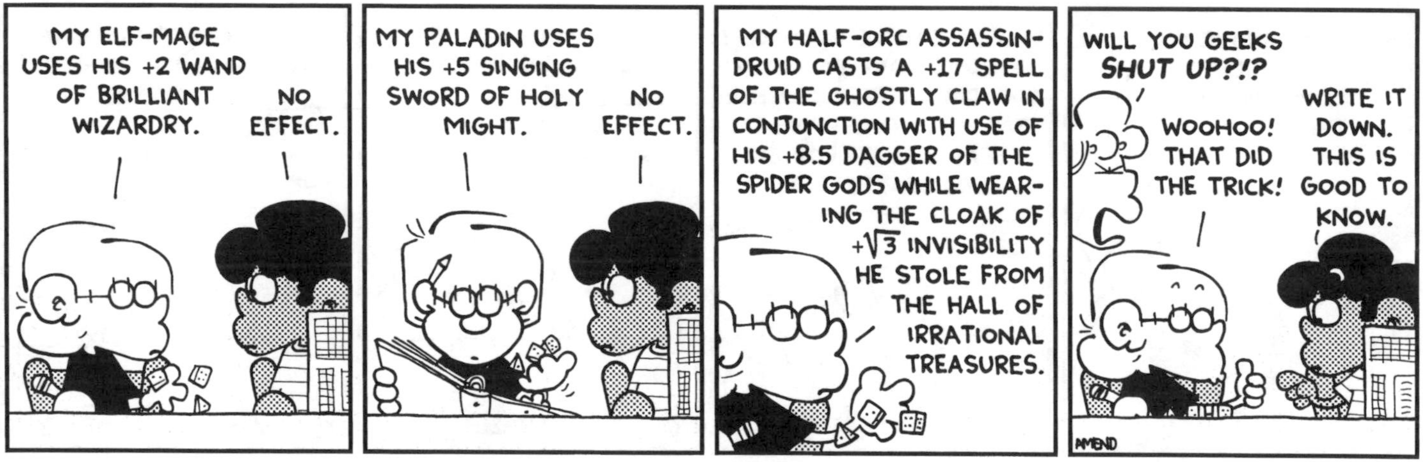
MY ELF-MAGE USES HIS +2 WAND OF BRILLIANT WIZARDRY.
NO EFFECT.
MY PALADIN USES HIS +5 SINGING SWORD OF HOLY MIGHT.
NO EFFECT.
MY HALF-ORC ASSASSIN-DRUID CASTS A +17 SPELL OF THE GHOSTLY CLAW IN CONJUNCTION WITH USE OF HIS +8.5 DAGGER OF THE SPIDER GODS WHILE WEARING THE CLOAK OF $+\sqrt{3}$ INVISIBILITY HE STOLE FROM THE HALL OF IRRATIONAL TREASURES.
WILL YOU GEEKS ***SHUT UP?!?***
WOOHOO! THAT DID THE TRICK!
WRITE IT DOWN. THIS IS GOOD TO KNOW.
AMEND

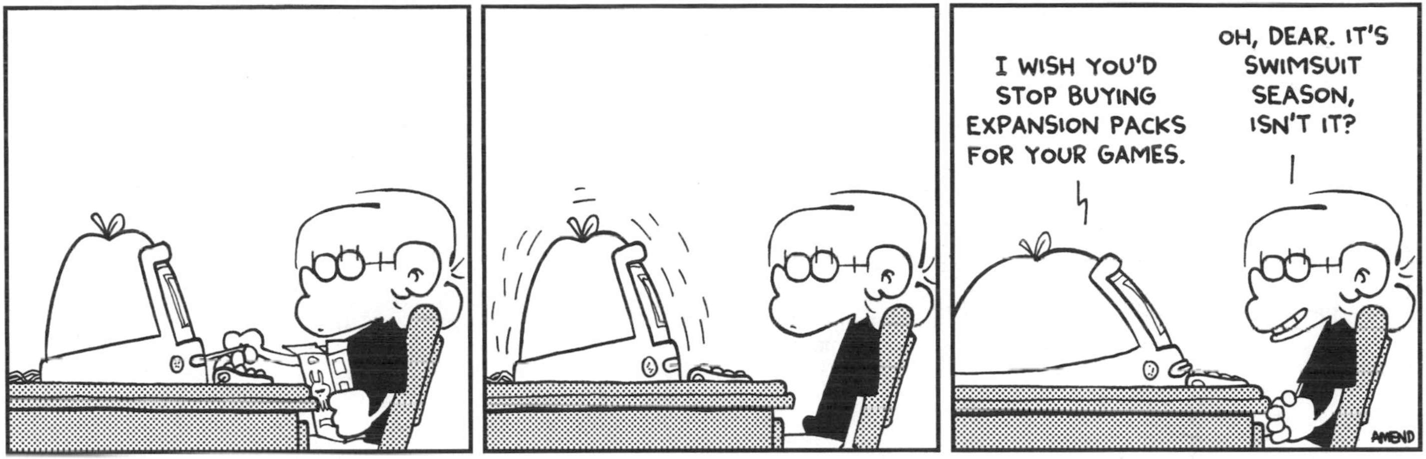
I WISH YOU'D STOP BUYING EXPANSION PACKS FOR YOUR GAMES.
OH, DEAR. IT'S SWIMSUIT SEASON, ISN'T IT?
AMEND

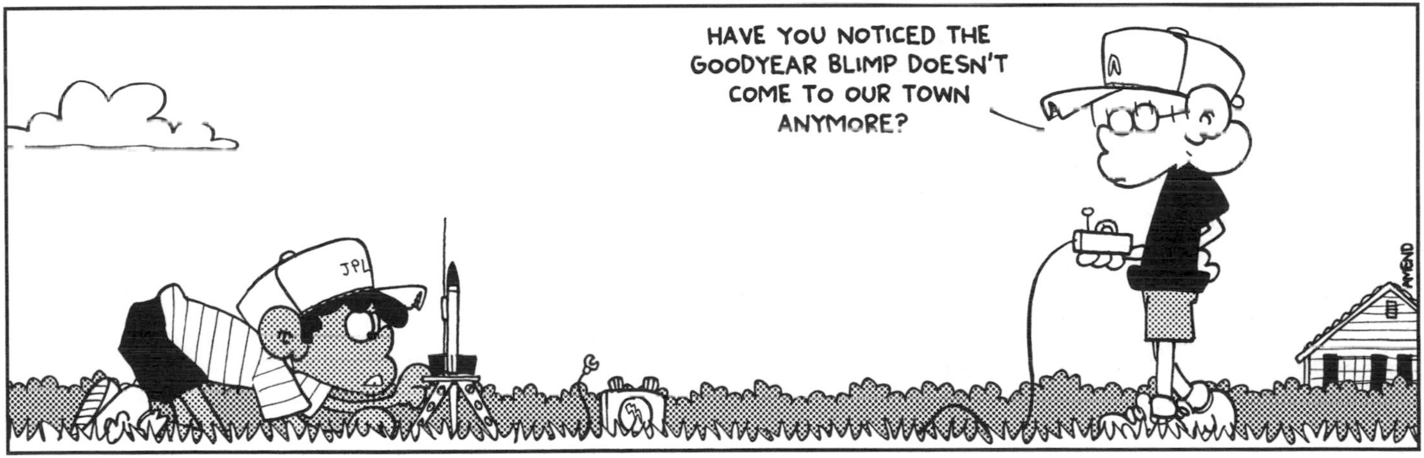
HAVE YOU NOTICED THE GOODYEAR BLIMP DOESN'T COME TO OUR TOWN ANYMORE?
JPL
AMEND

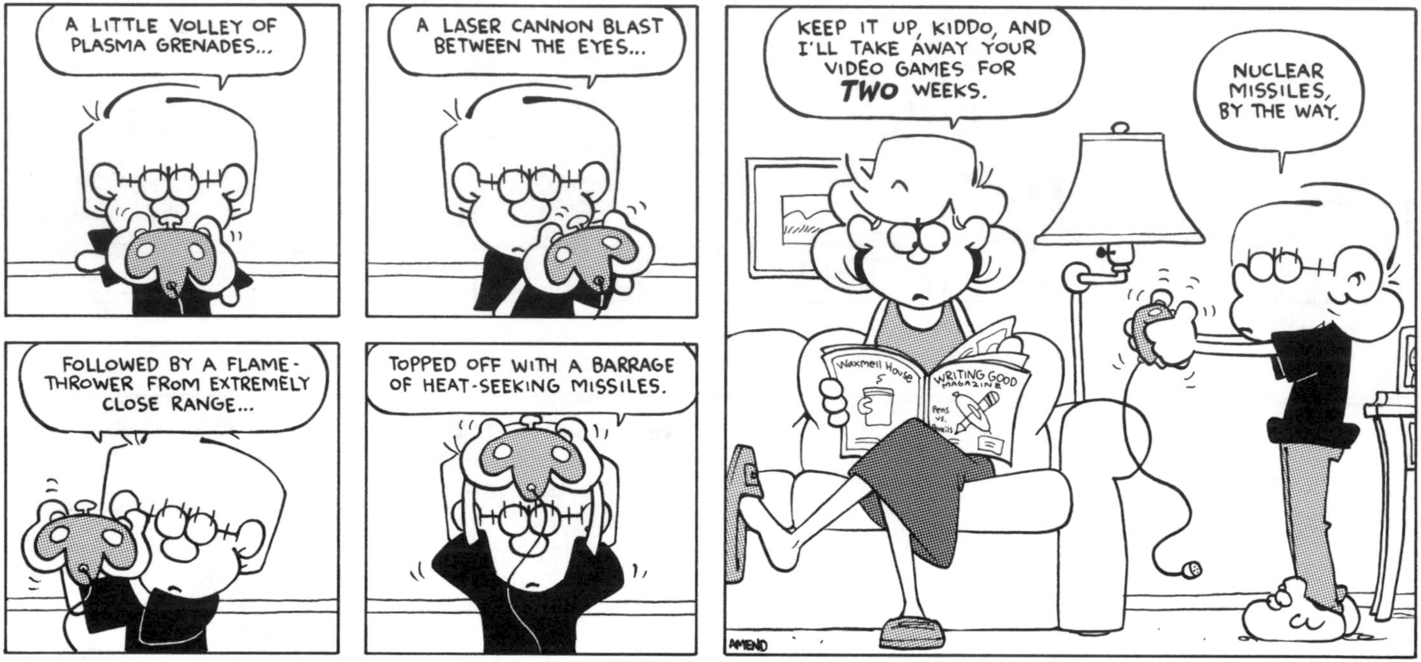
A LITTLE VOLLEY OF PLASMA GRENADES...
A LASER CANNON BLAST BETWEEN THE EYES...
FOLLOWED BY A FLAME-THROWER FROM EXTREMELY CLOSE RANGE...
TOPPED OFF WITH A BARRAGE OF HEAT-SEEKING MISSILES.
KEEP IT UP, KIDDO, AND I'LL TAKE AWAY YOUR VIDEO GAMES FOR TWO WEEKS.
NUCLEAR MISSILES, BY THE WAY.
Waxmell House
WRITING GOOD MAGAZINE
AMEND

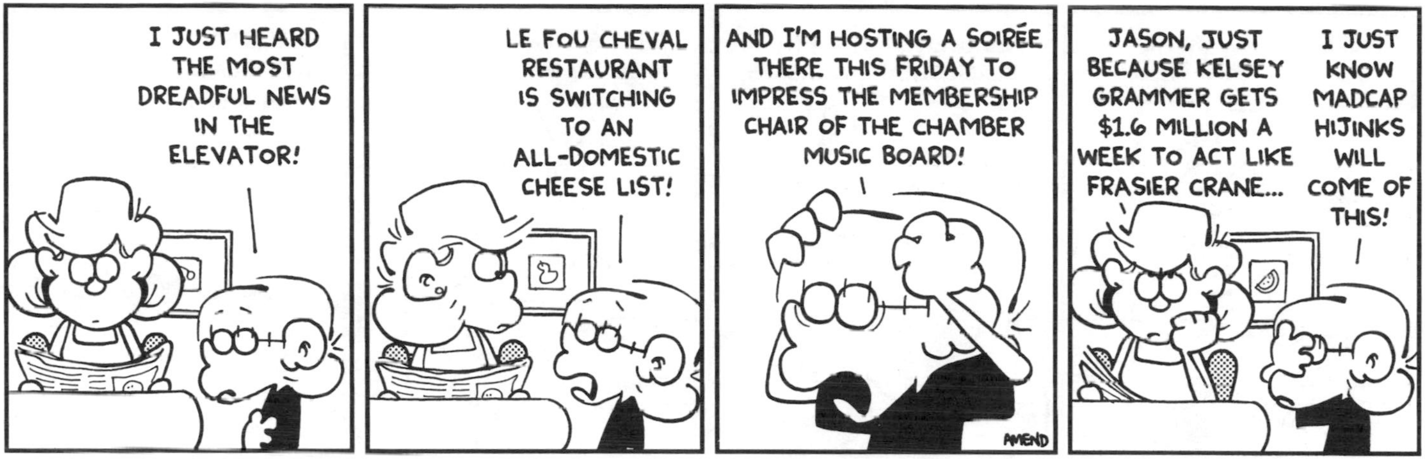
I JUST HEARD THE MOST DREADFUL NEWS IN THE ELEVATOR!
LE FOU CHEVAL RESTAURANT IS SWITCHING TO AN ALL-DOMESTIC CHEESE LIST!
AND I'M HOSTING A SOIRÉE THERE THIS FRIDAY TO IMPRESS THE MEMBERSHIP CHAIR OF THE CHAMBER MUSIC BOARD!
AMEND
JASON, JUST BECAUSE KELSEY GRAMMER GETS $1.6 MILLION A WEEK TO ACT LIKE FRASIER CRANE...
I JUST KNOW MADCAP HIJINKS WILL COME OF THIS!

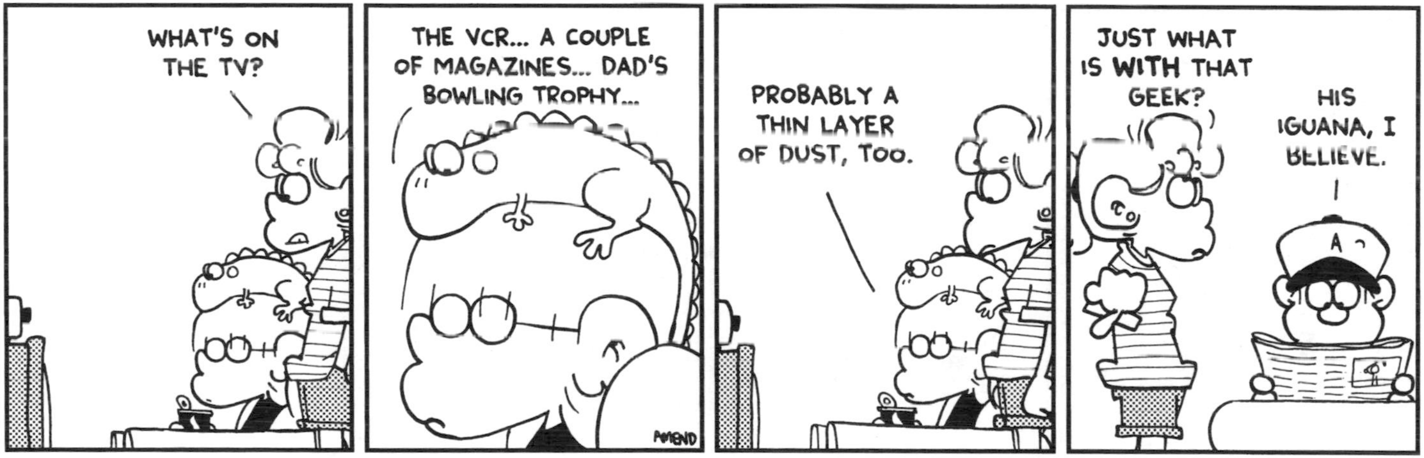
WHAT'S ON THE TV?
THE VCR... A COUPLE OF MAGAZINES... DAD'S BOWLING TROPHY...
AMEND
PROBABLY A THIN LAYER OF DUST, TOO.
JUST WHAT IS WITH THAT GEEK?
HIS IGUANA, I BELIEVE.

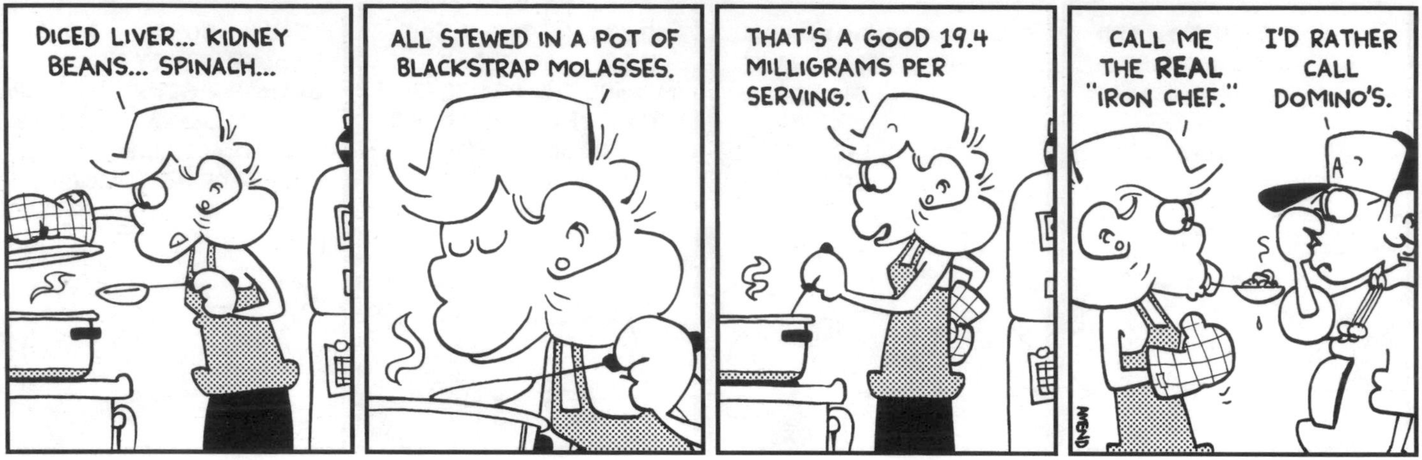
DICED LIVER... KIDNEY BEANS... SPINACH...
ALL STEWED IN A POT OF BLACKSTRAP MOLASSES.
THAT'S A GOOD 19.4 MILLIGRAMS PER SERVING.
CALL ME THE REAL "IRON CHEF."
I'D RATHER CALL DOMINO'S.
AMEND

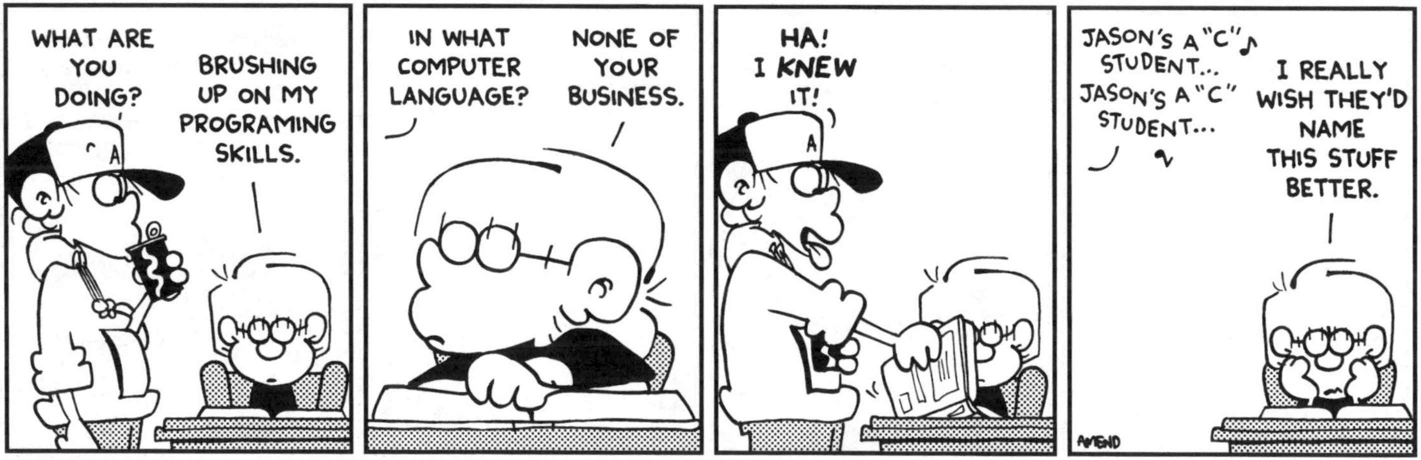
WHAT ARE YOU DOING?
BRUSHING UP ON MY PROGRAMING SKILLS.
IN WHAT COMPUTER LANGUAGE?
NONE OF YOUR BUSINESS.
HA! I KNEW IT!
JASON'S A "C" STUDENT... JASON'S A "C" STUDENT...
I REALLY WISH THEY'D NAME THIS STUFF BETTER.
AMEND

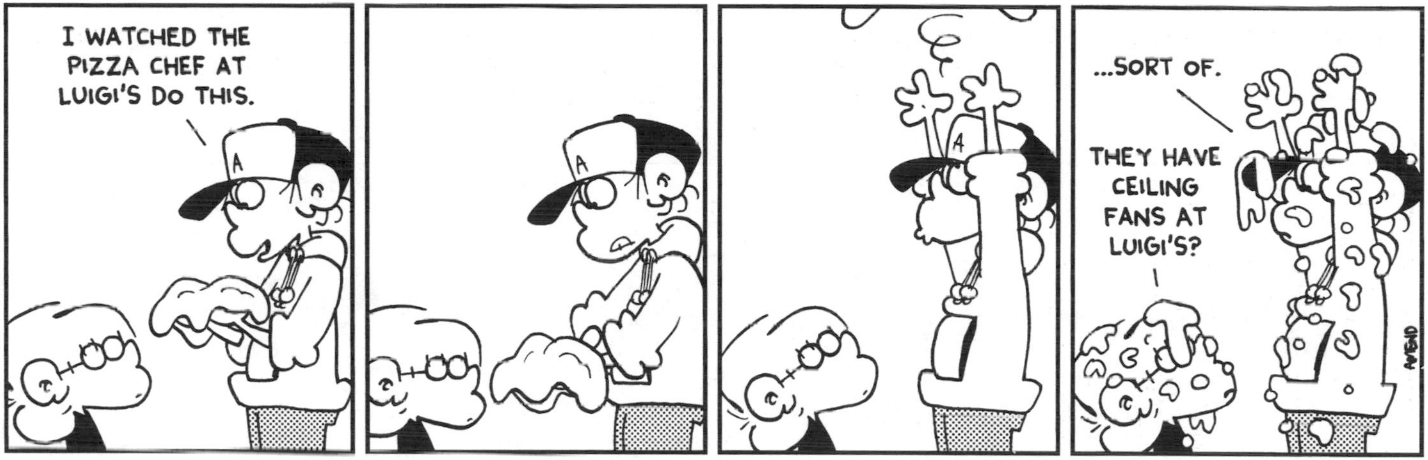
I WATCHED THE PIZZA CHEF AT LUIGI'S DO THIS.
...SORT OF.
THEY HAVE CEILING FANS AT LUIGI'S?
AMEND

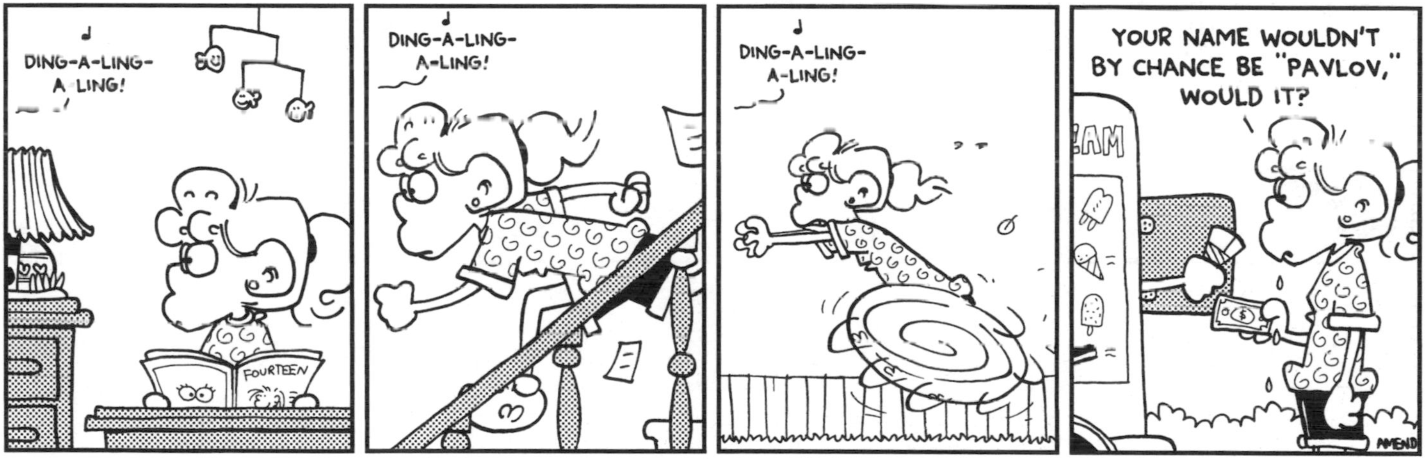
DING-A-LING-A-LING!
FOURTEEN
DING-A-LING-A-LING!
DING-A-LING-A-LING!
YOUR NAME WOULDN'T BY CHANCE BE "PAVLOV," WOULD IT?
AMEND

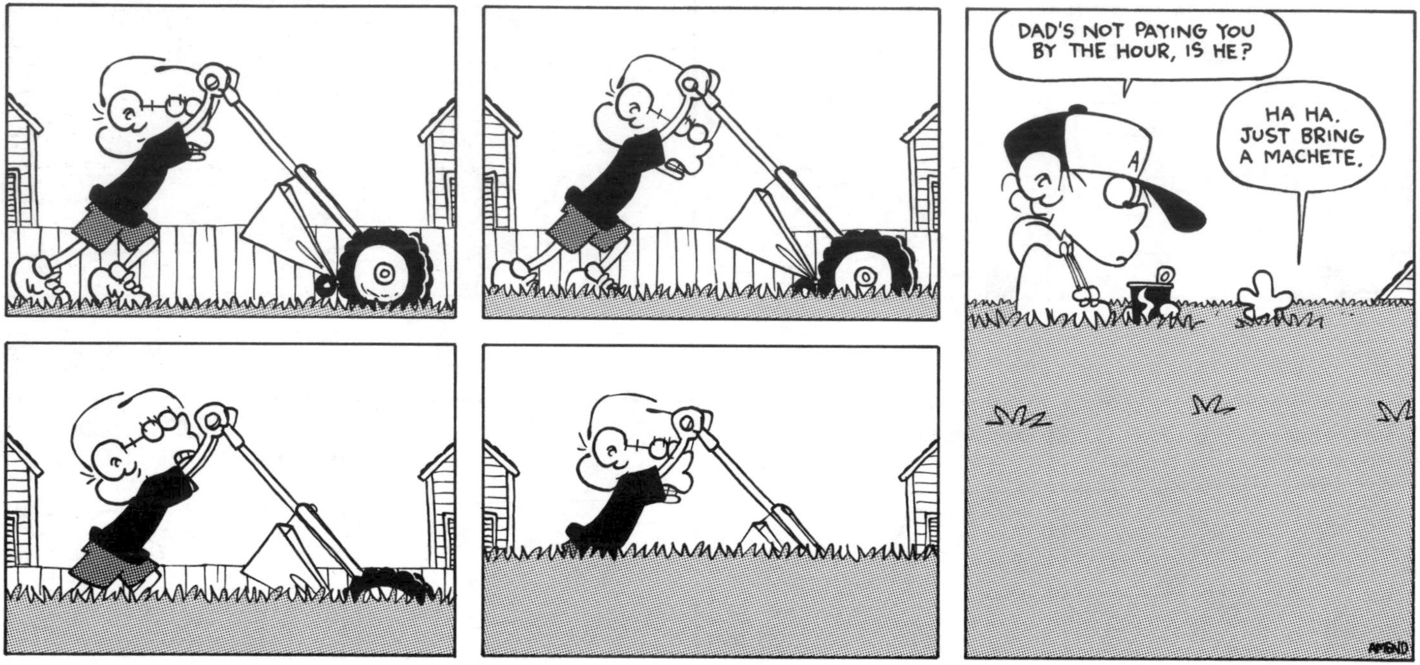
DAD'S NOT PAYING YOU BY THE HOUR, IS HE?
HA HA. JUST BRING A MACHETE.
AMEND

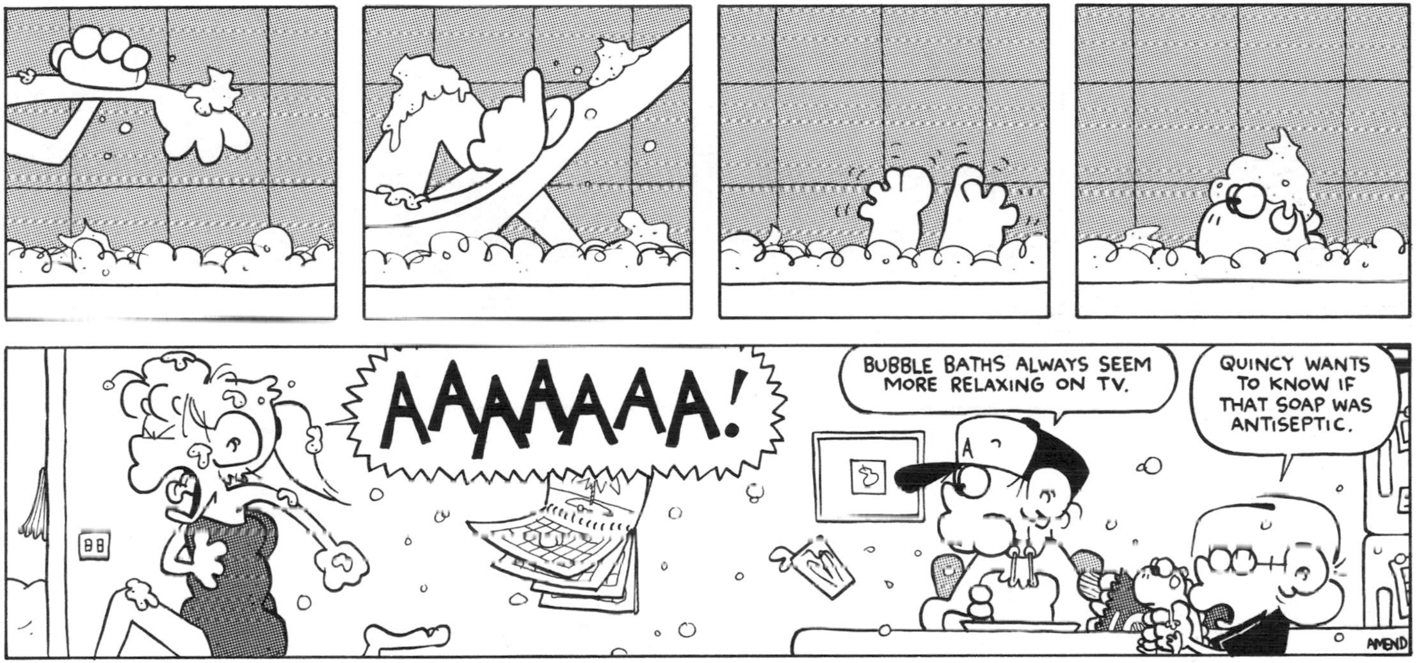
AAAAAAA!
BUBBLE BATHS ALWAYS SEEM MORE RELAXING ON TV.
QUINCY WANTS TO KNOW IF THAT SOAP WAS ANTISEPTIC.
AMEND

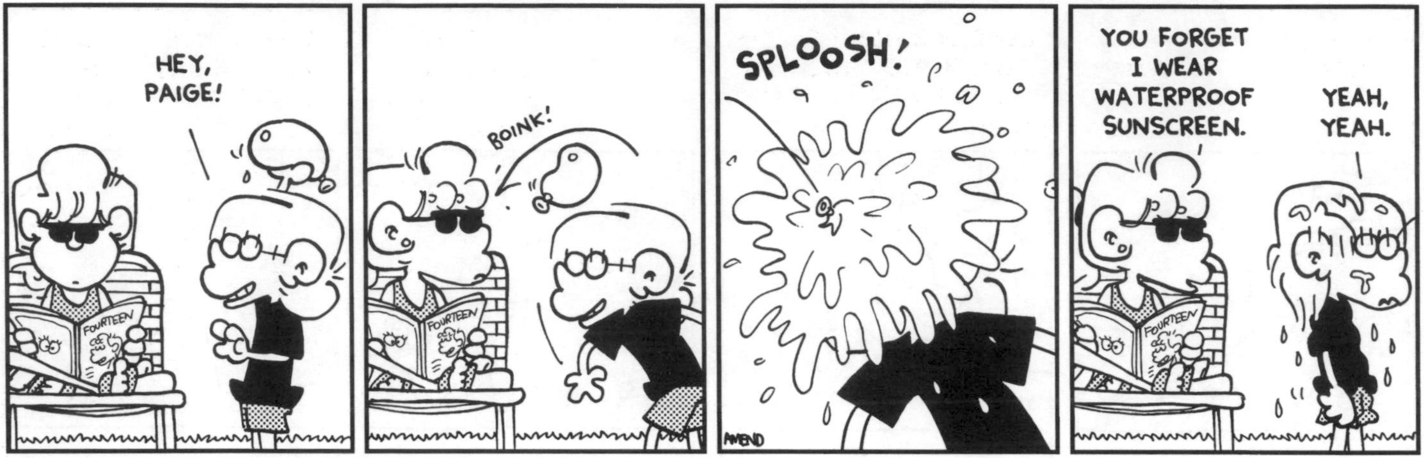
HEY, PAIGE!
BOINK!
SPLOOSH!
AMEND
YOU FORGET I WEAR WATERPROOF SUNSCREEN.
YEAH, YEAH.
FOURTEEN

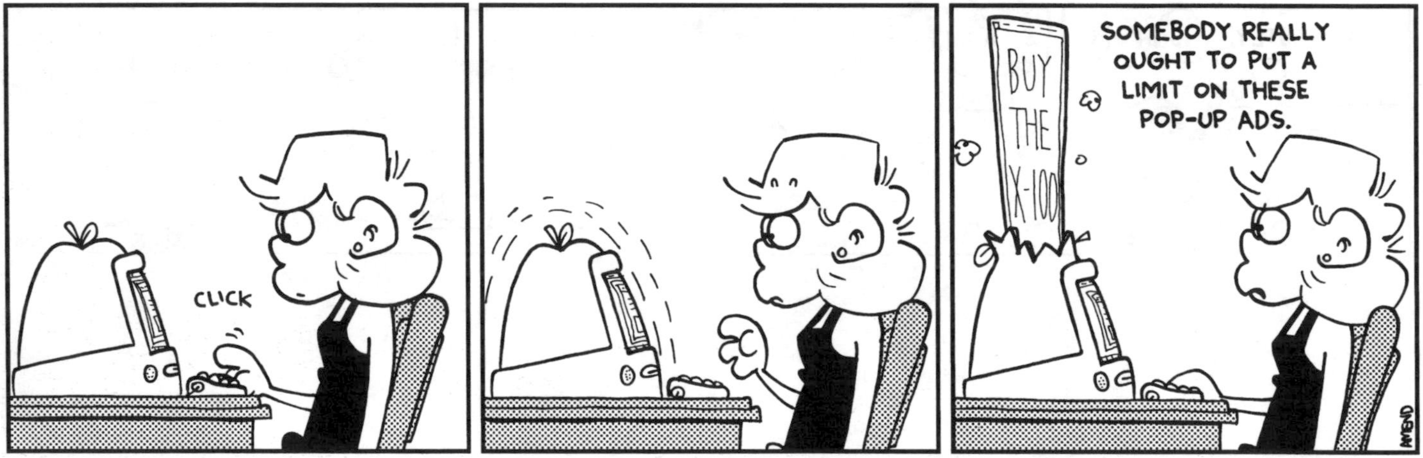
CLICK
BUY THE X-100
SOMEBODY REALLY OUGHT TO PUT A LIMIT ON THESE POP-UP ADS.
AMEND

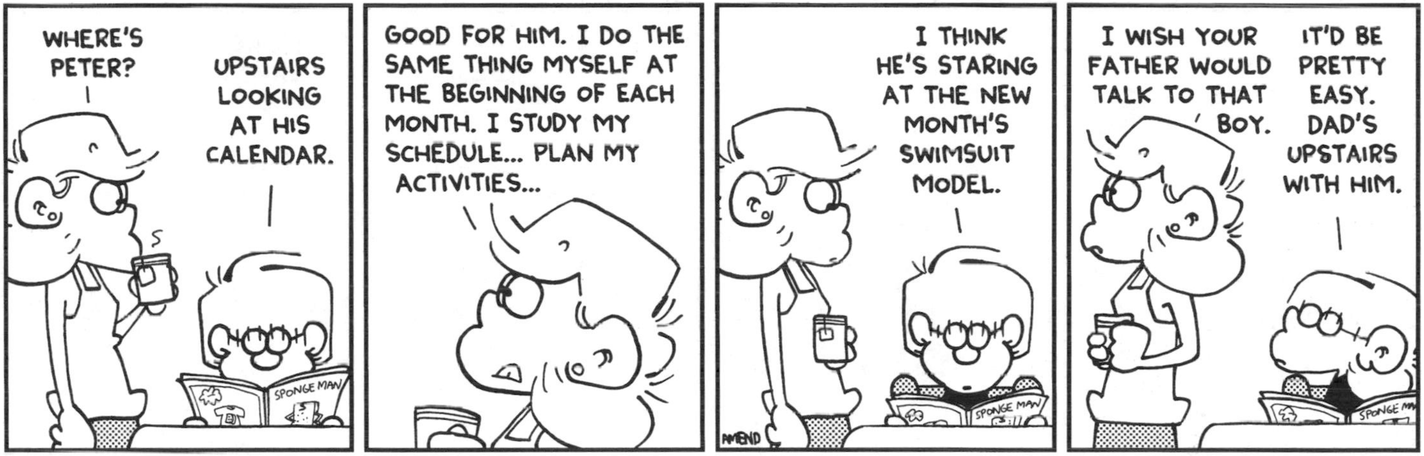
WHERE'S PETER?
UPSTAIRS LOOKING AT HIS CALENDAR.
SPONGE MAN
GOOD FOR HIM. I DO THE SAME THING MYSELF AT THE BEGINNING OF EACH MONTH. I STUDY MY SCHEDULE... PLAN MY ACTIVITIES...
I THINK HE'S STARING AT THE NEW MONTH'S SWIMSUIT MODEL.
AMEND
SPONGE MAN
I WISH YOUR FATHER WOULD TALK TO THAT BOY.
IT'D BE PRETTY EASY. DAD'S UPSTAIRS WITH HIM.

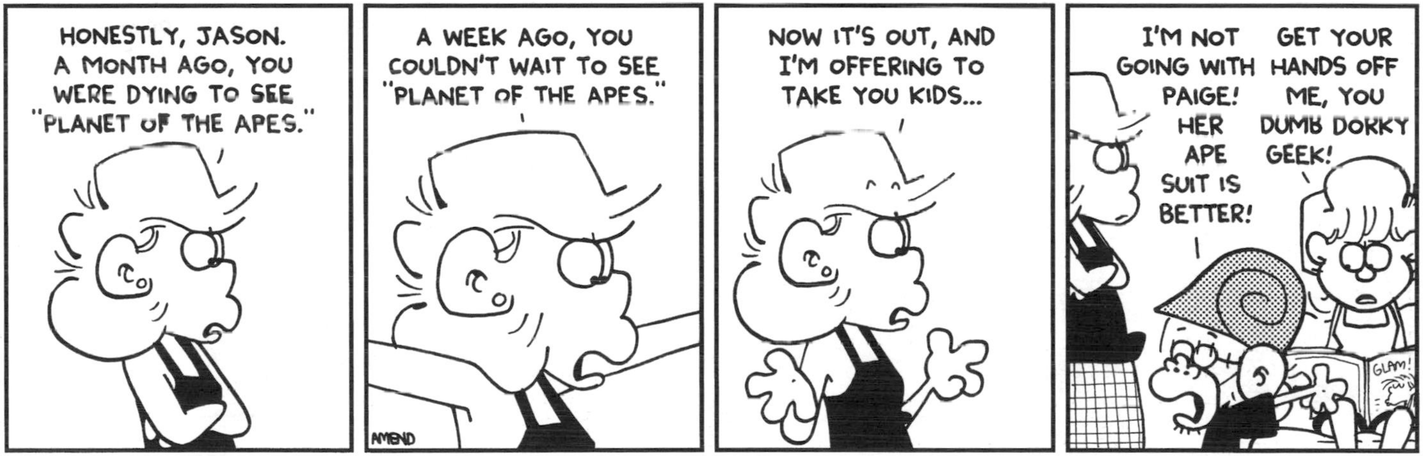
HONESTLY, JASON. A MONTH AGO, YOU WERE DYING TO SEE "PLANET OF THE APES."
A WEEK AGO, YOU COULDN'T WAIT TO SEE "PLANET OF THE APES."
AMEND
NOW IT'S OUT, AND I'M OFFERING TO TAKE YOU KIDS...
I'M NOT GOING WITH PAIGE! HER APE SUIT IS BETTER!
GET YOUR HANDS OFF ME, YOU DUMB DORKY GEEK!
GLAM!

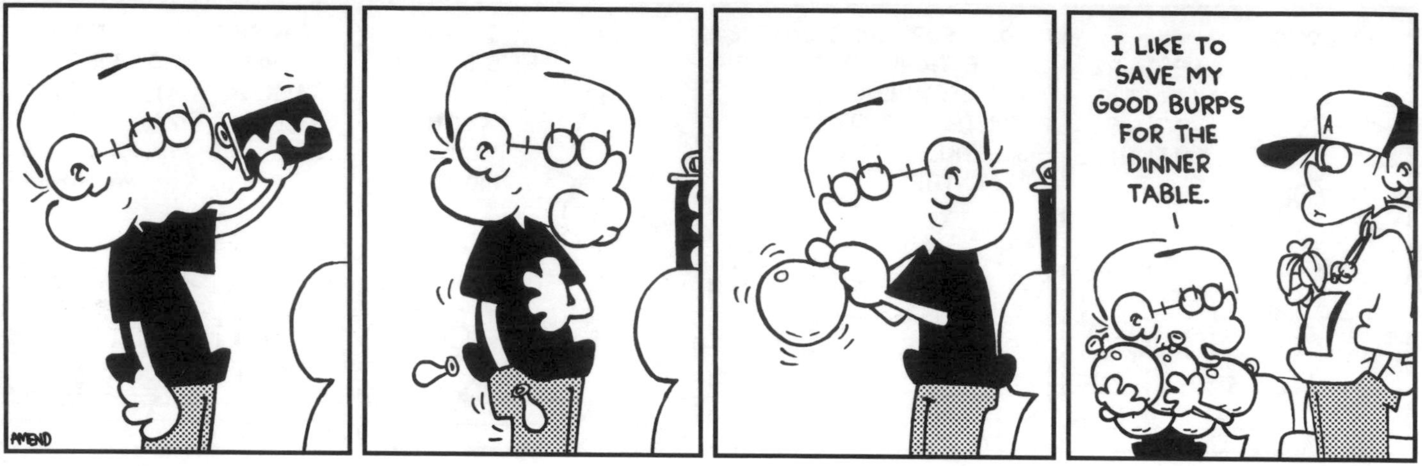
AMEND
I LIKE TO SAVE MY GOOD BURPS FOR THE DINNER TABLE.
A

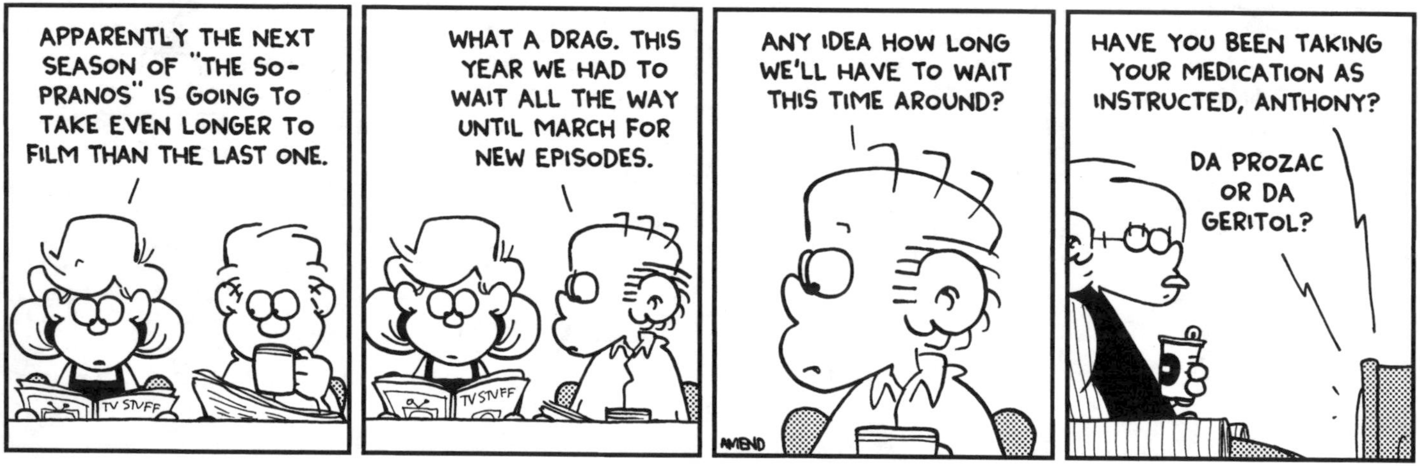
APPARENTLY THE NEXT SEASON OF "THE SOPRANOS" IS GOING TO TAKE EVEN LONGER TO FILM THAN THE LAST ONE.
TV STUFF
WHAT A DRAG. THIS YEAR WE HAD TO WAIT ALL THE WAY UNTIL MARCH FOR NEW EPISODES.
TV STUFF
ANY IDEA HOW LONG WE'LL HAVE TO WAIT THIS TIME AROUND?
AMEND
HAVE YOU BEEN TAKING YOUR MEDICATION AS INSTRUCTED, ANTHONY?
DA PROZAC OR DA GERITOL?

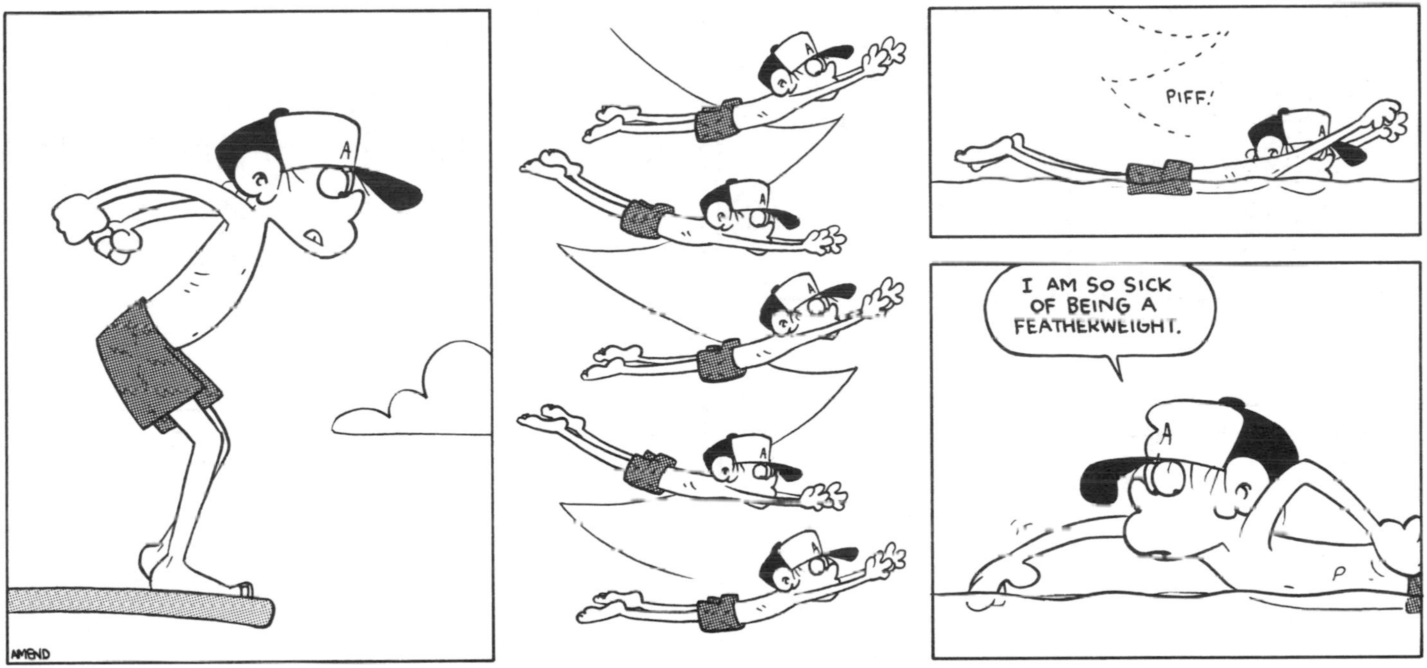
AMEND
PIFF!
I AM SO SICK OF BEING A FEATHERWEIGHT.

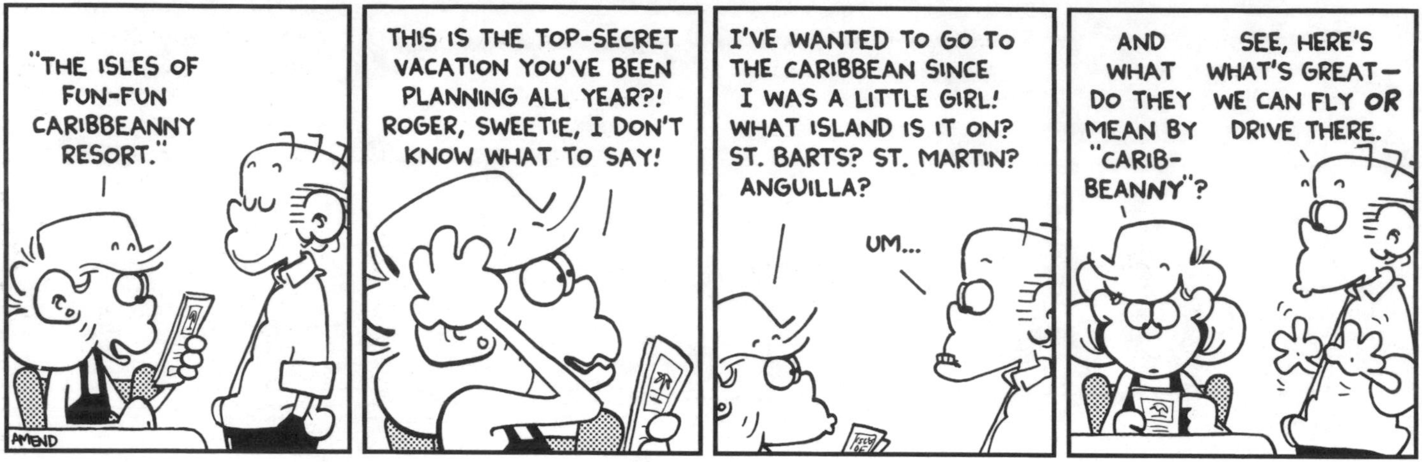
"THE ISLES OF FUN-FUN CARIBBEANNY RESORT."
THIS IS THE TOP-SECRET VACATION YOU'VE BEEN PLANNING ALL YEAR?! ROGER, SWEETIE, I DON'T KNOW WHAT TO SAY!
I'VE WANTED TO GO TO THE CARIBBEAN SINCE I WAS A LITTLE GIRL! WHAT ISLAND IS IT ON? ST. BARTS? ST. MARTIN? ANGUILLA?
UM...
AND WHAT DO THEY MEAN BY "CARIB-BEANNY"?
SEE, HERE'S WHAT'S GREAT— WE CAN FLY **OR** DRIVE THERE.
AMEND

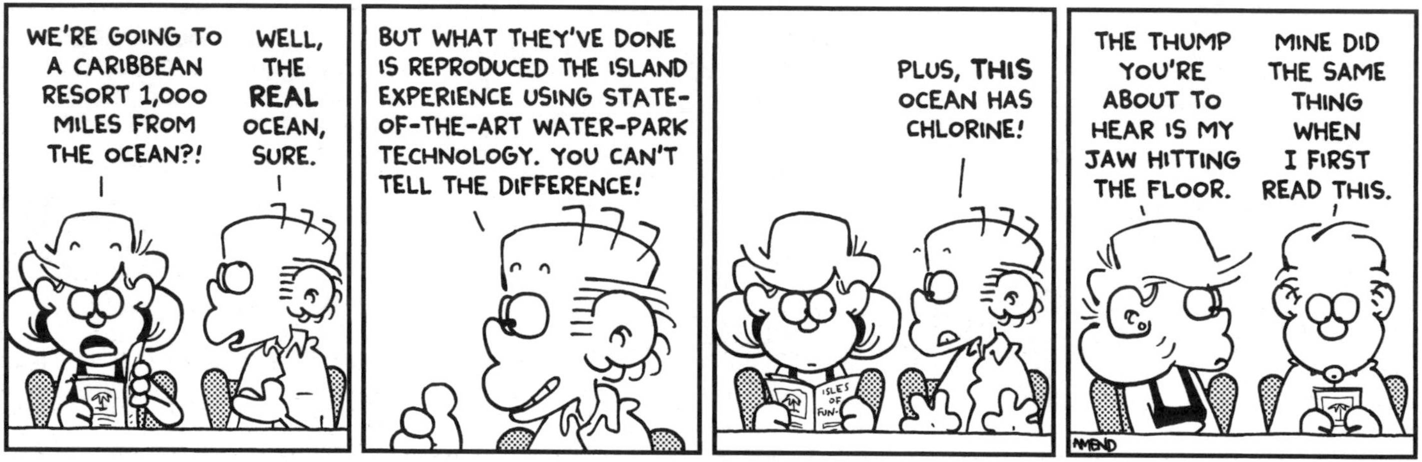
WE'RE GOING TO A CARIBBEAN RESORT 1,000 MILES FROM THE OCEAN?!
WELL, THE **REAL** OCEAN, SURE.
BUT WHAT THEY'VE DONE IS REPRODUCED THE ISLAND EXPERIENCE USING STATE-OF-THE-ART WATER-PARK TECHNOLOGY. YOU CAN'T TELL THE DIFFERENCE!
PLUS, **THIS** OCEAN HAS CHLORINE!
THE THUMP YOU'RE ABOUT TO HEAR IS MY JAW HITTING THE FLOOR.
MINE DID THE SAME THING WHEN I FIRST READ THIS.
AMEND

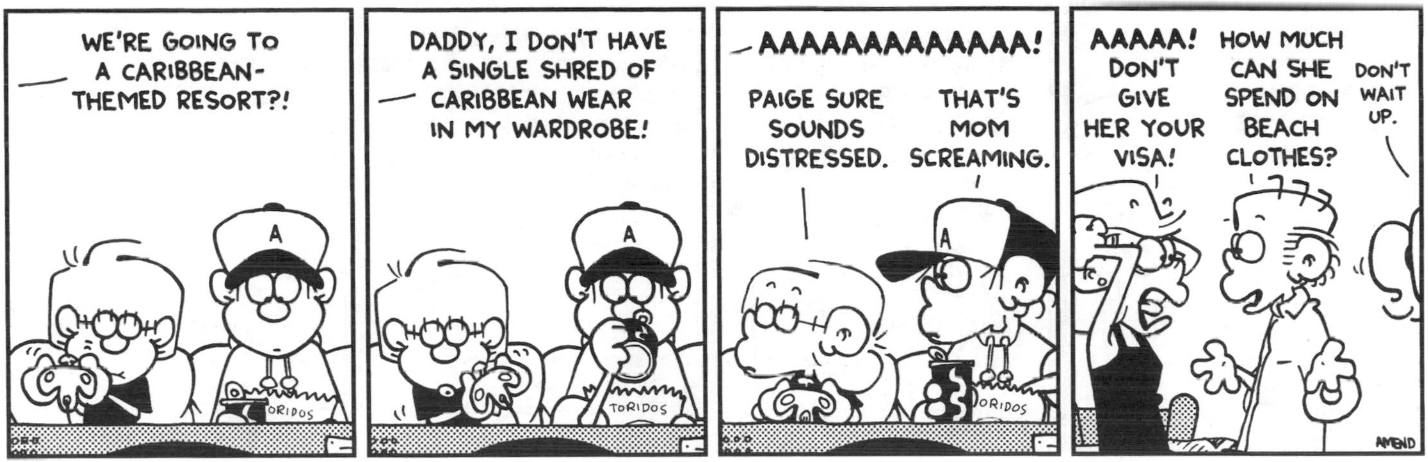
WE'RE GOING TO A CARIBBEAN-THEMED RESORT?!
DADDY, I DON'T HAVE A SINGLE SHRED OF CARIBBEAN WEAR IN MY WARDROBE!
AAAAAAAAAAAAA!
PAIGE SURE SOUNDS DISTRESSED.
THAT'S MOM SCREAMING.
AAAAA! DON'T GIVE HER YOUR VISA!
HOW MUCH CAN SHE SPEND ON BEACH CLOTHES?
DON'T WAIT UP.
AMEND

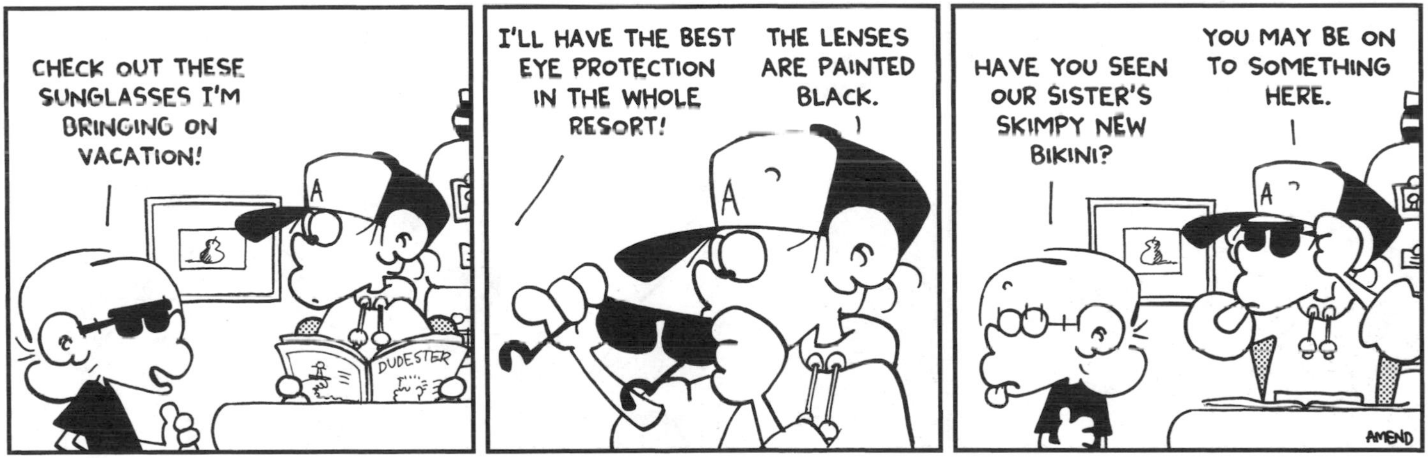
CHECK OUT THESE SUNGLASSES I'M BRINGING ON VACATION!
DUDESTER
I'LL HAVE THE BEST EYE PROTECTION IN THE WHOLE RESORT!
THE LENSES ARE PAINTED BLACK.
HAVE YOU SEEN OUR SISTER'S SKIMPY NEW BIKINI?
YOU MAY BE ON TO SOMETHING HERE.
AMEND

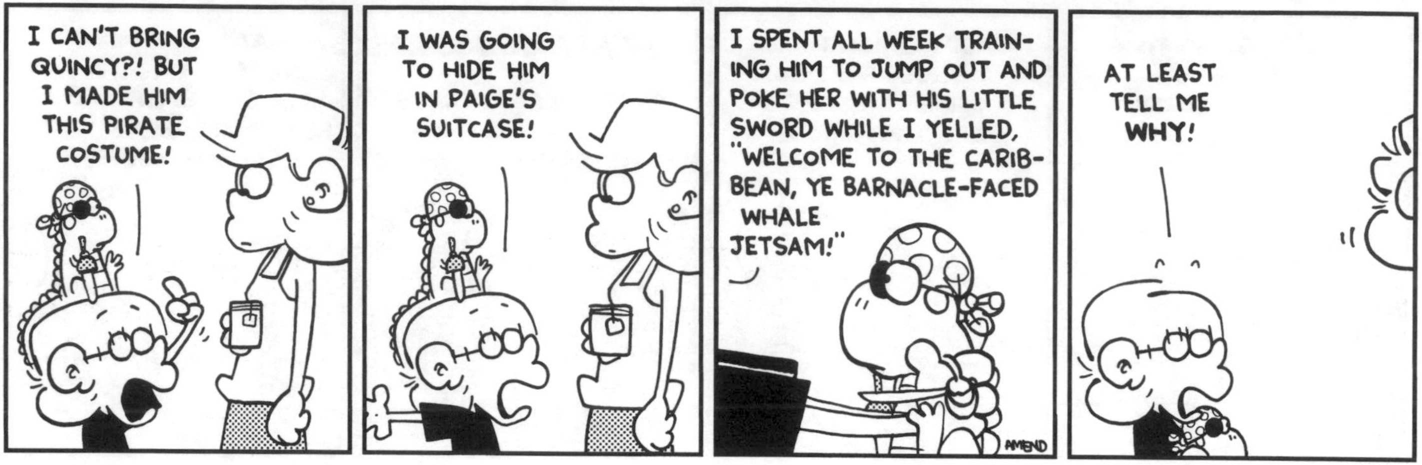
I CAN'T BRING QUINCY?! BUT I MADE HIM THIS PIRATE COSTUME!
I WAS GOING TO HIDE HIM IN PAIGE'S SUITCASE!
I SPENT ALL WEEK TRAINING HIM TO JUMP OUT AND POKE HER WITH HIS LITTLE SWORD WHILE I YELLED, "WELCOME TO THE CARIBBEAN, YE BARNACLE-FACED WHALE JETSAM!"
AT LEAST TELL ME WHY!
AMEND

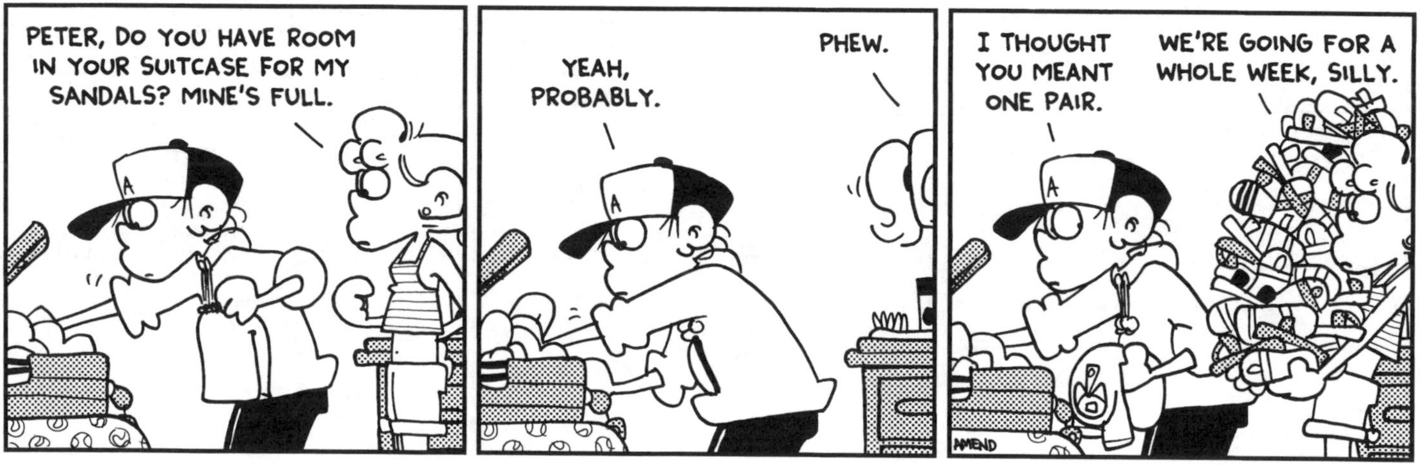
PETER, DO YOU HAVE ROOM IN YOUR SUITCASE FOR MY SANDALS? MINE'S FULL.
YEAH, PROBABLY.
PHEW.
I THOUGHT YOU MEANT ONE PAIR.
WE'RE GOING FOR A WHOLE WEEK, SILLY.
AMEND

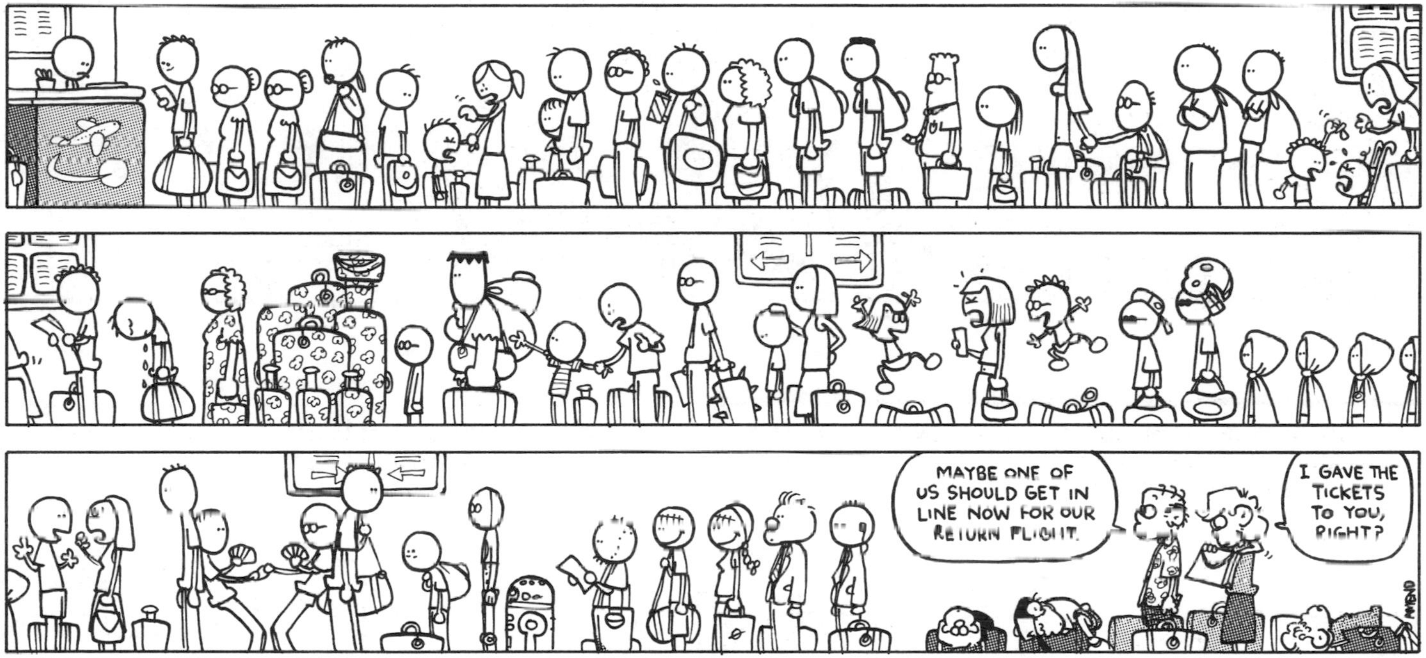
MAYBE ONE OF US SHOULD GET IN LINE NOW FOR OUR RETURN FLIGHT.
I GAVE THE TICKETS TO YOU, RIGHT?
PASTIS

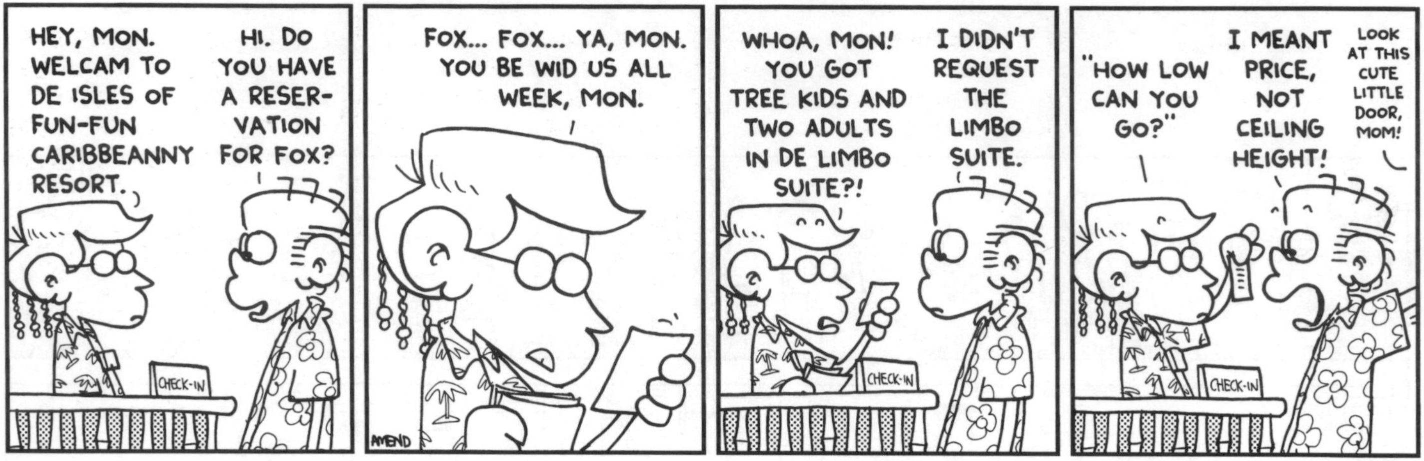
HEY, MON. WELCAM TO DE ISLES OF FUN-FUN CARIBBEANNY RESORT.
HI. DO YOU HAVE A RESER-VATION FOR FOX?
CHECK-IN
FOX... FOX... YA, MON. YOU BE WID US ALL WEEK, MON.
AMEND
WHOA, MON! YOU GOT TREE KIDS AND TWO ADULTS IN DE LIMBO SUITE?!
I DIDN'T REQUEST THE LIMBO SUITE.
"HOW LOW CAN YOU GO?"
I MEANT PRICE, NOT CEILING HEIGHT!
LOOK AT THIS CUTE LITTLE DOOR, MOM!

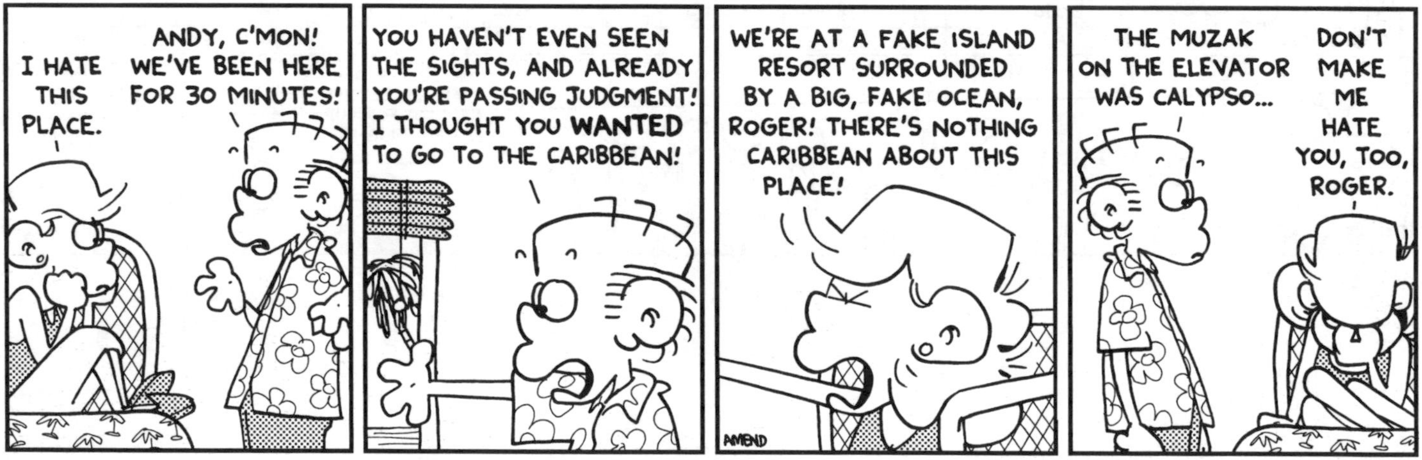
I HATE THIS PLACE.
ANDY, C'MON! WE'VE BEEN HERE FOR 30 MINUTES!
YOU HAVEN'T EVEN SEEN THE SIGHTS, AND ALREADY YOU'RE PASSING JUDGMENT! I THOUGHT YOU WANTED TO GO TO THE CARIBBEAN!
WE'RE AT A FAKE ISLAND RESORT SURROUNDED BY A BIG, FAKE OCEAN, ROGER! THERE'S NOTHING CARIBBEAN ABOUT THIS PLACE!
AMEND
THE MUZAK ON THE ELEVATOR WAS CALYPSO...
DON'T MAKE ME HATE YOU, TOO, ROGER.

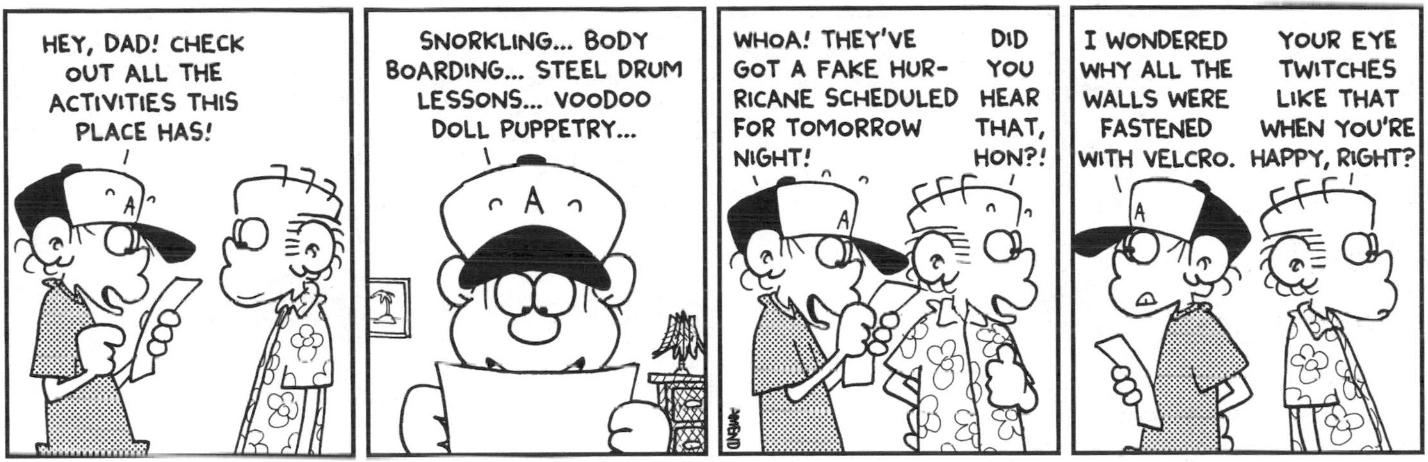
HEY, DAD! CHECK OUT ALL THE ACTIVITIES THIS PLACE HAS!
SNORKLING... BODY BOARDING... STEEL DRUM LESSONS... VOODOO DOLL PUPPETRY...
WHOA! THEY'VE GOT A FAKE HUR-RICANE SCHEDULED FOR TOMORROW NIGHT!
DID YOU HEAR THAT, HON?!
I WONDERED WHY ALL THE WALLS WERE FASTENED WITH VELCRO.
YOUR EYE TWITCHES LIKE THAT WHEN YOU'RE HAPPY, RIGHT?
AMEND

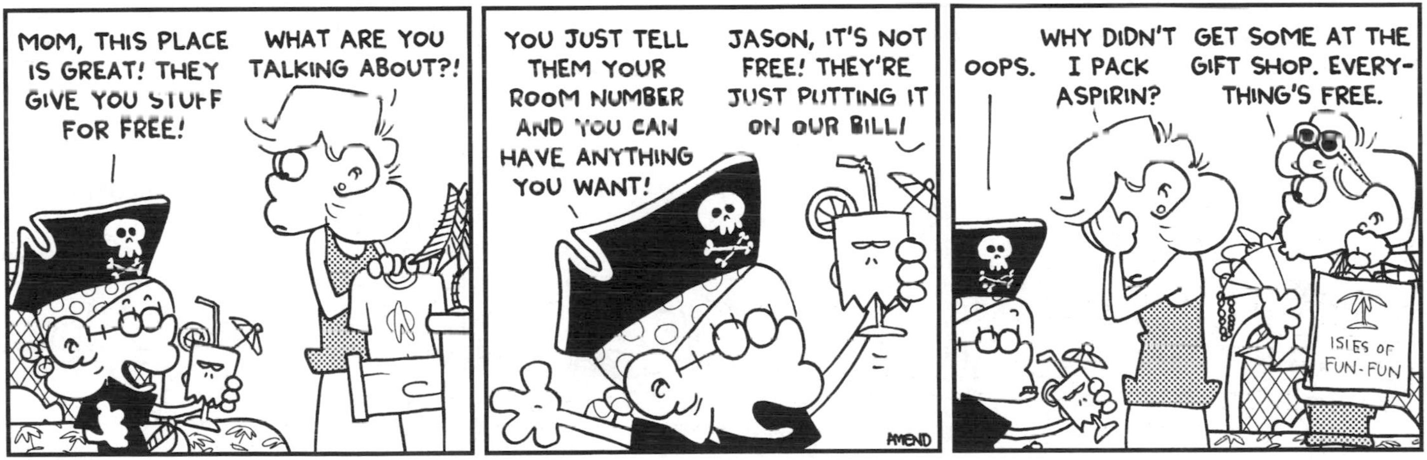
MOM, THIS PLACE IS GREAT! THEY GIVE YOU STUFF FOR FREE!
WHAT ARE YOU TALKING ABOUT?!
YOU JUST TELL THEM YOUR ROOM NUMBER AND YOU CAN HAVE ANYTHING YOU WANT!
JASON, IT'S NOT FREE! THEY'RE JUST PUTTING IT ON OUR BILL!
AMEND
OOPS.
WHY DIDN'T I PACK ASPIRIN?
GET SOME AT THE GIFT SHOP. EVERY-THING'S FREE.
ISLES OF FUN-FUN

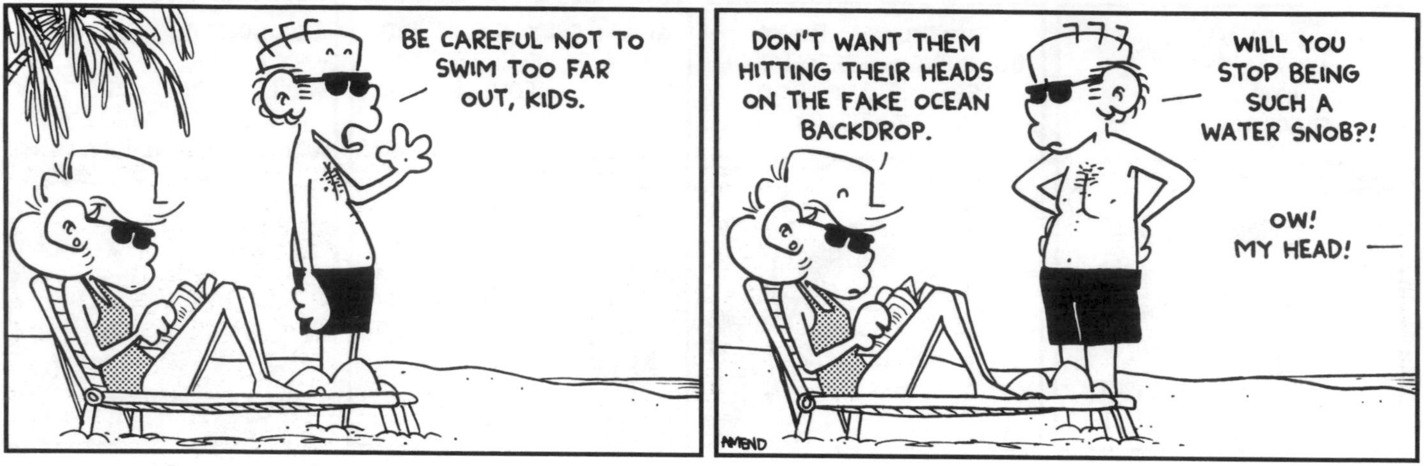
BE CAREFUL NOT TO SWIM TOO FAR OUT, KIDS.
DON'T WANT THEM HITTING THEIR HEADS ON THE FAKE OCEAN BACKDROP.
WILL YOU STOP BEING SUCH A WATER SNOB?!
OW! MY HEAD!
AMEND

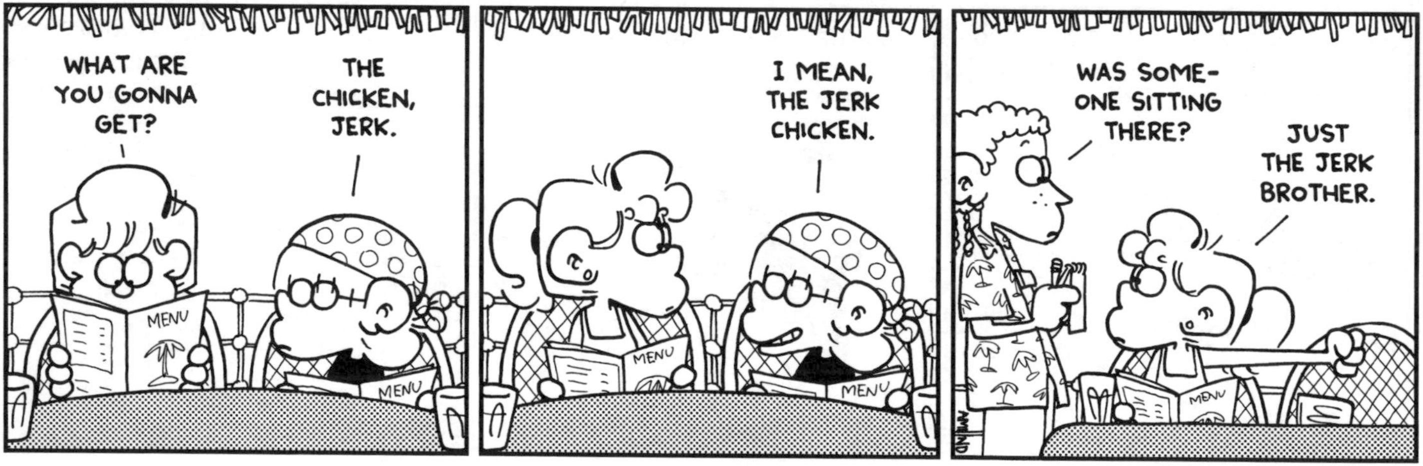
WHAT ARE YOU GONNA GET?
THE CHICKEN, JERK.
MENU
MENU
I MEAN, THE JERK CHICKEN.
MENU
MENU
WAS SOME-ONE SITTING THERE?
JUST THE JERK BROTHER.
MENU
AMEND

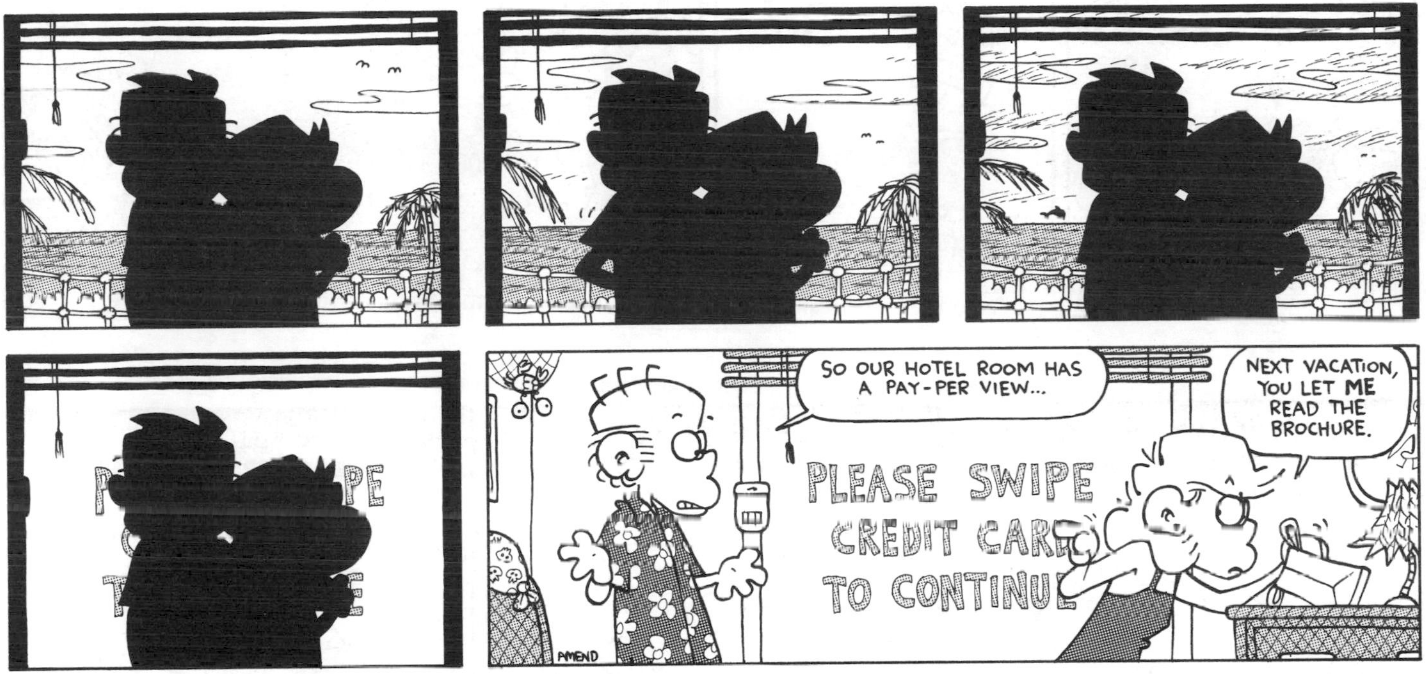
SO OUR HOTEL ROOM HAS A PAY-PER VIEW...
NEXT VACATION, YOU LET **ME** READ THE BROCHURE.
PLEASE SWIPE
AMEND

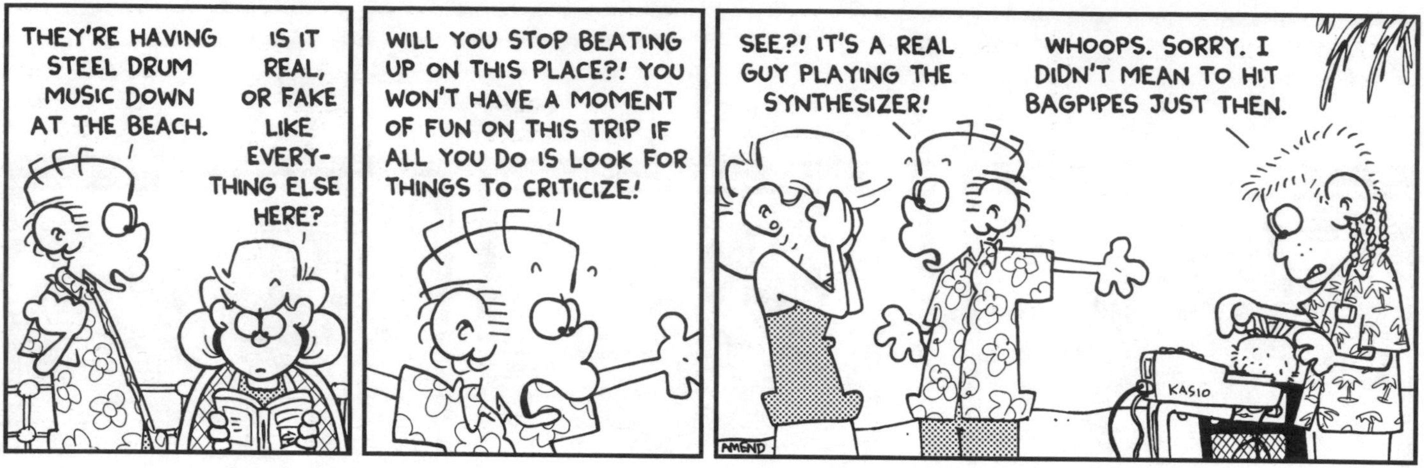
THEY'RE HAVING STEEL DRUM MUSIC DOWN AT THE BEACH.
IS IT REAL, OR FAKE LIKE EVERYTHING ELSE HERE?
WILL YOU STOP BEATING UP ON THIS PLACE?! YOU WON'T HAVE A MOMENT OF FUN ON THIS TRIP IF ALL YOU DO IS LOOK FOR THINGS TO CRITICIZE!
SEE?! IT'S A REAL GUY PLAYING THE SYNTHESIZER!
WHOOPS. SORRY. I DIDN'T MEAN TO HIT BAGPIPES JUST THEN.
KASIO
AMEND

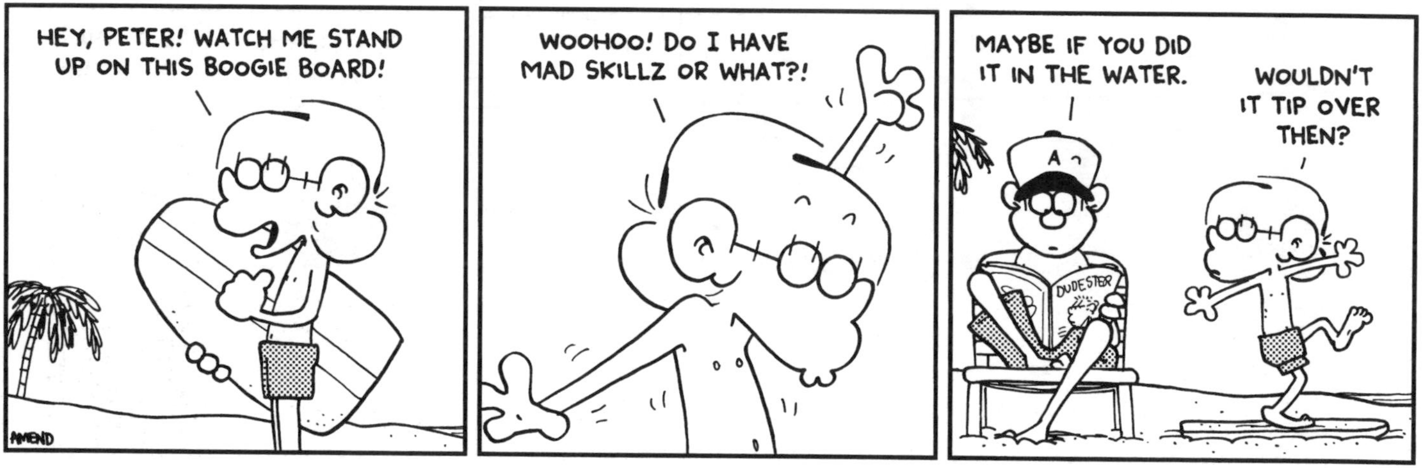
HEY, PETER! WATCH ME STAND UP ON THIS BOOGIE BOARD!
AMEND
WOOHOO! DO I HAVE MAD SKILLZ OR WHAT?!
MAYBE IF YOU DID IT IN THE WATER.
WOULDN'T IT TIP OVER THEN?
DUDESTER

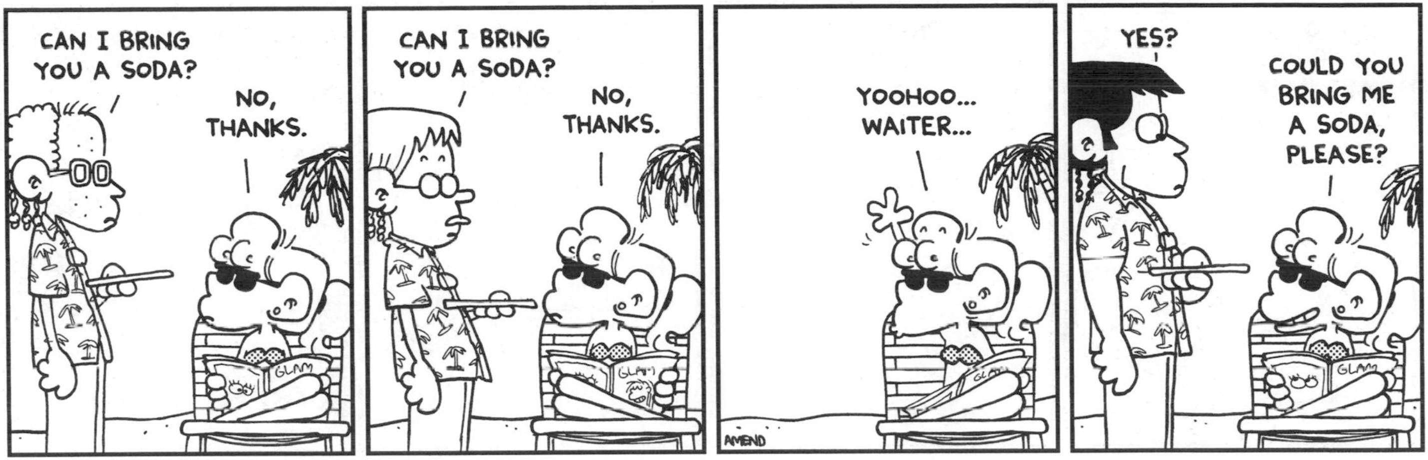
CAN I BRING YOU A SODA?
NO, THANKS.
CAN I BRING YOU A SODA?
NO, THANKS.
YOOHOO... WAITER...
YES?
COULD YOU BRING ME A SODA, PLEASE?
GLAM
AMEND

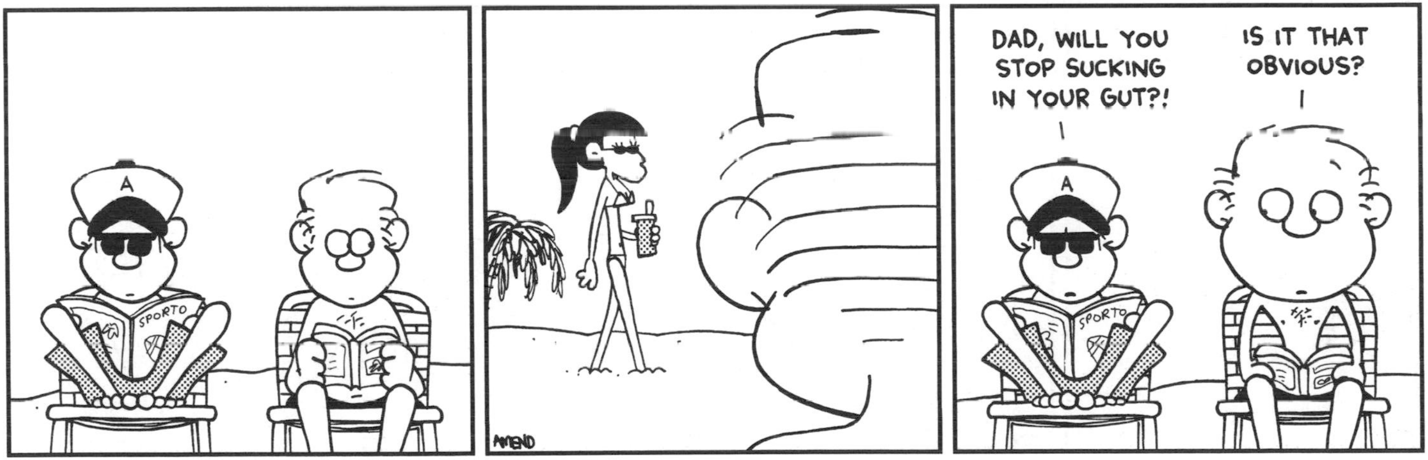
SPORTO
AMEND
DAD, WILL YOU STOP SUCKING IN YOUR GUT?!
IS IT THAT OBVIOUS?

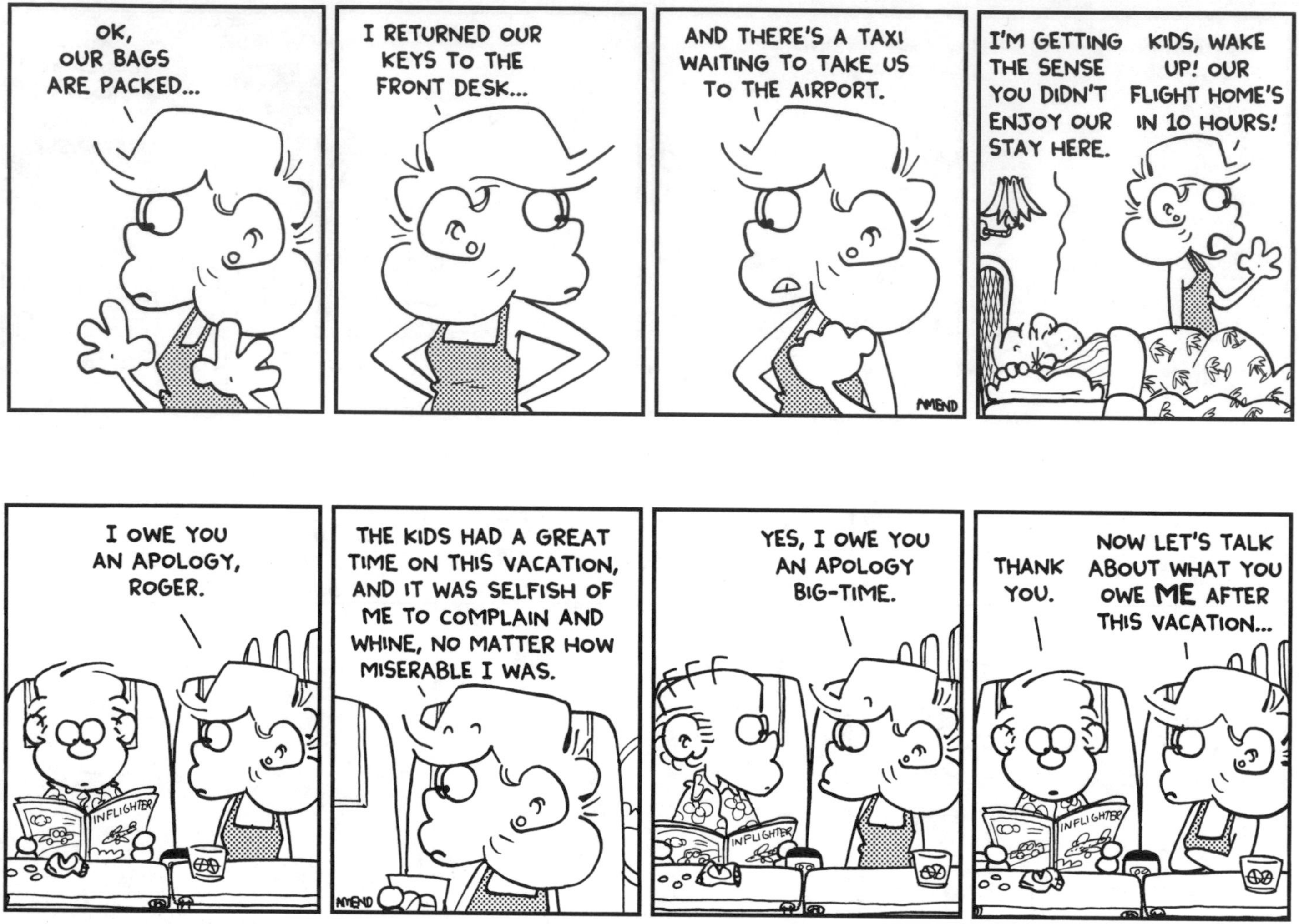
OK, OUR BAGS ARE PACKED...
I RETURNED OUR KEYS TO THE FRONT DESK...
AND THERE'S A TAXI WAITING TO TAKE US TO THE AIRPORT.
AMEND
I'M GETTING THE SENSE YOU DIDN'T ENJOY OUR STAY HERE.
KIDS, WAKE UP! OUR FLIGHT HOME'S IN 10 HOURS!
I OWE YOU AN APOLOGY, ROGER.
INFLIGHTER
THE KIDS HAD A GREAT TIME ON THIS VACATION, AND IT WAS SELFISH OF ME TO COMPLAIN AND WHINE, NO MATTER HOW MISERABLE I WAS.
AMEND
YES, I OWE YOU AN APOLOGY BIG-TIME.
INFLIGHTER
THANK YOU.
NOW LET'S TALK ABOUT WHAT YOU OWE ME AFTER THIS VACATION...
INFLIGHTER